Southern Living

NO TASTE LIKE
HOME

Southern Living

NO TASTE LIKE
HOME

A Celebration of Regional Southern Cooking and Hometown Flavor

Kelly Alexander

OXMOOR
HOUSE®

Contents

It's easy to get sentimental when we talk about our hometowns. Whenever someone mentions my own—Atlanta, Georgia—I feel the warm cinnamon sting of my mema's mandelbrot cookies on my tongue, smell her slow-simmered pot roast in the air, and see my sweet stepfather coming in from the yard with a handful of boiled peanuts and an ice-cold bottle of Coca-Cola. I'm not alone, of course: From *The Wizard of Oz* to *As I Lay Dying,* literature the world over echoes with the tug of home.

While we all reserve a special space in our hearts for the places that raise us, we carry some of our fondest memories a bit deeper: in our bellies. Nothing transports you faster—to your parents' dinner table, your favorite hangout, your elementary school bake sale—than the flavor of a dish you enjoyed there.

All hometown food is special, of course, but I daresay Southern hometown food is extraordinary. Down here when we talk about what's for dinner, we're talking about so much more than fried chicken and biscuits, pulled pork, or pots of bubbling burgoo. We're talking about race and class and religion and music and our unique slice of the collective Southern culture.

This book is devoted to exploring not only the food but the appetites and traditions of tasty hometowns across six Southern regions that have more than geography in common: The big-hearted cooking of the heart of Dixie. The musical, French-tinged, high-low, melting-pot cuisine of the Cajun country. The Tex-Mex flair and big-money swagger of big, bold Texas. The sweet-hot, smoky charms of the bluegrass, bourbon, and barbecue trail. The pure, clear-as-a-mountain-stream flavors of the Piedmont. And the harbor-influenced tables of the wide-ranging coastal South.

The chapters are chock-full of delicious recipes inspired and contributed by *Southern Living* readers, chefs, and locals-done-good in each region—from Texas brisket, New Orleans gumbo, and Carolina barbecue to Miranda Lambert's mama's meatloaf, Charles Frazier's soup beans, and Eva Longoria's mint lemonade. Each is served up in the company of the people, places, and stories that make every bite and sip so incredible. You'll get the lowdown on favorite dishes and also a genuine taste of the regions where the recipes and their keepers grew up.

I hope these pages bring you the unparalleled pleasure of enjoying local specialties the way the natives, including some very celebrated ones, do. And wherever it is that you call home, may the rich history and enduring character of these unforgettable places inspire you to discover and appreciate the magic of your own hometown.

Bon voyage, and welcome home.

K Alexander

Kelly Alexander
Chapel Hill, North Carolina

P.S. For me, nothing says Atlanta like my late grandmother's mandelbrot, which we ate at every birthday party, Jewish holiday, and "just because" occasion. (You might not equate Atlanta with Jewish culture, but the city has had a vibrant Jewish community since right after the Civil War, when newspaperman Henry Grady's vision of the "New South" lured many Jewish businessmen there. My grandparents arrived after World War II, when my grandfather was stationed nearby at Fort Benning.) My grandmother, Lillian Pachter, sent me wax-paper-lined shoeboxes of mandelbrot until she became too old to bake, well after I'd graduated from college. I make it for my children today. Turn the page for the recipe.

Mema's Mandelbrot

Mandelbrot are the twice-or-thrice-baked cookies popularized in Ashkenazi Jewish cooking (mandel *means almond and* brot *means bread in Yiddish*) *that bear more than passing resemblance to Italian biscotti. This is perhaps because a large population of Jews lived in Italy's Piedmont region, where biscotti is said to have originated. It probably originally appealed to the Jews because it's made with flour, sugar, eggs, and oil—not butter—and thus is pareve, or kosher, for the Sabbath. Noted for their distinctive, addictive crunchiness, mandelbrot are terrific with coffee or, on a warm day, a tall glass of iced sweet tea.*

Makes about 3 dozen
Hands-On Time 15 min.   Total Time 1 hour, 5 min.

5½ cups all-purpose flour, divided	1 tsp. orange zest (optional)
2 heaping tsp. baking powder	¼ cup pulp-free orange juice
Pinch of table salt	1 tsp. vanilla extract
4 large eggs	½ cup finely crushed almonds
1½ cups sugar	1 Tbsp. sugar
¾ cup vegetable oil	1½ tsp. ground cinnamon

1. Preheat the oven to 350°. Sift 4 cups flour, baking powder, and salt into a large bowl. Make a well in the center; set aside. In another bowl, gently beat together the eggs, 1½ cups sugar, oil, orange zest (if using), orange juice, and vanilla. Pour the egg mixture into the well in the dry ingredients in 2 additions, stopping to stir in between. Add the almonds, and stir until a very sticky dough forms. Turn dough out onto a heavily floured surface, and knead with floured hands, adding remaining 1½ cups flour if necessary, until dough is smooth. Divide into 4 (13- x 1½-inch) logs. Place on generously greased baking sheets. In a small bowl, mix together the 1 Tbsp. sugar and cinnamon; dust top of each log with cinnamon-sugar mixture.

2. Bake at 350° for 22 to 25 minutes or until tops are dark blond but not yet golden. Remove from the oven (leave oven on), and cool 5 minutes. While still warm, slice diagonally into even strips about 1½ inches wide to make individual cookies. Place cookies, cut sides down, on the baking sheets; return to oven, and bake 20 minutes, turning cookies over after 10 minutes to crisp and brown the other side.

Kelly Alexander
Chapel Hill, North Carolina

Piedmont Park
Atlanta, Georgia

Birmingham Botanical Gardens
Birmingham, Alabama

The Heart of Dixie

To call an area the *heart* of something is to say that it is a hub in the traditional sense—a place where important materials are concentrated and a center through which people pass on their way to somewhere else. But the phrase also implies an emotional pull, and the heart of Dixie is the bull's-eye of the collective Southern soul.

In this Georgia-Alabama-Mississippi constellation, the largest star, shining big and bright, is **Atlanta, Georgia.** The distinguished journalist and former *New York Times* editor R.W. "Johnny" Apple, Jr., once described Atlanta as "a Deep South version of Los Angeles." He may have been referring to both cities' legendary traffic problems, but what he likely meant was that swirling around Atlanta's historic core is a constant state of reinvention and evolution. The city's roots aren't as deep as those of some other Southern towns.

Originally called Terminus because it was the southeastern end of the Western & Atlantic Railroad line, Atlanta served as a link between Southern seaports and Chattanooga, Tennessee, and thus to the cities of the North.

What sprang up from the red Georgia clay to serve the railroad business quickly emerged and has forever after thrived as a city of commerce: Atlanta is home to corporate headquarters for Coca-Cola, Home Depot, and Delta Air Lines. Its airport is routinely ranked the busiest in the world, as measured by the number of passengers that parade through it each day. (Hence the old Southern adage: To get to heaven, you have to change planes in Atlanta first.)

Perhaps the most important thing to happen to Atlanta occurred in 1864 when Union General William Tecumseh Sherman and his forces burned the city. The carnage marked the beginning of the end of the Civil War (Sherman concluded his "March to the Sea" a month later in Savannah), and it set the tone for Atlanta's character ever afterward. Visionary Atlantans rebuilt their city on the back of an idea called the "New South." This meant a city willing to do business with anybody willing to do business in it, further contributing to Atlanta's commerce-centric present.

Of course, Atlanta's image as a New South city also was built in part by the Reverend Dr. Martin Luther King, Jr. He was born and is now buried on Auburn Avenue, where both he and his father preached at Ebenezer Baptist Church. King won the Nobel Peace Prize in 1964 when

11

The Varsity
Atlanta, Georgia

Georgian Terrace Hotel
Atlanta, Georgia

Atlanta diners are democratic. They like barbecue
and chili dogs as well as pomegranate martinis and milk
shakes made with liquid nitrogen.

he was 35, the youngest person to do so at the time. (Another Georgian, former President Jimmy Carter, a native of Plains, Georgia, and a current Atlantan who works tirelessly for Habitat for Humanity, won the prize in 2002.) In the annals of colorful Atlantans one must also mention Ted Turner, the entrepreneur who began his career selling billboards and later almost single-handedly created what we now consider cable television.

There are 32 streets with "Peachtree" in their titles within the Atlanta metropolitan area. And on those 32 streets, what do the people find to eat? Atlantans have money to spend and sophisticated palates to tend. The city has produced one winner of the television reality cooking program *Top Chef*, the faux-hawked Richard Blais, he of the liquid nitrogen canisters and Krispy Kreme doughnut milk shakes. It also has

helped produce the "winningest man in barbecue," the outspoken Myron Mixon, from the town of Unadilla just two hours south. Together, Blais and Mixon represent the Atlanta food scene.

Do Atlantans like to eat barbecue and fried chicken and grits? You bet. Do they like pomegranate martinis and smoked salmon pizza? Yes, sir. And if they can get all of those dishes at the same place? They're all for it. Atlanta diners are democratic; they are not encumbered by notions of what things are "supposed" to taste like—a virtue, perhaps, of existing in a relatively new town.

About 150 miles west sits another big-time, big-name Southern city: **Birmingham, Alabama.** Like Atlanta, Birmingham owes its existence to railroads. The city was incorporated in 1871—after the Civil War and during

Reconstruction—where the old South & North Railroad met up with the Alabama & Chattanooga Railroad. This was a strategic spot, indeed: The Alabama soil is laced with natural deposits of coal, iron ore, and limestone—the essentials of making steel and iron.

In those days and in that place, labor was cheap, and the steel and iron flowed. The city's founders named the spot Birmingham after the United Kingdom's industrial capital, and Alabama's Birmingham so quickly became a foundation of industry that it acquired the nickname "Magic City"—because it seemingly grew up out of nothing overnight. (Another nickname, "The Pittsburgh of the South," suggests steel but is less romantic.)

For most of its first 100 years Birmingham was a steel town, a boomtown, and presiding over it

Birmingham, the "Magic City," thrives as a tourist destination for other Southerners—a place that has grown up and yet still feels familiar.

since 1906 has been a massive 56-foot cast-iron statue of Vulcan, the Roman god of fire and molten arts (including blacksmithing). Considered the planet's largest cast-iron statue, Vulcan was commissioned by the city's Commerce Club and sent to the historic 1904 World's Fair in St. Louis to represent Birmingham. He still stands tall atop Red Mountain overlooking the downtown skyline, a living testament to industry (and to a time before gods wore pants).

Iron and steel carried Birmingham until the 1970s, when the industry began to decline—but there were some other problems before that. The Great Depression took a

significant toll on the city's economy and morale, laying the groundwork, some historians believe, for the massive Civil Rights unrest that took place there in the 1950s and 1960s. It's been an uphill battle for Birmingham to overcome its image as a place where the U.S. government had to force the integration of schools and the Ku Klux Klan bombing of the Sixteenth Street Baptist Church killed four young girls.

When the metals petered out and the racial tensions eased, "Bombingham" had to reinvent itself. Today, Birmingham has a second life as a major banking center that competes with Charlotte, North Carolina,

for the number of corporate bank headquarters within city limits, and also, thanks to the University of Alabama at Birmingham Medical Center, a healthcare epicenter.

This is a city that is neither an air traffic hub nor an enjoining point of a major north-south interstate; and yet Birmingham is quietly thriving as a tourist destination for other Southerners, a place that has grown up and yet still feels familiar.

When it comes to food, one of Alabama's signatures is "white barbecue sauce," a concoction of mayonnaise, pepper, and vinegar traditionally served with smoked barbecued chicken. The owners of

Birmingham, Alabama

Big Bob Gibson's famous barbecue joints claim to have invented the stuff in 1925 at their outpost in Decatur, Alabama, and it's beloved all over the state.

In cosmopolitan Birmingham it's not all barbecue. A sea change came to the city's dining scene—and Alabama's—in 1982, when native son Frank Stitt opened Highlands Bar and Grill. In that high-end, chic restaurant you can reliably find fresh Gulf seafood—black grouper, Gulf shrimp, swordfish—brought straight from the water to the dining room, and upscale ingredients like veal sweetbreads and venison accented by the distinctly Southern flavors of bourbon, pork belly, and delicate lady peas.

Oxford, Mississippi, is not among the South's biggest cities, not by a long shot; only about 19,000 or so people live there. But it is one of its most interesting. No conversation about what's special in Mississippi, about what makes up the heart of Dixie, is complete without mention of Oxford.

Incorporated in May 1837, it was built on land that had once belonged to the Chickasaw Indian Nation. In a bid for greatness—and specifically to convince the state government that it should situate a new university there—the town's forefathers named it after the vaunted British university. "Incredibly," marveled *New York Times* editor Dwight Garner, "this scheme— the equivalent of naming your child Jefferson and hoping he will become president— actually worked."

The University of Mississippi opened its doors in Oxford in 1848. What has gone on since is a perfect storm of three Southern pastimes: literature, football, and food.

Let's start with the first: Oxford is the hometown of that lion of Southern letters, William Faulkner, and thus a seat of the great Southern literary tradition. "I discovered that my own little postage stamp of native soil was worth writing about and that I would never live long enough to exhaust it," Faulkner told the *The Paris Review* in 1956.

The religion in Oxford is Ole Miss football, and it is practiced during home games at what is often referred to as "the biggest tailgate party in the country" in an area of the Ole Miss campus known as The Grove. This 10-acre lawn lined with old oaks and magnolias at the center of campus is where folks take the business of eating before a football game very, very seriously.

Rowan Oak
Oxford, Mississippi

The Grove at Ole Miss
Oxford, Mississippi

City Grocery
Oxford, Mississippi

Thanks largely to the University of Mississippi, Oxford
enjoys a perfect storm of three major Southern pastimes:
literature, football, and food.

Tailgating at Ole Miss has been going on since at least the 1930s and attracts an estimated 60,000 fans on game days. Along the way, the food moved beyond hamburgers-and-hot dogs-and-picnic basket territory. By 1992, when cars were banned from the lawn, it had become downright fancy.

What you see today are waves upon waves of billowy tents hoisted up, each housing a miniature upscale living room. Some people bring flat-screen televisions, chandeliers, chafing dishes, china, and real silver to the proceedings. All the folks dress up—men in jackets and khakis, ladies in dresses and pearls. And they consume Southern staples like hot crab dip, carved pork loin roasts with rich gravy, and giant old-fashioned layer cakes (caramel is a favorite) in the most genteel form of rooting for a team you can imagine.

That's not to say that Ole Miss fans don't get loud—they get plenty loud, singing their "Hotty Toddy" cheer every 30 seconds or so. ("Are you ready? Hell, yes! Damn right! Hotty Toddy, Gosh almighty. Who the hell are we? Hey! Flim flam, bim bam, Ole Miss, by damn!")

But they don't paint their faces or naked bellies or anything, and as soon as the players make their procession across campus (known as The Walk), they clean up and get themselves into the stadium to watch their team.

Whether or not Ole Miss is any good on any given year is immaterial; when they're not, fans simply sustain themselves by talking about the glory years with the Mannings—the great quarterbacks Archie and his son Eli (son Peyton went to the University of Tennessee).

College towns often boast good dives, and Oxford is no exception. Proud Larry's is the favorite local music bar, and there's also a local blues record label, Fat Possum Records.

The restaurants on the square are by and large very good, especially if you're in one of the four owned by chef John Currence. The New Orleans transplant trained at Crook's Corner, the famed "New Southern" North Carolina temple where the great chef Bill Neal allegedly invented upscale dishes of shrimp 'n' grits.

Currence settled in Oxford in 1992 and opened City Grocery with hopes of making a mark in another beloved Southern college town. That he has: City Grocery's menu includes shrimp 'n' grits, along with delicacies like Tabasco-cured duck leg confit and Mississippi Bo Ssam, his take on the Korean roasted pork shoulder

Taylor Grocery & Restaurant
Taylor, Mississippi

specialty that comes with a garnish of fried oysters.

The only other thing to know about Oxford is that it is prime catfish-loving territory. In North American waters there are at least 39 species of catfish (so named because of their whiskers, which they use to feel around for food). The *Ictalurus punctatus*, or the channel catfish, is what they like in Mississippi. The beloved fish are farmed in the nearby Delta, which is the heart of the American catfish industry.

If you want to try them just so, which is to say battered in cornmeal and flash-fried, drive 8 or so miles outside of town to the site of a former dry goods store in rural Taylor. There you'll find the Taylor Grocery & Restaurant, which serves up catfish (and, sometimes, live music) at communal tables.

They don't serve alcohol, so folks bring their own and sip away on the front porch. It's the kind of scene that reminds you exactly what *heart* means.

Atlanta is a spread-out sprawl, a city of neighborhoods loosely knit together by a famously clogged highway system.

Its skyscraper-peppered downtown is notable as the home of Centennial Olympic Park (created for the 1996 games) and for the fact that it's open only as long as a typical business day: In Atlanta, folks may work downtown, but they don't live there.

Atlanta's list of noteworthy neighborhoods feels endless because there are so many, but some are more famous outside the city's borders than others. One is Midtown, a once down-and-out area that's enjoying a magnificent architectural and cultural revival—all restored antebellum homes, art galleries, cafes, and multicultural throngs.

Another is the Virginia Highland area, a series of walkable streets lined with antiques joints, boutiques, and agreeably twee Southern bars (think boiled peanuts, tin roofs, PBR in the can, and a combination of Lynyrd Skynyrd and Mumford & Sons on the jukebox).

And, of course, there is the dogwood-strewn Inman Park, an "in town" neighborhood listed on the National Register of Historic Places and one of the nation's oldest "garden suburbs." Its venerable neighborhood association bills Inman Park as Atlanta's first "official planned community."

The Woodruff Arts Center at the High Musueum of Art
Atlanta, Georgia

Farmers' Market Pizza

Decatur's Dekalb Farmers Market inspired the vegetable medley for this pizza.

Makes 6 servings Hands-On Time 30 min. Total Time 1 hour, 50 min.

Plain white cornmeal
1   lb. bakery pizza dough
½   to ¾ cup Quick Tomato Sauce
1   (8-oz.) package sliced fresh
     mozzarella cheese

¼   lb. mild Italian sausage, cooked
     and crumbled
1 ½ cups Farmers' Market Roasted
     Vegetables

1. Preheat oven to 500°. Heat a pizza stone or baking sheet in oven 30 minutes.

2. Meanwhile, lightly dust a second baking sheet with cornmeal. Stretch pizza dough into a 12- to 14-inch circle on baking sheet.

3. Spread Quick Tomato Sauce over dough. Top with mozzarella slices and Italian sausage. Arrange Farmers' Market Roasted Vegetables over pizza; season with kosher salt and freshly ground black pepper to taste.

4. Slide pizza from baking sheet onto hot pizza stone or baking sheet in oven. Bake at 500° for 15 minutes or until crust is thoroughly cooked, edges are golden, and cheese melts.

Quick Tomato Sauce

Makes 3 cups Hands-On Time 5 min. Total Time 5 min.

1   (28-oz.) can whole peeled
     tomatoes with basil

1 ½ Tbsp. extra virgin olive oil
1   tsp. kosher salt

1. Stir together tomatoes, olive oil, and salt. Process with a handheld blender until smooth.

Farmers' Market Roasted Vegetables

Makes 3 cups Hands-On Time 15 min. Total Time 1 hour, 10 min.

1   medium eggplant, cut into 1-inch
     pieces
2   large red bell peppers, cut into
     1-inch pieces
1   fennel bulb, cut into ¼-inch slices
3   garlic cloves, thinly sliced

3   Tbsp. extra virgin olive oil
1   tsp. kosher salt
½   tsp. freshly ground black pepper
2   Tbsp. chopped fresh basil
1   Tbsp. white balsamic vinegar

1. Preheat oven to 450°. Toss together first 7 ingredients in a bowl until coated. Spread eggplant mixture in a single layer in a 15- x 10-inch jelly-roll pan. Bake 45 to 50 minutes or until vegetables are tender and slightly charred, stirring halfway through. Cool slightly (about 10 minutes). Toss with basil and vinegar. Serve immediately. Store in an airtight container in refrigerator up to 2 days.

Butternut Squash Bake

Each fall, people across the South decorate their homes with pretty gourds and their tables with delicious squash dishes. This scrumptious side, perfect for a holiday dinner with roasted turkey or pork, has a soufflé-like quality.

**Makes 4 to 6 servings   Hands-On Time 25 min.
Total Time 1 hour, 30 min**

Roasted Winter Squash, coarsely chopped	2 Tbsp. honey
¾ cup egg substitute	⅛ tsp. table salt
2 Tbsp. butter, melted	Dash of ground nutmeg
2 Tbsp. frozen orange juice concentrate, thawed	

1. Preheat oven to 350°. Toss together chopped roasted squash and remaining ingredients in a large bowl. Process mixture, in batches, in a blender or food processor until smooth, stopping to scrape down sides. Pour mixture into a lightly greased 1½-qt. baking dish.

2. Bake at 350° for 35 to 40 minutes or until mixture is set.

Roasted Winter Squash

Makes 6 servings   Hands-On Time 10 min.   Total Time 40 min.

3 lb. butternut squash	¼ tsp. table salt
1 Tbsp. butter, melted	¼ tsp. black pepper
½ Tbsp. honey	

1. Preheat oven to 450°. Remove stem from squash. Cut squash in half lengthwise; remove and discard seeds. Cut each half into 4 wedges, and place on an aluminum foil-lined jelly-roll pan.

2. Stir together butter and honey until blended. Brush squash evenly with butter mixture; sprinkle evenly with salt and pepper.

3. Bake at 450° for 30 to 35 minutes or until tender, turning once. Cut skins from squash wedges, and discard.

**Dorothy Roberts
Hiawassee, Georgia**

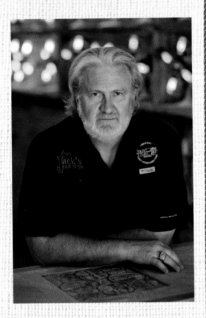

Meet Pitmaster Myron Mixon

Quite literally born into barbecue, Myron Mixon is the top dog on the professional barbecue circuit.

Raised in Vienna, Georgia, Mixon helped his father, Jack, run a barbecue restaurant that featured Jack's Old South BBQ Sauce. After his father died in 1996, Mixon figured that competing in barbecue contests could help the family business sell some sauce.

He has won more than 180 grand championships, 30 state championships, 11 national championships, and more than 1,800 barbecue trophies. The chief cook of the Jack's Old South Competition Bar-B-Que Team, the star of Destination America's *BBQ Pitmasters* and CBS's *Ultimate Barbecue Showdown*, he is author of the *New York Times* best-selling cookbook *Smokin' with Myron Mixon*.

The owner of the popular Pride and Joy barbecue restaurants in Miami and New York, he is widely recognized not only as the most successful man in barbecue but also one of the most charismatic. He lives in Unadilla, Georgia, and abides by the motto: "Barbecue is a simple food. Don't mess it up."

"Smoking a whole chicken is probably the easiest thing you can master. My solution to never having dry chickens: a small pan of apple juice. It steams up and circulates, keeping the meat tender and ensuring a melt-in-your-mouth texture." —Myron Mixon

Pitmaster Smoked Whole Chicken

The skin on this chicken is delicious and soft enough to bite through. If you prefer crunchy skin, you should make yourself some fried chicken instead.

Makes 4 servings   Hands-On Time 20 min.
Total Time 3 hours, 20 min., plus 1 day for marinating

1	(3 ¼ -lb.) whole chicken, giblets removed
4	cups chicken broth
1	(1-oz.) envelope dry onion soup mix
⅔	cup chili powder
½	cup sugar
¼	cup kosher salt
¼	cup onion powder
¼	cup garlic powder
1	tsp. ground red pepper
2	cups apple juice

1. Rinse the chicken inside and out, and pat it dry thoroughly. Stir together the chicken broth and dry onion soup mix in a deep bowl. Add the chicken to the bowl, coating it well with the mixture; marinate it, covered, in the refrigerator overnight. In a small bowl, combine the chili powder and next 5 ingredients to make a rub.

2. Preheat a charcoal grill or a smoker to about 250° (medium-low) heat. Remove the chicken from the bowl, and discard the marinade. Pat chicken dry with paper towels. Sprinkle rub liberally on chicken, patting to adhere (you can store any unused rub in an airtight container up to 1 year). Place the chicken, breast side up, on a meat rack inside a 13- x 9- x 2-inch disposable aluminum pan (be sure the rack raises the bird above the surface of the pan). Pour the apple juice into another disposable pan or into your smoker's water pan.

3. Bank ashed-over charcoals on the left and right sides of the grill, and place the pan of apple juice between the banked coals or on the water-pan shelf of your smoker. Place the pan with the chicken on the center of the grill grates, above the apple juice, or on the top shelf of the smoker. Cover and cook, maintaining heat at 225° to 250°, for 2 hours and 45 minutes or until a meat thermometer inserted into the thickest portion of the breast meat registers 165°.

4. Remove chicken from grill or smoker, and let rest, loosely covered with foil, 15 minutes. Quarter the chicken—or, for sandwiches, pull the meat from the bones, and serve on buns with hickory sauce, creamy coleslaw, and sliced pickles.

Grilled Pork Porterhouse with Peach Agrodolce

Agrodolce, a traditional Italian sweet–and–sour sauce made with vinegar and sugar (or sweet ingredients such as peaches and raisins), adds fresh summer flavor to the granddaddy of all pork chops.

Makes 4 servings   Hands-On Time 15 min.   Total Time 1 hour, 25 min.

4	(1 ½-inch-thick) pork porterhouse chops (about 2 ½ lb.)	¾	tsp. kosher salt
1	Tbsp. olive oil	½	tsp. freshly ground black pepper
			Peach Agrodolce

1. Let pork stand at room temperature 30 minutes. Light one side of grill, heating to 350° to 400° (medium-high) heat; leave other side unlit. Brush pork with olive oil, and sprinkle with salt and pepper.

2. Grill pork over lit side of grill, covered with grill lid, 4 minutes on each side; transfer pork to unlit side, and grill, covered with grill lid, 10 minutes on each side or until a meat thermometer registers 150°. Let stand 5 minutes. Arrange pork on a serving platter, and top with Peach Agrodolce.

Peach Agrodolce

2	Tbsp. raisins	1	Tbsp. olive oil
2	Tbsp. tawny port wine	2	large fresh, ripe peaches, peeled and diced into 1-inch pieces
1	Tbsp. chopped fresh parsley		
1	Tbsp. balsamic vinegar		

1. Cook raisins, port, and 2 Tbsp. water in a small saucepan over medium heat, stirring occasionally, 5 minutes. Remove from heat; whisk in parsley, vinegar, and oil. Stir in peaches, and add salt and freshly ground pepper to taste.

Chef Hugh Acheson, Five & Ten
Athens, Georgia

Meet Songwriter Matthew Sweet

A pioneer in the Athens rock scene, singer and songwriter Matthew Sweet rose to widespread fame on the college music circuit in the early and mid 1980s.

Originally from Lincoln, Nebraska, Sweet arrived in Athens in 1983 to attend college and, he hoped, join in the local music scene. His breakthrough 1991 album *Girlfriend*, written in Athens, included a Top Ten single (the title track) that was on massive rotation on MTV.

Sweet writes and produces music now, has written songs for Hanson and with Susanna Hoffs of The Bangles, and still performs "Girlfriend" live.

"I remember taking out-of-town visitors to the Bluebird and having many a fine breakfast with members of R.E.M., Pylon, the B-52s, Oh-OK, and others. I still consider its Bulldog Tofu a classic." —Matthew Sweet

Bluebird Cafe Bulldog Tofu Stir-Fry with Grits

Originally named the El Dorado, the Bluebird Cafe (now closed) was Athens's oldest vegetarian restaurant. Back in the 1970s, many Athens musicians and artists hung out and drank coffee there.

Makes 4 to 6 servings   Hands-On Time 35 min.   Total Time 35 min.

GRITS
- ½ tsp. table salt
- 1 cup uncooked stone-ground yellow grits
- 2 Tbsp. butter
- ¼ tsp. freshly ground black pepper
- Nutritional yeast* (optional)

STIR-FRY
- 1 (14-oz.) package extra-firm tofu, drained
- 2 Tbsp. canola oil
- 1 onion, coarsely chopped
- 1 red bell pepper, sliced
- 4 garlic cloves, minced
- 1 Tbsp. minced fresh ginger
- 2 tomatoes, chopped
- ⅓ cup soy sauce
- ¼ cup nutritional yeast
- 2 cups firmly packed fresh baby spinach

1. Prepare the Grits: Bring 4 cups water and salt to a boil in a medium saucepan; add grits. Reduce heat, and simmer, stirring constantly, 18 to 20 minutes. Add butter and pepper at the end. You can add a pinch of nutritional yeast to the grits, as well, for seasoning.

2. Prepare the Stir-Fry: Place tofu on layers of paper towels; cover with additional layers of paper towels. Weight the top with a dinner plate to release all of the moisture. (Sides of tofu should be bulging slightly but not cracking.) Let stand 10 minutes; discard paper towels. Cut into ½-inch cubes. Fry tofu in hot oil in a large skillet over medium-high heat, stirring often, 8 minutes or until browned on all sides. Remove to a paper towel-lined plate, reserving oil in skillet. Add onion, bell pepper, garlic, and ginger to skillet; sauté 6 minutes. Add tomato, and sauté 2 minutes. Add soy sauce and yeast; sauté 1 minute. Add spinach; sauté 1 minute. Serve over grits.

Note: We tested with Lewis Labs Brewer's Yeast.

Tiny Caramel Tarts

For extra indulgence, sprinkle with finely chopped chocolate, crystallized ginger, toffee bits, or toasted and buttered pecans just before serving.

Makes 6 dozen   Hands-On Time 30 min.   Total Time 4 hours, 30 min.

2 cups sugar, divided	2 cups milk
½ cup cold butter, sliced	Cream Cheese Pastry Shells
6 Tbsp. all-purpose flour	Sweetened whipped cream
4 egg yolks	

1. Cook 1 cup sugar in a medium-size heavy skillet over medium heat, stirring constantly, 6 to 8 minutes or until sugar melts and turns golden brown. Stir in butter until melted.

2. Whisk together flour, egg yolks, milk, and remaining 1 cup sugar in a 3-qt. heavy saucepan; bring just to a simmer over low heat, whisking constantly. Add sugar mixture to flour mixture, and cook, whisking constantly, 1 to 2 minutes or until thickened. Cover and chill 4 hours.

3. Meanwhile, prepare Cream Cheese Pastry Shells. Spoon caramel mixture into pastry shells, and top with whipped cream.

Cream Cheese Pastry Shells

Makes 6 dozen   Hands-On Time 55 min.   Total Time 2 hours, 20 min.

1 cup butter, softened	3 ½ cups all-purpose flour
1 (8-oz.) package cream cheese, softened	

1. Beat butter and cream cheese at medium speed with a heavy-duty electric stand mixer until creamy. Gradually add flour to butter mixture, beating at low speed just until blended. Shape dough into 72 (¾-inch) balls, and place on a baking sheet; cover and chill 1 hour.

2. Preheat oven to 400°. Place dough balls in cups of lightly greased miniature muffin pans; press dough to top of cups, forming shells.

3. Bake at 400° for 10 to 12 minutes. Remove from pans to wire racks, and cool completely (about 15 minutes).

Note: Baked pastry shells may be made up to 1 month ahead and frozen in an airtight container. Thaw at room temperature before filling.

Telia Johnson
Birmingham, Alabama

Meet Actress Donna D'Errico

Perhaps best known for her role as Donna Marco on one of the world's most-watched television shows, Donna D'Errico is an actress, documentarian, and professional adventurer.

Since her *Baywatch* days, she has appeared in independent films and worked as a producer, writer, director, and videographer.

Born in Dothan, Alabama, and raised in Columbus, Georgia, D'Errico decided recently to do what she had dreamed of since she was a child: climb Mount Ararat in Turkey in search of the Biblical Noah's Ark. She embarked on the dangerous expedition up the mountain in late 2012 and is producing a documentary about the search.

When she's not exploring, the single mother of two takes pride in domestic pursuits: cleaning, doing laundry, washing windows, tending a vegetable garden, and re-creating the Southern flavors she grew up eating.

"Country Captain took hold back in the 1920s, after Mary Bullard of Columbus served it to President Franklin D. Roosevelt. Knowing that Roosevelt was a frequent guest there always intrigued me and made me feel proud to be from Columbus." —Donna D'Errico

Country Captain

Bullard also served this mildly curried chicken–and–rice dish to the likes of Supreme Court Justice Thomas Murphy and Army generals John Pershing, Dwight D. Eisenhower, Omar Bradley, George Marshall, and even George Patton. Once, while on his way to nearby Fort Benning, Patton famously sent a telegram to the Bullard family, stating: "If you can't give me a party and have Country Captain, meet me at the train with a bucket of it."

Makes 4 to 6 servings   Hands-On Time 30 min.
Total Time 1 hour, 15 min.

1 cup sliced almonds	1 small garlic clove, minced
½ cup shortening or cooking oil	1 Tbsp. curry powder
1 cup all-purpose flour	½ tsp. ground white pepper
1½ tsp. table salt, divided	2 (14½-oz.) cans diced tomatoes, undrained
¾ tsp. freshly ground black pepper	
1 (4-lb.) whole chicken, cut up (or 3 lb. skinned, bone-in chicken breasts)	1½ tsp. chopped fresh parsley, plus more for garnish
	½ tsp. fresh thyme leaves
2 Tbsp. unsalted butter	4 to 6 cups cooked long-grain rice
2 onions, finely chopped	3 Tbsp. dried currants
2 green bell peppers, chopped	

1. Preheat oven to 350°. Bake almonds in a single layer in a shallow pan 6 to 8 minutes or until toasted and fragrant, stirring halfway through.

2. Heat shortening or oil in large cast-iron or other ovenproof skillet over medium-high heat. Season flour with ½ tsp. salt and ¼ tsp. black pepper. Remove skin from chicken pieces, and sprinkle pieces with ½ tsp. salt and remaining ½ tsp. black pepper on all sides. Roll chicken pieces in the flour, coating each piece well. Place chicken pieces in skillet, and fry 12 to 15 minutes or until browned, turning after 6 minutes. Remove chicken after browning, and keep hot.

3. Reduce heat to medium; add butter to skillet. Add onion, bell pepper, and garlic; cook, stirring frequently, 8 minutes or until onion is very soft and transparent. Add curry powder, white pepper, and remaining ½ tsp. salt. Add tomatoes, parsley, and thyme. Season to taste with additional salt, white pepper, and curry.

4. Return chicken to skillet. Cover tightly, and bake at 350° for 45 minutes or until chicken reaches desired degree of doneness. To serve, place chicken in center of a large serving dish surrounded by hot cooked rice. Add the currants to the sauce mixture, and pour over rice. Sprinkle toasted almonds over the top.

Welcome to
Birmingham

✿✿✿

What to say about a city presided over by the world's largest cast-iron statue, a visage with a fiery expression and no pants? It's a place with colossal aspiration.

Birmingham residents, justifiably proud of their six-ton wonder, want you to know that Vulcan is more than just a statue. It's a place to go to celebrate Birmingham. Complete with a 6-acre park and a museum, the Vulcan Center makes an ideal first stop for visitors. In addition to being able to climb the tower to the base of the statue, park visitors enjoy interactive exhibits and great spots to picnic while overlooking downtown Birmingham.

What's more: Vulcan helps visitors interpret Birmingham's history through the lens of the American experience—how the great themes of westward expansion, reconstruction, industrialization, the Great Depression, and the Civil Rights era played out in this "Magic City."

In 1901, James A. McKnight, the manager of the Alabama State Fair, commissioned the statue to highlight Birmingham's growing industrial might. Italian sculptor Giuseppe Moretti had only months to complete the project. It was dedicated on June 7, 1904, at the St. Louis World's Fair, and later taken apart and brought back by train to Birmingham.

Alabama White Barbecue Sauce

In northern Alabama they like "regular" barbecue sauce (the spicy tomato-based sort with hickory-smoked flavor) just fine. But what they're most famous for, the thing that is uniquely theirs, is Alabama white barbecue sauce.

Don McLemore, whose grandfather opened Big Bob Gibson's in Decatur in 1925, says his granddaddy came up with the combination of mayonnaise, fresh-cracked black pepper, fresh lemon juice, and cider vinegar. Big Bob's has popularized it ever since.

'Cue aficionados use it specifically to douse their smoked chicken. The place to try it in Birmingham is the beloved Miss Myra's Pit Bar-B-Q, which has the typical pig-inspired decor, devoted folks lining up at lunchtime for rib platters and the like, and bottles of both red and white sauces on the tables.

Grilled Chicken with White Barbecue Sauce

Makes 5 servings   Hands-On Time 20 min.   Total Time 4 hours, 35 min.

1	Tbsp. dried thyme	½	tsp. table salt
1	Tbsp. dried oregano	½	tsp. black pepper
1	Tbsp. ground cumin	10	chicken thighs (about 3 lb.)
1	Tbsp. paprika		White Barbecue Sauce
1	tsp. onion powder		

1. Combine first 7 ingredients. Rinse chicken, and pat dry; rub mixture evenly over chicken. Place chicken in a zip-top plastic freezer bag. Seal and chill 4 hours. Remove chicken from bag, discarding bag.

2. Preheat grill to 350° to 400° (medium-high) heat. Grill, covered with grill lid, 8 to 10 minutes on each side or until a meat thermometer inserted into thickest portion registers 180°. Serve with White Barbecue Sauce.

Note: Four chicken leg quarters (about 3 lb.) may be substituted for chicken thighs. Increase cooking time to 20 to 25 minutes on each side.

White Barbecue Sauce

Makes 1 ¾ cups   Hands-On Time 10 min.   Total Time 2 hours, 10 min.

1 ½	cups mayonnaise	1	Tbsp. spicy brown mustard
¼	cup white wine vinegar	1	tsp. sugar
1	garlic clove, minced	1	tsp. table salt
1	Tbsp. coarse, ground black pepper	2	tsp. horseradish

1. Stir together all ingredients until well blended. Refrigerate in an airtight container up to 1 week.

The Heart of Dixie

Not Yo' Mama's Mac 'N' Cheese

Decadent is the only word to describe this top-rated mac 'n' cheese from John's City Diner in Birmingham. The smoked Gouda adds marvelous flavor, but you can substitute regular Gouda.

Makes 8 to 10 servings   Hands-On Time 1 hour
Total Time 1 hour, 20 min.

1. Preheat oven to 400°. Bake breadcrumbs in a single layer on a baking sheet 5 to 7 minutes or until golden, stirring once after 2½ minutes.

2. Cook prosciutto, in batches, in a lightly greased large skillet over medium heat 3 to 4 minutes on each side or until crisp. Drain on paper towels; crumble.

3. Prepare pasta according to package directions.

4. Meanwhile, melt butter in a Dutch oven over medium heat; add shallot, and sauté 3 minutes or until tender. Add wine, stirring to loosen particles from bottom of Dutch oven, and cook 1 minute.

5. Gradually whisk in flour until smooth; cook, whisking constantly, 2 minutes. Gradually whisk in milk and next 4 ingredients; cook, whisking constantly, 12 to 14 minutes or until mixture thickens and begins to bubble. Remove and discard bay leaf.

6. Place 4 cups (16 oz.) Cheddar cheese in a large heatproof bowl; reserve remaining Cheddar cheese for another use. Add Gouda and Parmesan cheeses to bowl.

7. Gradually pour white sauce over cheeses, whisking until cheeses melt and sauce is smooth.

8. Stir in pasta and prosciutto until blended. Pour into a lightly greased 13- x 9-inch baking dish; sprinkle with breadcrumbs.

9. Bake at 400° for 15 minutes or until bubbly. Serve immediately.

Note: Don't use preshredded cheese; it doesn't melt as smoothly. You can shred the cheese and crisp the prosciutto up to 1 day ahead and chill. You can also toast the breadcrumbs ahead and store them in a zip-top plastic bag.

For No-Bake Mac 'N' Cheese: Omit breadcrumbs. Prepare recipe as directed in Steps 2 through 6. Stir pasta, prosciutto, and cheeses into white sauce. Serve immediately.

Executive Chef Shannon Gober, John's City Diner
Birmingham, Alabama

1	cup panko (Japanese breadcrumbs)
1	(4-oz.) package thinly sliced prosciutto
1	(16-oz.) package penne or cavatappi pasta
½	cup butter
1	shallot, minced
¼	cup dry white wine
¼	cup all-purpose flour
2	cups milk
2	cups whipping cream
1	bay leaf
½	tsp. table salt
¼	tsp. ground red pepper
2	(10-oz.) blocks sharp white Cheddar cheese, shredded
1	cup (4 oz.) shredded smoked Gouda
½	cup (2 oz.) shredded Parmesan cheese

Fried Green Tomato Stacks

For bacon drippings, fry three to four bacon slices in a skillet until crisp; remove bacon from skillet, and reserve bacon for another use.

Makes 6 servings   Hands-On Time 25 min.   Total Time 1 hour, 15 min.

3	tomatillos, husked
2	Tbsp. bacon drippings
1	garlic clove, pressed
1½	tsp. table salt, divided
1	tsp. black pepper, divided
½	tsp. paprika
¼	cup thinly sliced fresh basil
1½	cups self-rising yellow cornmeal mix
4	large green tomatoes, cut into 18 (¼-inch) slices

1	cup buttermilk
	Peanut oil
1	(8-oz.) package cream cheese, softened
1	(4-oz.) package goat cheese, softened
⅓	cup milk
1	tsp. sugar

1. Bring tomatillos and water to cover to a boil in a small saucepan; reduce heat, and simmer 10 minutes. Drain tomatillos, and cool.

2. Process tomatillos, bacon drippings, garlic, ½ tsp. salt, ½ tsp. pepper, and paprika in a food processor or blender until smooth; stir in basil. Cover and chill until ready to serve.

3. Stir together cornmeal mix, ¾ tsp. salt, and remaining ½ tsp. pepper. Dip tomato slices in buttermilk, shaking off excess; dredge in cornmeal mixture.

4. Pour oil to a depth of ½ inch in a skillet; heat to 375°. Fry tomato slices, in batches, in hot oil 1 to 2 minutes on each side; drain on a wire rack over paper towels. Keep warm.

5. Combine cream cheese, next 3 ingredients, and remaining ¼ tsp. salt. Place 1 fried tomato slice on each of 6 salad plates; top each evenly with half of cream cheese mixture. Top each with 1 fried tomato slice and remaining cream cheese mixture. Top with remaining 6 fried tomato slices; drizzle with tomatillo dressing.

Cathedral Chicken Salad

Serve this deliciously simple recipe like they do during the Lenten lunches at Birmingham's Cathedral Church of the Advent: on a lettuce leaf with a sprinkle of paprika.

Makes about 3½ cups   Hands-On Time 10 min.   Total Time 10 min.

½	cup mayonnaise
1	Tbsp. fresh lemon juice
2	tsp. Dijon mustard
½	tsp. ground white pepper

½	tsp. seasoning salt
3	cups chopped cooked chicken
½	cup chopped celery

1. Stir together first 5 ingredients until blended.

2. Place chicken and celery in a large bowl; add mayonnaise mixture, and toss to combine.

Summer Grilled Peach Salad

Gorgonzola cheese gets gooey and delicious when it's melted over the grilled peaches in this amazing summer salad.

Makes 4 servings   Hands-On Time 20 min.   Total Time 30 min.

1 cup pecans	2 cups arugula
4 large fresh, ripe peaches, halved	¼ cup honey*
3 Tbsp. extra virgin olive oil, divided	2 Tbsp. finely chopped chives
1 (4-oz.) wedge Gorgonzola cheese, broken into 8 pieces	

1. Preheat oven to 350°. Bake pecans in a single layer in a shallow pan 10 to 12 minutes or until toasted and fragrant, stirring halfway through.

2. Preheat grill to 350° to 400° (medium-high) heat. Gently toss peach halves in 1 Tbsp. olive oil; sprinkle with salt and pepper to taste. Grill peaches, cut sides down, covered with grill lid, 2 to 3 minutes or until golden. Turn peaches, and place 1 cheese piece in center of each peach; grill, covered with grill lid, 2 to 3 minutes or until cheese begins to melt.

3. Toss arugula with remaining 2 Tbsp. olive oil and salt and pepper to taste. Arrange arugula on a serving platter; sprinkle with toasted pecans, and top with grilled peach halves. Drizzle peaches with honey, and sprinkle with chives.

Note: Aged balsamic vinegar may be substituted.

Executive Chef Haller Magee, Satterfield's Restaurant
Birmingham, Alabama

Niki's West
Birmingham, Alabama

Order a "Meat-and-Three" Like a Local

Meat-and-three restaurants are old-fashioned fixtures of the South, vestiges of rural country cooking.

They're either sit-down eateries or cafeteria-style setups that allow each diner to select one protein and three sides from a seemingly endless array of choices: for the meat, you can expect barbecued or fried chicken, brisket, meatloaf, or catfish; for the sides, selections often include macaroni and cheese, collard greens, squash casserole, and congealed salads, plus cornbread and sweet tea.

Take Niki's West, a big cafeteria that has been serving Birmingham its meat-and-threes since 1957 and steers as many as 2,000 diners through its line at lunch. The pace is one reason so many folks always order the same thing. You don't want to be still mulling the choices when you grab your tray and the kindly but superefficient folks ask: "Serve you?"

Meet Chef Frank Stitt

Deemed "the father of Birmingham's gourmet new wave" by *The New York Times*, chef Frank Stitt is an Alabama native and a chef through and through.

He put Birmingham on the culinary map when he opened Highlands Bar and Grill in the Five Points South neighborhood in 1982.

Stitt originally left his small northern Alabama town of Cullman to study philosophy in Berkeley, California. Instead, he fell in love with the cooking of Alice Waters at her venerable Chez Panisse restaurant and soon was off to France to devote himself to studying with the great cooking teacher and cookbook writer Richard Olney.

Eventually Stitt came home and gave Birmingham what it didn't even know it needed: a glorious fine-dining destination, housed in a 1920s building decorated with vintage French posters. To this day, Highlands applies classic French technique to the local and coastal Alabama bounty.

Stitt owns three other nearby restaurants—the French bistro Chez Fonfon, the Italian restaurant Bottega, and the more casual Bottega Café next door.

"The delicacy of flounder fillets is complemented here by tiny, tender, pale green lady peas, which are the most delicate of the pea world. Basil, dill, and chives make this nontraditional succotash very special." —Frank Stitt

Flounder with Lady Pea Succotash

Makes 4 servings   Hands-On Time 45 min.   Total Time 45 min.

SUCCOTASH

1   small red onion, cut into 1-inch-thick slices
2   ears fresh corn
1   cup cooked lady peas*, drained, plus ¼ cup reserved pot liquor (cooking liquid from the peas)
2   tomatoes, seeded and cut into ¼-inch dice
½   small shallot, finely minced
4   basil leaves, torn into pieces
1   Tbsp. chopped fresh dill weed
1   Tbsp. finely chopped fresh chives
3   Tbsp. extra virgin olive oil
1   Tbsp. sherry vinegar

FLOUNDER

4   (6- to 8-oz.) flounder fillets, skin on or skinless
½   tsp. kosher salt
¼   tsp. freshly ground black pepper
5   tsp. vegetable oil
1   lemon, cut into wedges
Extra virgin olive oil (optional)

1. Prepare the Succotash: Preheat grill to 350° to 400° (medium-high) heat or preheat broiler with oven rack 5½ inches from heat. Grill onion slices, covered with grill lid, or broil onion slices 4 minutes on each side or until lightly charred. Cool slightly, and cut into ¼-inch dice. Cook corn in boiling water to cover 4 minutes; drain. Cut kernels from cobs; discard cobs. Combine charred onion, corn, peas, tomatoes, shallot, basil, dill, and chives in a large bowl. Stir in 3 Tbsp. olive oil, sherry vinegar, and reserved pot liquor. Add kosher salt and freshly ground white pepper to taste.

2. Prepare the Flounder: Season the fish with salt and pepper. Heat 3 tsp. oil in a large heavy skillet over medium-high heat until shimmering. Reduce heat to medium, place 2 fillets (skin side up, if they have skin) in the skillet, and cook 3 minutes on each side or until golden brown and fish flakes with a fork. (Peek inside one fillet to check for doneness—the thickest part should have turned pearly white.) Remove fish from skillet; keep warm. Heat remaining 2 tsp. oil in skillet, and repeat procedure with remaining fillets. Place succotash in a large sauté pan, and cook over medium heat 2 minutes or until heated through. Transfer fish to plates, and serve with succotash and lemon wedges. Drizzle each fillet with olive oil, if desired.

Note: If lady peas are not available, substitute pink-eyes, white acres, crowders, cranberry beans, fresh fava beans, or sweet peas.

Meet Country Singer
Sara Evans

The eldest of seven kids, Sara Evans sang and played in a family band from the age of 5.

She started playing professionally only to help pay the bills after a car accident left her with two broken legs.

It was soon apparent that her music could do more than earn her a little extra cash, and Evans moved from Missouri to Nashville to try her luck singing in nightclubs.

She signed a contract with RCA, which released her first album, *Three Chords and the Truth*, in 1997. Her next record, *No Place That Far*, took off, thanks in part to a chart-topping duet with Vince Gill. More hits followed, including *Restless* in 2003, *Real Fine Place* in 2005, and *Stronger* in 2011.

Today, Evans makes her home in Birmingham with husband, Jay Barker, a former University of Alabama quarterback and current football commentator, and enjoys cooking for their combined seven kids and sharing recipes.

"It's not hard to cook for your family. I think people are intimidated by it. It's not about making gourmet meals but about sitting down as a family and having that meal together. There's something important about that."

—Sara Evans

Cheesy Potato Soup

Makes 8 servings   **Hands-On Time 20 min.**   **Total Time 40 min.**

3	lb. baking potatoes (6 to 8 medium)
1	small white onion, finely chopped
4	cups milk or half-and-half
1	(10 ¾-oz.) can cream of mushroom, chicken, or potato soup
1	(8-oz.) package processed cheese (such as Velveeta), cubed
	Round buttery crackers or saltine crackers, crushed
¼	cup (1 oz.) shredded sharp Cheddar cheese

1. Peel potatoes, and cut into bite-size pieces. Boil potatoes and onion together in a 6-qt. Dutch oven of salted water (1 tsp. salt to 12 cups water) 15 to 20 minutes or until tender. Drain potato mixture in a fine wire-mesh strainer, and return to pot.

2. Add milk, can of soup, and cheese to potato mixture; bring to a simmer over medium heat, and cook, stirring occasionally, 4 minutes or until cheese melts. Add salt and pepper to taste.

3. Divide among serving bowls. Top with crushed crackers and Cheddar cheese.

Honey-Ginger Tea

This hot tea has Southern personality: sweet as honey with a peppery kick.

Makes 1 cup   Hands-On Time 5 min.   Total Time 10 min.

1	(1-inch) piece fresh ginger, peeled
1	regular-size green tea bag

1	Tbsp. fresh lemon juice
2	Tbsp. honey
1	cup boiling water

1. Grate ginger, using the large holes of a box grater, to equal 1 Tbsp. Squeeze juice from ginger into a teacup; discard solids. Place tea bag, lemon juice, and honey in teacup; add boiling water. Cover and steep 3 minutes. Remove and discard tea bag, squeezing gently.

Rose Marie Crowe
Trussville, Alabama

Vanilla-Rosemary Lemonade

Fresh herbs add verve to freshly squeezed lemon juice in this aromatic drink.

Makes 6 cups   Hands-On Time 30 min.   Total Time 4 hours

1 ½	cups sugar
1	vanilla bean, split
3	small fresh rosemary sprigs

3	cups fresh lemon juice (26 to 30 lemons)*

1. Combine sugar, vanilla bean, rosemary, and 3 cups water in a medium saucepan. Bring to a light boil over medium heat, stirring occasionally. Simmer 5 minutes. Remove from heat, and cool 30 minutes.

2. Pour through a fine wire-mesh strainer into a large pitcher, discarding solids. Stir in fresh lemon juice. Cover and chill 3 to 48 hours. Stir just before serving over ice.

Note: Three (7.5-oz.) containers frozen lemon juice, thawed, may be substituted.

Maureen Holt, Little Savannah Restaurant
Birmingham, Alabama

Visit the Moto-Museum Like a Local

When in Birmingham, you'll want to vroom over to the Barber Vintage Motorsports Museum, the largest motorcycle collection in North America.

Its holdings include 84 Harley-Davidsons and 21 of the bikes the Guggenheim Museum borrowed for its historic "Art of the Motorcycle" exhibit in 1998.

After a tour, go to the adjacent Barber Motorsports Park for a chance to see the machines roar. Every October, the park hosts the Barber Vintage Festival, an event featuring antique motorcycle road racing plus motocross, cross-country events, an airshow, and a "swap meet" with 250 vendors.

Barber also has a very popular Indy car race series and Grand-Am racing, which includes Grand Touring class cars, muscle cars and BMWs—not to mention Porsches, the favorite of owner George Barber.

A Birmingham dairy and real estate magnate, and, most pertinently, a former driver for the Sports Club of America—Barber parlayed his passion for vintage cars (and later motorcycles) into this terrific museum and park.

If you're walking in Oxford, you are walking on literary ground tilled for half a century by the American writer and novelist William Faulkner.

Though he was born in New Albany, Mississippi, in 1897, Faulkner moved with his family to Oxford shortly before his fifth birthday and lived there off and on, when he wasn't traveling or on loan to a university's literature department, for the rest of his life. He attended the University of Mississippi, albeit briefly; famously, he earned a D in English and dropped out. He based many of the characters in his fictional Yoknapatawpha County around ones he knew in and around Lafayette County, of which Oxford is the county seat.

By 1930, he'd written *The Sound and the Fury* and *As I Lay Dying* and achieved enough success to buy an antebellum Oxford home, which he named Rowan Oak and owned until his death in 1962. Faulkner won the 1949 Nobel Prize for Literature, and two of his lesser-known novels won Pulitzer Prizes in 1955 and 1963. Rowan Oak was sold by Faulkner's estate to the university in 1972 and is meticulously maintained as a museum—complete with his old typewriter in his office and mud-caked boots at his doorway. This literary landmark is open for tours most Tuesdays through Sundays.

Many other beloved writers have taken up residence in and around Oxford: Eudora Welty, Tennessee Williams, Richard Ford, Shelby Foote, Willie Morris, Barry Hannah, Walker Percy, Larry Brown, Donna Tartt, and John Grisham. First editions of the works of lots of these folks can be found in another Oxford landmark: Square Books, so named because it's on the town square. Open since 1979, it's routinely listed among the country's top independent booksellers.

Rowan Oak, home of William Faulkner
Oxford, Mississippi

Honeysuckle-Watermelon Cocktails

Makes 8 cups   **Hands-On Time 20 min.**   **Total Time: 20 min.**

8 cups seeded and cubed watermelon (about 1 [6-lb.] watermelon)
1 cup honeysuckle vodka*
½ cup fresh lime juice
¼ cup sugar
4 cups ice cubes
2 cups lemon-lime soft drink
Garnishes: lime slices, diced water
melon, fresh mint leaves

1. Process watermelon in a blender or food processor until smooth. Pour through a fine wire-mesh strainer into a large pitcher, using back of a spoon to squeeze out juice; discard solids.

2. Stir vodka and next 2 ingredients into watermelon juice. Add ice, and top with soft drink; gently stir. Serve immediately.

Note: We tested with Mississippi's Cathead Honeysuckle Flavored Vodka. Light rum or plain vodka may by substituted.

Double-Stuffed Barbecue Potatoes

What's better than a stuffed baked potato? One that's additionally stuffed with barbecued pork. You'll find versions of it at barbecue restaurants all over Dixie.

Makes 8 servings   Hands-On Time 30 min.   Total Time 1 hour, 10 min.

8	large baking potatoes
1	(8-oz.) container cream cheese, softened
½	cup mayonnaise
1	Tbsp. white wine vinegar
1	tsp. seasoned pepper
2	tsp. fresh lemon juice
¾	tsp. table salt
3	cups chopped barbecued pork, warmed
1	cup (4 oz.) shredded Cheddar cheese
¼	cup chopped fresh chives

1. Preheat oven to 425°. Wrap each potato in a piece of aluminum foil; place potatoes on a baking sheet. Bake potatoes at 425° for 45 minutes or until tender. Reduce oven temperature to 375°.

2. Cut a 4- x 2-inch strip from top of each baked potato. Carefully scoop out pulp into a large bowl, leaving 8 shells intact; set aside about 2 cups of pulp for another use.

3. Mash together remaining potato pulp, cream cheese, and next 5 ingredients; stir in 2 cups of the pork. Spoon mixture evenly into shells; top evenly with remaining 1 cup of pork, Cheddar cheese, and chives. Place on a lightly greased baking sheet.

4. Bake at 375° for 20 to 25 minutes or until thoroughly heated.

Carolyn Walthall
Oxford, Mississippi

Mississippi Bourbon Punch

Makes about 14 cups   Hands-On Time 10 min.   Total Time 10 min.

2	(750-milliliter) bottles dry muscadine wine, chilled
1	(12-oz.) bottle grenadine, chilled
1½	cups chilled bourbon
1	cup chilled fresh orange juice
1	cup chilled cranberry juice
⅓	cup fresh lime juice
8	cups ice cubes
1	(12-oz.) can lemon-lime soft drink, chilled
1	cup chilled club soda

1. Pour muscadine wine, grenadine, bourbon, orange juice, cranberry juice, and lime juice into a punch bowl. Stir in ice cubes, lemon-lime soft drink, and club soda.

Note: We tested with Morgan Creek Vineyards Cahaba White Alabama muscadine wine and Stirrings Authentic Grenadine. Chardonnay may be substituted.

Bartender Jayce McConnell, Snackbar
Oxford, Mississippi

"I grew up with an unholy love for freezer-section chicken pot pie, so it only made sense to gravitate toward a tweaked-up version. I keep a stash of these around in the winter months. They are my favorite after-work meal."

—John Currence

Chicken and Duck Pot Pies

Rich duck, good mushrooms, fresh thyme, and potatoes cooked in duck fat add depth in Currence's version of a favorite Southern comfort food.

Makes 4 (2-cup) pies　Hands-On Time 1 hour, 20 min.
Total Time 2 hours, 40 min.

4	carrots, cut into ½-inch pieces	4	(6-oz.) boned duck breast halves with skin
2	medium onions, chopped		
8	oz. assorted mushrooms, such as cremini and stemmed shiitake, sliced ½ inch thick	8	oz. small red potatoes, coarsely chopped
1	Tbsp. fresh thyme leaves	3	cups reduced-sodium fat-free chicken broth, divided
2	Tbsp. olive oil	3	Tbsp. unsalted butter
6	garlic cloves, thinly sliced	6	Tbsp. all-purpose flour
1	(3 ½-lb.) whole chicken	1	package frozen puff pastry, thawed
2	tsp. table salt, divided		
1 ½	tsp. freshly ground black pepper, divided	1	large egg, lightly beaten

1. Preheat oven to 400°. In a large roasting pan, toss together first 6 ingredients; spread the vegetables in an even layer. Season the chicken inside and out with 1½ tsp. salt and 1 tsp. pepper. Place the chicken, breast side up, on top of the vegetables. Bake at 400° for 55 to 60 minutes or until the chicken is cooked through and the vegetables are tender. Increase oven temperature to 450°.

2. Meanwhile, make ¼-inch-deep cuts in duck skin with a sharp knife; pat dry. Season duck with remaining ½ tsp. salt and ½ tsp. pepper. Heat a large skillet over medium-high heat; add duck, skin side down, and cook 5 minutes or until skin is well seared and fat is rendered. Turn breast halves over, and cook 7 minutes or until duck is just cooked through. Remove duck, reserving drippings in skillet. Add potatoes to hot duck drippings in skillet, and sauté 6 to 7 minutes or until tender and browned. Remove from heat. Spoon potatoes into a large bowl using a slotted spoon; reserve duck drippings in skillet.

3. Remove chicken from roasting pan; place on a platter. Add 1 cup chicken broth to roasting pan, stirring to loosen browned bits from bottom of pan. Pour chicken broth and vegetables out of roasting pan through a fine wire-mesh strainer, reserving broth in a bowl. Add drained vegetables to potatoes. Add remaining 2 cups chicken broth to reserved broth in bowl to measure 3 cups.

4. Discard skin from the chicken and duck; remove the meat from chicken, and shred. Coarsely chop duck. Add chicken and duck to

potatoes and vegetables. Melt butter in skillet with reserved duck drippings over medium-high heat. Add flour, and cook 2 minutes, whisking constantly. Add reserved broth; cook, stirring often, 10 minutes or until thickened. Stir in meat and vegetables.

5. Spoon mixture into 4 (2-cup) ramekins or baking dishes. Roll puff pastry to ⅛-inch thickness on a lightly floured surface; cut into 4 circles using a 6-inch round cutter. Place 1 circle of pastry on top of each ramekin, pressing to seal. Brush with beaten egg. Place ramekins on an aluminum foil-lined jelly-roll pan; bake at 450° for 20 minutes or until pastry is browned.

Mississippi Mudslides

Makes about 4 cups   **Hands-On Time 10 min.**   **Total Time 10 min.**

1	pt. chocolate ice cream	½	cup bourbon
1	pt. coffee ice cream		Toppings: whipped cream, chocolate
1	cup milk		syrup, marshmallows

1. Process first 4 ingredients in a blender until smooth. Serve with desired toppings.

Peanut Butter Mississippi Mud Brownies

Makes about 2½ dozen
Hands-On Time 20 min.   **Total Time 1 hour, 15 min.**

4   (1-oz.) unsweetened chocolate
     baking squares
1⅓ cups butter, softened and divided
2½ cups granulated sugar, divided
4   large eggs
2   cups all-purpose flour, divided
1   tsp. vanilla extract
½   cup creamy peanut butter
½   cup firmly packed light brown sugar
2   large eggs
1   tsp. baking powder
3   cups miniature marshmallows
1½ cups lightly salted roasted peanuts
Chocolate Frosting

1. Preheat oven to 350°. Microwave chocolate in a microwave-safe bowl at MEDIUM (50% power) 1½ minutes or until melted and smooth, stirring at 30-second intervals.

2. Beat 1 cup butter and 2 cups granulated sugar at medium speed with an electric mixer until light and fluffy. Add 4 eggs, 1 at a time, beating just until blended after each addition. Add melted chocolate, beating just until blended. Add 1 cup flour, beating at low speed just until blended. Stir in vanilla. Spread half of batter in a greased and floured 13- x 9-inch pan.

3. Beat peanut butter, brown sugar, and remaining ⅓ cup butter and ¼ cup granulated sugar at medium speed with an electric mixer until light and fluffy. Add 2 eggs, 1 at a time, beating just until blended after each addition. Stir together baking powder and remaining 1 cup flour; add to peanut butter mixture, beating at low speed just until blended.

4. Spoon peanut butter mixture over brownie batter; top with remaining brownie batter, and swirl together.

5. Bake at 350° for 45 to 55 minutes or until a wooden pick inserted in center comes out with a few moist crumbs. Remove from oven to a wire rack; sprinkle with marshmallows and peanuts. Prepare Chocolate Frosting, and drizzle over brownies. Cool completely.

Chocolate Frosting

Makes about 3 cups   **Hands-On Time 10 min.**   **Total Time 10 min.**

¼	cup butter	2	cups powdered sugar
3	Tbsp. unsweetened cocoa	½	tsp. vanilla extract
3	Tbsp. milk		

1. Cook butter, cocoa, and milk in a saucepan over medium heat, whisking constantly, 4 minutes or until slightly thickened; remove from heat. Whisk in powdered sugar and vanilla until smooth.

Mississippi Mudslides

Atchafalaya River
South-Central Louisiana

Cafe Du Monde
New Orleans, Louisiana

Cajun Country

Small but feisty, southern Louisiana is home to about 700,000 people, about a third of the state, and about 300 miles of coastline. Its heart is 40 miles from the Gulf of Mexico, 70 miles from Texas, and 80 miles from New Orleans. And it's a world unto itself.

Originally called Acadiana, Cajun country was named for its French-Canadian settlers who fled Canadian colonies after the British wrested those colonies from the French in the late 1750s.

Exiles from the prosperous French New World colony of Acadia (which included Nova Scotia, New Brunswick, and Prince Edward Island in Canada, and part of the state of Maine) moved south—all the way south, to Louisiana—to hook up with what was then the largest of the French colonies in the Americas.

They first settled upriver of New Orleans in the area named St. James Parish, and later spread west and founded settlements along Bayou Teche and Bayou Lafourche.

This trio came to be known as Acadiana, and the Acadians who lived there were called "Cajuns."

Today we know that Cajun is not really about geography: It is a culture with its own distinct food, music, economic conditions (both very high and very low), and even governmental traditions. The Cajun culture makes this especially active, vibrant region of Louisiana distinct from all others. It's home to zydeco music, curtains of Spanish moss, hurricane cocktails, and just plain hurricanes. It has streetcars and oyster po'boys. Folks here drink coffee with chicory and eat Tabasco sauce on most things.

The area is also renowned for its Mardi Gras celebrations, its amazing Garden District, and the Audubon Zoo. When people doubt what America has contributed to the world, we would do well to show them this particularly zesty slice of our collective pie.

New Orleans, Louisiana, was founded in 1718 by the Montreal-born French colonist Jean-Baptiste Le Moyne. Called the Crescent City because it sits on a crescent-shaped bend in the Mississippi River, it was ruled variously by Spain and France until the Americans got hold of it in the Louisiana Purchase of 1803, still known as "the greatest land bargain in U.S. history" (more than 800,000 square miles from Mississippi to the Rockies sold for between 3 and 4 cents an acre).

New Orleans constantly ranks in polls, novice-run and expert-produced alike, as one of the nation's top dining destinations. Indeed New Orleanians take food very seriously;

71

Cochon restaurant
New Orleans, Louisiana

When people doubt what America has contributed to
the world, we would do well to show them Cajun Country,
a particularly zesty slice of our collective pie.

it is the local obsession that not even Saints football can compete with—and that's saying a lot in the Drew Brees era.

From the beginning, New Orleans has been a place with its own mind, a rugged individualist among American cities. It has its own vernacular: The streets are *rues*; the counties are parishes. It has its own customs: The dead are buried in above-ground mausoleums (the city is below sea level). It has its own religion: The city has always been predominantly Catholic, as opposed to the Anglo-Saxon Protestant norm of the day in which it was founded. And it has also always been heavily populated by African-Americans.

Well before the Civil War, Africans who entered New Orleans in shackles had the chance to live free and work for themselves. As Lolis Eric Elie, a columnist for the New Orleans *Times-Picayune*, put it: "The French in New

Orleans had different conceptions about slavery than the English in the rest of the country." Slaves could own property, and those who could afford it were allowed to buy their freedom and establish their own part of town.

Tremé (treh-MAY), the first of those areas for freed slaves, today is widely considered the oldest black neighborhood in the United States. Established in the late 1700s and incorporated into New Orleans in 1812, it's where the country's first African-American daily newspaper was born. (Since 2010, the neighborhood has been the subject of a fictional TV program that shares its name and explores the city's long road to recovery and flood-proof culture in the wake of Hurricane Katrina.)

For a time before the Civil War, New Orleans was one of the richest cities in America, and you can see evidence of what that wealth was like

in the Garden District, the premier neighborhood lined with Greek Revival and Victorian-style homes that were built in antebellum days.

New Orleans was firmly with the Confederacy for economic reasons: Slave labor enabled the sugar and cotton plantations of the Mississippi Valley. When the war came, New Orleans was one of the jewels in the Confederacy's crown because it controlled access to the Mississippi River from the Gulf of Mexico.

Despite this, New Orleans wasn't particularly well protected, and the Union took it over in the late spring of 1862. This was a turning point in the War: When the Mississippi River was claimed by the Union forces, the Confederacy was essentially cut in two, making it significantly weaker.

Historians say that brunch was invented in this town: Madame Bégué, a German immigrant to the city who married a Frenchman,

No Taste Like Home

72

Spotted Cat Music Club
New Orleans, Louisiana

Audubon Park
New Orleans, Louisiana

Jackson Square
New Orleans, Louisiana

Historians say that brunch was invented in New Orleans.
So was Bananas Foster, which came about at Brennan's, and
Oysters Rockefeller, which first showed up at Antoine's.

opened a restaurant in 1863 that became famous for its "second breakfast," a multicourse affair served at 11 a.m. daily. (Other dishes invented in New Orleans include Bananas Foster, which came about at Brennan's, and Oysters Rockefeller, which first showed up at Antoine's.)

Parties in New Orleans are legendary. The king is Mardi Gras. Based on thousand-year-old pagan fertility rites including the Roman Saturnalia, Mardi Gras has become one of the great American festivities. (When Christianity came to Rome, the Catholics adopted these festivals. That's why Mardi Gras is associated with Catholicism, why it's held as a precursor to Lent, and how it got its name. In French, *Mardi Gras* means "Fat Tuesday"—a day of feasting before the start of Lenten fasts.)

Mardi Gras has been going on in New Orleans since the city's first days; the earliest one was

held in 1703. Since then it has been dominated by "krewes," local nonprofit crews or clubs financed by dues and fund-raising projects.

It actually starts two weeks before the big Mardi Gras day with parades galore (most follow the same route: St. Charles Avenue through the Uptown, Garden District and Lower Garden District neighborhoods, before proceeding through the Central Business District and disbanding at the border of the French Quarter.)

Notable paraders include the so-called Mardi Gras Indians—African-Americans who feel tied to Native Americans by bloodlines and a history of resistance—who have paraded informally, in terrifically decorated, feathered, beaded, and brightly winged costumes, at Mardi Gras for more than a century.

Everything is purple (for justice), gold (for power), and green (for

faith)—buntings, flags, tinsel displays, masks, wreaths, beads thrown from floats, and the icing on the famous Mardi Gras king cake. Find the little gold or plastic baby Jesus inside for good luck or, some say, the obligation to bring the king cake next year.

The other important New Orleans party is Jazz Fest, officially known as the New Orleans Jazz & Heritage Festival, first held in 1970. When it was founded, Jazz Fest was a very deliberate thing, an attempt by city leaders to recognize New Orleans as the birthplace of jazz.

To that end, they hired George Wein, jazz impresario and the founder of the Newport Jazz Festival, to come down and orchestrate something suitable.

Wein delivered, producing an all-day concert with various acts playing on different stages in a "something for everyone" approach that quickly became an annual tradition.

Today there are some 12 stages, the event lasts four days, and headliners include the likes of Fleetwood Mac. (Previous Jazz Fest performers have included Aretha Franklin, Bob Dylan, Santana, Paul Simon, B.B. King, Lenny Kravitz, Linda Ronstadt, Willie Nelson, and many more legends.)

There's no way to talk about New Orleans without mentioning August 29, 2005, the day Hurricane Katrina—one of the strongest storms to impact the United States in a century—struck the city and breached its levees. "New Orleans will forever exist as two cities," declared a *Times-Picayune* headline. "The one that existed before that date, and the one after."

New Orleans's many fans around the globe watched in horror as the beloved city sank beneath the water, its Superdome filling with more than 10,000 evacuees, boats washing onto highways, residents stranded and trapped in their homes, hundreds dead, and thousands displaced.

Our collective party capital, the Crescent City, was dealt a bracing blow. But New Orleans is a town with a special spirit, and it has risen again—if not exactly to its former carefree glory, then at least to a place where the good times are even more cherished.

In Cajun country proper, the big city is **Lafayette, Louisiana,** about two hours west of New Orleans. How do you know you're in Lafayette? The street signs say Rue instead of Street. You spot herons and ibises, alligators and yellow-bellied turtles along the bayou. Lacy curtains of Spanish moss hang down from the trees, and rows of okra grow in fields nearby.

A bona fide oil boom has made once-poor Lafayette fairly prosperous, though, so now instead of seeing swamp houses you're more likely to find tidy suburbs. (It helps that Hurricane Katrina didn't much touch the town, too.)

In nearby Breaux Bridge, about 10 minutes away from Lafayette, you can experience what is quite possibly the best amalgam of music and food anyplace, anywhere: the "zydeco breakfast" held at Café Des Amis every Saturday from 8:30 to 11:30 a.m. It's a bit early for some, but it's always packed. They garnish your Bloody Mary with pickled green beans and serve platters of cheese grits with andouille sausage and floorboard-shaking, accordion-driven dance music.

Cajun food is defined by its unique mixture of French home-cooking techniques and bayou ingredients. The latter refers to everything from the okra that the African slaves brought over and the cayenne

New Orleans is a town with a special spirit, and it has risen again—
if not exactly to its former carefree glory, then at least to a place
where the good times are even more cherished.

The Whirlybird dance hall
St. Landry Parish, Louisiana

Spotted Cat Music Club
New Orleans, Louisiana

Folklore suggests that only Louisianans can tell the difference between Creole and Cajun. But of course that doesn't stop people from trying.

pepper imported from the Caribbean to the native Louisiana blue crabs, crawfish ("suck the head, and eat the tail"), oysters, and shrimp. It's a heady combination that has naturally led to the headiest and most aromatic and richly spiced dish in the American food canon: gumbo.

Another regional favorite is jambalaya. "Jambalaya and a crawfish pie and filé gumbo / 'Cause tonight I'm gonna see my *ma cher amio*. / Pick guitar, fill fruit jar and be gay-o / Son of a gun, we'll have big fun on the bayou." So sang the late, great Hank Williams Sr. in 1952.

In many ways, jambalaya is the ultimate fusion dish: It was first made by Spanish settlers in New Orleans who were seeking to re-create their own paella—but the Cajuns quickly adopted it and made it their own.

Jambalaya is one of those robust, throw-everything-in-the-pot meals, a crowd-pleaser with especially bright,

zesty flavors, that's just designed to feed a group. Traditionally, it features shellfish, chicken giblets, spicy andouille sausage, and tasso ham (the peppery smoked pork made not from the hind leg but from the fattier shoulder).

It's made by browning the meat in a cast-iron pot; adding onions, celery, and green peppers, and sautéing until they are soft; adding rich stock and seasonings and uncooked rice; and simmering over very low heat until the rice is fully cooked.

Variations of the dish and theories on the origin of the name abound. Some say it's a cross between *jamon* and *paella*. Some suspect it comes from the African term *ya* for rice. Others hold that it came from the Provençal word *jambalaia*, meaning mishmash. In Cajun country everybody claims this dish.

Now is a good time to talk about Creole cooking, which is essentially

the other thing that goes on in New Orleans and its surroundings. The distinction between Creole and Cajun is difficult to define. Folklore suggests that only Louisianans can tell the difference. But of course that doesn't stop people from trying.

"Creole cooking is more refined than Cajun," concluded *New York Times* food editor Craig Claiborne in a 1987 column on gumbo. "While its origins are also classic French, it was influenced by Spanish, African, Italian, and Native American cuisines—that is, by the culinary practices of the ethnic groups that settled in Louisiana." And indeed there is a New Orleans proverb that goes something like this: "A Creole can feed one family with three chickens, and a Cajun can feed three families with one chicken."

In general, Creoles lived in the city and had access to better markets and ingredients, while Cajuns lived in the country and had to make do with

what was available beyond the city limits. The famous New Orleans chef Paul Prudhomme has said that the difference comes down to African-American people who, as cooks in many Louisiana homes, incorporated the various styles of cooking into their own. In Creole homes, there were servants; in Cajun homes, there were not.

Cajun and Creole cuisines have grown up together and informed each other so much that it's easier to talk about what they have in common than how they differ. The main conjoiner, as it were, is roux. The base for almost all of the classic French sauces, roux is the starter for the classic gumbos and stews of both Cajun and Creole kitchens.

A classic French chef would say that a roux is a blend of butter (or some other fat, such as lard) and flour. Cajun and Creole chefs take the formula and make it their own, creating a veritable rainbow of roux colors, cooking it until it is dark blond to flavor chicken and other light-meat dishes, sautéing it until it is medium-brown to flavor

game dishes, and roasting it until it is almost mahogany for gumbo. Louisiana's chefs say this proprietary, much-sweated-over roux gives a good gumbo its characteristic richness and nutty flavor.

While some argue that Creole roux is made from butter and the Cajun variety is made from lard, others swear by the opposite. Both sides tend to agree that when you want to make a roux, you can't even think about leaving the stove to stop stirring until the entire gumbo or stew has come together. Then you get to leave it alone for hours so the flavors will meld and marry.

In Cajun country, the supper club tradition is alive and well—only these aren't dress-up, stuffy, cocktail party-type affairs. You can don your cowboy boots and eat your crawfish and do the two-step.

In fact, music is integral to enjoying the food in Cajun country. Along with their roux, the Cajuns fleeing Canada for Louisiana brought their French folk music traditions.

These, like the food, became mingled with the local ingredients

and customs and took on many variations.

The fiddle drives traditional Cajun music, which in general has lyrics and a woeful tone. Though born of the same roots, zydeco is something different altogether. It's basically what happens when the blues meet French traditions, and it's a party: Hard-driving accordions chime in with the fiddles, basses, guitars, and percussion instruments.

The best thing that can happen to you when eating in these parts is to find yourself in a place with great examples of both the food and the sound.

Cajun country is the kind of place where a certain authenticity of spirit is prized.

As the infamously freewheeling political consultant James "The Ragin' Cajun" Carville once advised, "stand for yourself, be for something, and the hell with it."

Down here, folks are going to have a good time, dance well, and eat the best that they can for as long as they can. Let the good times roll, indeed.

Welcome to
the Bayou

Ki ça di? That's "what's up?" in Louisiana Creole, one of three French-based languages in Cajun country. The others are straight-up French and Cajun Creole, and when you go to New Orleans and parts nearby, you will hear all of these spoken.

Also sometimes called Haitian Creole, Louisiana Creole is heavily influenced by aspects of west and central African linguistics. It's the language of some natives of Cajun country.

Cajun Creole, on the other hand, derives more from the language spoken in the French colony of Acadia at the time the Acadians were expelled. But even it is not pure, deriving some of its vocabulary from the Spanish, German, Portuguese, and Haitian Creole that it met when it got to Louisiana.

None of these holds allegiance to any one tradition in Louisiana, and all are wildly entertaining to hear, though they can be a barrier to the uninitiated. You already know ki ça di (kee-sah-DEE) means "what's up." Here are a few more to help you get your bearings:

Cher is an abbreviation of the French *cherie,* meaning "sweetheart" or "dear." Pronounced "sha," you'll hear it in calls from friendly business owners when you walk in—as in, "How ya doin', cher?" *Dat* means "that," and *dey* means "they." To crawfish means to "back out of a deal."

It only adds to the region's charm when you decipher what someone means when he says: *"Fisça da Geda ywum ywum doun bayeou!"* (Loose translation: "We relish hunting alligators in the bayou—and eating them, too.")

~ A Recipe from a Local ~

Hurricane Punch

Sweep away your cares with this fruity but potent cocktail.

Makes 8 ¼ cups   Hands-On Time 5 min.   Total Time 5 min.

½ (64-oz.) bottle red fruit punch

½ (12-oz.) can frozen limeade
   concentrate, thawed

1 (6-oz.) can frozen orange juice
   concentrate, thawed

1 ⅔ cups light rum

1 ⅔ cups dark rum

1. Stir together all ingredients. Serve over ice.

Kathy Bowes
Metairie, Louisiana

Crab Cake Hush Puppies

Hush puppies were perhaps the original dog treat. Legend has it that Southern fishermen and Civil War soldiers made the golden nuggets from scraps and tossed them to barking and begging dogs with the simple command: "Hush, puppy." This version is bound to hush your mouth, too.

Makes 8 servings (about 32 hush puppies)
Hands-On Time 30 min.   Total Time 40 min.

1	cup self-rising white cornmeal mix	¼	tsp. table salt
½	cup self-rising flour	8	oz. fresh lump crabmeat, drained
3	green onions, thinly sliced	1	large egg
½	cup finely chopped red bell pepper	¾	cup beer
1	Tbsp. sugar		Vegetable oil

1. Stir together cornmeal mix, flour, green onions, bell pepper, sugar, and salt in a large bowl.

2. Pick crabmeat, removing any bits of shell. Stir in crabmeat, egg, and beer until just moistened. Let stand 10 minutes.

3. Pour oil to depth of 2 inches into a Dutch oven; heat to 360°.

4. Drop batter by tablespoonfuls into hot oil, and fry, in batches, 2 to 3 minutes or until golden brown, turning once. Serve with your favorite rémoulade or cocktail sauce.

Rémoulade

You can make this sauce ahead to serve with boiled shrimp, spread on sandwiches, or use as a dip for hush puppies. Leftover sauce will keep in the refrigerator up to two weeks.

Makes 5 cups   Hands-On Time 10 min.   Total Time 10 min.

6	garlic cloves, peeled	¼	cup yellow mustard
3	celery ribs, chopped	2	Tbsp. mild paprika
⅓	cup white vinegar	2	Tbsp. Worcestershire sauce
½	cup egg substitute	1	Tbsp. hot sauce or to taste
¼	cup ketchup	1	tsp. ground red pepper
¼	cup prepared horseradish	1½	cups vegetable oil
¼	cup Creole mustard	6	green onions, sliced

1. Process first 12 ingredients in a blender or food processor until smooth. With blender running, pour oil in a slow, steady stream until thickened. Stir in green onions; add kosher salt and black pepper to taste. Cover and chill until ready to serve.

Meet Chef John Besh

The face most associated with the post-Katrina modern food scene in New Orleans belongs to John Besh.

Born in Meridian, Mississippi, and raised in southern Louisiana, Besh was cooking at the highest level at his New Orleans restaurant August long before the hurricane. But it was afterward that he came to symbolize the city's dedication to getting back on its feet, starting first at the table. A former Marine who led an infantry squad in the Persian Gulf War, Besh toured his flooded city in a little speedboat delivering food.

His efforts earned him just about every award there is for feeding people, including a "best new chef" moniker from *Food & Wine* and a best restaurant award for August from the James Beard Foundation.

He's now busy raising four boys and running nine restaurants (eight in New Orleans and one in San Antonio, Texas.) His eateries range from upscale French-Cajun canteen August to Soda Shop, a cafe inside the National World War II Museum.

"This recipe requires high-quality wild shrimp. Of course, I prefer wild Gulf shrimp from the waters I know. You can mix up your vegetables with the shrimp, using whatever's fresh and local." —John Besh

Pickled Shrimp

Makes 10 servings   Hands-On Time 40 min.
Total Time 1 hour, 15 min., plus 1 day for pickling

BRINE
2   cups rice vinegar
Zest and juice of 1 lemon
Zest and juice of 1 orange
½   cup sugar
1   Tbsp. coriander seeds
1   Tbsp. mustard seeds
1   Tbsp. black peppercorns
1   Tbsp. dried crushed red pepper
5   garlic cloves, thinly sliced
2   bay leaves
Pinch of kosher salt

REMAINING INGREDIENTS
2   lb. unpeeled large wild Gulf shrimp
12   small carrots with tops
12   fresh green beans
12   pearl onions, peeled
12   small fresh okra

1. Prepare the Brine: Combine all brine ingredients in a large nonreactive saucepan. Add 2½ cups water, and bring to a boil. Remove pan from heat, and cool 10 minutes.

2. Prepare the Remaining Ingredients: Bring a large pot of salted water to boil; add shrimp, and remove pan from heat. Let stand 1 minute or until shrimp turn pink. Drain and rinse with cold water. Peel and devein. Peel carrots, trim greenery to 1 inch, and halve lengthwise. Pack shrimp, carrots, green beans, pearl onions, and okra in alternating layers into a 1-gal. glass jar or very large glass bowl. Pour hot brine to cover over the shrimp and vegetables. Cover and cool. Refrigerate overnight. Serve right from the jar when you're ready.

~ You've Gotta Try ~
Gumbo

Gumbo defines Cajun cooking; it is the iconic dish, the sterling example of what "melting pot cuisine" looks like. A soup-stew that evolved over many years and many stoves. Gumbo means a different thing in every kitchen in which it's cooked.

It almost always involves crabmeat and shrimp, sometimes oysters, sometimes chicken, sometimes okra (the name is said to come from the African word for okra), and always a dark brown sauce with a roux (a combination of fat and flour that thickens and enriches many dishes in and beyond Cajun country).

Gumbo may be seasoned and further thickened with filé (the powdered, dried leaves of the sassafras tree), spiked with spicy tasso or Spanish chorizo or both, scented with bay leaf, and bruised with plenty of black pepper.

~ A Recipe from a Local ~

Chicken-Tasso-Andouille Sausage Gumbo

Tasso is a spicy, cayenne-rubbed, smoked pork popular in many Cajun dishes.

**Makes 5 qt. (about 20 servings)   Hands-On Time 45 min.
Total Time 5 hours**

1. Cut first 3 ingredients into bite-size pieces. Place in a large Dutch oven over medium heat, and cook, stirring often, 20 minutes or until browned. Drain on paper towels. Wipe out Dutch oven with paper towels.

2. Heat oil in Dutch oven over medium heat; gradually whisk in flour, and cook, whisking constantly, 25 minutes or until mixture is a dark mahogany.

3. Stir in onion and next 3 ingredients; cook, stirring often, 18 to 20 minutes or until tender. Gradually add broth. Stir in chicken, sausage, tasso, thyme, black pepper, and ground red pepper.

4. Bring mixture to a boil over medium-high heat. Reduce heat to medium-low, and simmer, stirring occasionally, 2 1/2 to 3 hours. Stir in parsley. Remove from heat; serve over hot cooked rice.

For Shrimp-Tasso-Andouille Sausage Gumbo: Omit chicken thighs and, in Step 4, stir in 4 lb. medium-size raw shrimp, peeled and deveined, during the last 15 minutes of cooking.

Philip Elliott
Baton Rouge, Louisiana

4	lb. skinned and boned chicken thighs
1	lb. andouille or smoked sausage
1	lb. tasso or smoked ham
1	cup vegetable oil
1	cup all-purpose flour
4	medium onions, chopped
2	large green bell peppers, chopped
2	large celery ribs, chopped
4	large garlic cloves, minced
4	(32-oz.) boxes chicken broth
1 1/2	tsp. dried thyme
1	tsp. black pepper
1/2	tsp. ground red pepper
1/3	cup chopped fresh parsley

Hot cooked rice

Garnishes: sliced green onions or chopped fresh parsley, filé powder

Meet Chef Emeril Lagasse

Easily one of the most well-known and well-loved chefs in America, Emeril Lagasse became an early star on the Food Network while cooking in New Orleans.

The South was, perhaps, an unlikely destination for Lagasse, a native of Fall River, Massachusetts, who found his passion for cooking in high school while working in a Portuguese bakery. After culinary school in Rhode Island, and stints in France and the Northeast, Lagasse was hired in 1982 by the famed Brennan family of New Orleans restaurateurs, to take over their flagship Crescent City restaurant, Commander's Palace, from Paul Prudhomme.

He left Commander's Palace in 1990 to open Emeril's. It was an instant hit, a fusion of all of the flavors Emeril himself loved best, including Cajun, Portuguese, and Italian. It was named Restaurant of the Year by *Esquire* that year.

Today, Lagasse has an empire of restaurants (13 at last count), a line of cookware, and a thick stack of best-selling cookbooks. In addition, he runs a foundation that supports children's enrichment programs in and around New Orleans.

These oyster po'boys are from his 2012 cookbook, *Emeril's Kicked-Up Sandwiches.*

"Oh, baby. The crispy fried 'ersters,' the salty bacon, and the creamy avocado all come together in this ultimate oyster sandwich. If you've ever wanted to re-create the experience of a fried oyster po'boy from New Orleans, save the flight—this is it!" —Emeril Lagasse

Fried Oyster Po'Boys with Jalapeño Mayonnaise and Avocado

Traditional New Orleans po'boy loaves are airy, long French breads. If you cannot find po'boy bread in your area, substitute any long Italian or French bread loaves that are not too dense. If the only bread you can find is very dense, consider pinching out the center doughy portions so that your po'boy is not overly bready.

Makes 4 servings   Hands-On Time 40 min.   Total Time 1 hour, 10 min.

1¼ cups buttermilk	4 (8-inch) lengths po'boy bread or French or Italian loaves, split lengthwise
½ cup your favorite Louisiana red hot sauce	
¼ ·cup Emeril's Original Essence or Creole seasoning, divided	3 Tbsp. butter, melted
	Jalapeño Mayo
4 dozen oysters, shucked and drained [or 2 (16-oz.) containers]	1 cup shredded lettuce
	1 medium tomato, thinly sliced
1½ cups masa harina (corn flour)	1 avocado, thinly sliced
1½ cups all-purpose flour	8 to 12 cooked bacon slices
Vegetable oil	

1. Combine the buttermilk, hot sauce, and 2 Tbsp. of the Essence in a medium mixing bowl, and stir to combine. Add the oysters, and marinate in the refrigerator up to 30 minutes.

2. In a separate medium bowl, combine the masa harina, all-purpose flour, and remaining 2 Tbsp. Essence; stir to blend.

3. Pour oil to depth of 2½ inches into a medium-size heavy pot or deep-fryer; heat to 360°. Working in batches, remove the oysters from the buttermilk marinade, and transfer them to the masa harina mixture. Dredge to coat, shaking to remove any excess breading. Cook the oysters in small batches in the hot oil 2 to 3 minutes or until golden brown and crispy. Remove with a slotted spoon, and transfer to paper towels to drain. Sprinkle with salt and black pepper to taste.

4. To assemble: Spread the bottom halves of the bread with the melted butter. Generously spread the top halves of the bread with Jalapeño Mayo. Divide the oysters evenly among the bottom halves, followed by the lettuce, tomato, avocado, and bacon. Place the top halves of the bread over the fillings and press lightly. Cut each sandwich in half, and serve immediately.

Jalapeño Mayo

Keep this in the fridge to wake up your old standby roast beef or turkey-and-cheese sandwich, or use it with fried seafood, such as the oyster po'boy.

Makes 1³⁄₄ cups   Hands-On Time 15 min.   Total Time 15 min.

1. In a food processor or a blender, combine the egg, egg yolk, cilantro (if using), lemon juice, garlic, mustard, and jalapeños; process until smooth. With the motor still running, add the oil in a thin stream until a thick emulsion is formed. Add the salt and pepper, and transfer the mayonnaise to a nonreactive container. Cover and refrigerate until ready to use or up to 3 days.

Note: This recipe is prepared with raw eggs. Consuming raw eggs may increase your risk of foodborne illness. For a cooked alternative, omit the egg, egg yolk, and salt, and blend the remaining ingredients into 1¹⁄₂ cups prepared mayonnaise (such as Hellmann's).

1   large egg, at room temperature
1   large egg yolk, at room temperature
2   Tbsp. chopped fresh cilantro leaves (optional)
1   Tbsp. freshly squeezed lemon juice
1   tsp. minced garlic
½   tsp. Dijon mustard
2   to 3 jalapeños, stemmed, seeded, and chopped
1   cup vegetable oil
¾   tsp. table salt
¼   tsp. freshly ground black pepper

Welcome to
the Boudin Trail

Boudin is distinctive to Cajun country. What's special about this sausage is not just how it's made and how delicious it is, but also how it's eaten.

If you think you already know what boudin (BOO-dan) is, you're probably thinking of its French ancestors, *boudin blanc* (a white-meat-only sausage made of pork and chicken) and *boudin noir* (a darker, richer version of the same, made with pig blood). In Cajun country, boudin is something else altogether, a sausage made from the shoulder, neck, and sometimes trotters (that means feet) and liver of the hog, combined with rice, onion, lots of freshly ground black pepper, and a bit of cayenne.

The meat is coarsely ground, mixed with the other ingredients, usually by hand, and either rolled into sausage balls and fried ("boudin balls") or pumped into casings, and then either gently simmered or smoked until done. Here's where it gets interesting: To eat boudin like a Cajun, you bite a hunk off the link, and then, using your fingers or, preferably, just your teeth, you pull the meat out of the casing. This is often but not always accompanied with bracing Creole mustard (like Dijon, but spicier), a cold beer, and maybe some crackers. It is messy, it is visceral, and it is not for the faint of heart; that said, it is singularly delicious.

Although Cajun country is not exactly enormous, it offers a TON of boudin joints to choose from. Lots of folks like the Eunice Superette & Slaughter House. Others swear by Johnson's Boucaniere in Lafayette. The Lafayette Parish Convention and Visitors Commission's website (www.cajunboudintrail.com) lists the best places to get your boudin on.

T-Boy's
Mamou, Louisiana

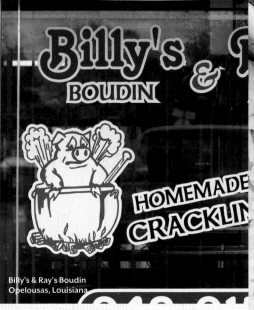

Billy's & Ray's Boudin
Opelousas, Louisiana

John's Red Beans & Rice

This one–dish meal is a favorite comfort food served throughout Louisiana. Long simmering helps the flavor develop.

Makes 10 to 12 servings
Hands-On Time 30 min.
Total Time 3 hours, 55 min.

1   (16-oz.) package dried red kidney beans
1   lb. mild smoked sausage, cut into ¼-inch-thick slices
1   (½-lb.) smoked ham hock, cut in half
¼   cup vegetable oil
3   celery ribs, diced
1   medium-size yellow onion, diced
1   green bell pepper, diced
3   bay leaves
3   garlic cloves, chopped
2   Tbsp. salt-free Cajun seasoning
1   tsp. kosher salt
1   tsp. dried thyme
1   tsp. ground black pepper
3   (32-oz.) boxes reduced-sodium chicken broth
Hot cooked rice

1. Place beans in a large Dutch oven; add water 2 inches above beans. Boil 1 minute; cover, remove from heat, and let stand 1 hour. Drain.

2. Cook sausage and ham in hot oil in Dutch oven over medium-high heat 8 to 10 minutes or until browned. Drain sausage and ham on paper towels, reserving 2 Tbsp. drippings. Add celery and next 8 ingredients to drippings; cook over low heat, stirring occasionally, 15 minutes.

3. Add broth, beans, sausage, and ham to Dutch oven. Bring to a simmer. Cook, stirring occasionally, 2 hours or until beans are tender. Discard ham hock and bay leaves. Serve over hot cooked rice.

Chef-Owner John Harris, Lilette Restaurant New Orleans, Louisiana

New Orleans Barbecue Shrimp

When you see the words barbecue and shrimp together in New Orleans, don't be looking for the grill. Barbecue shrimp here is actually a lot more like a Belgian mussels dish, with the main ingredient cooked up a skillet at a time in a flavorful sauce, served in bowls, and eaten with your hands and plenty of good bread to sop up the sauce. This version involves marinating the shrimp ahead of time for maximum flavor and finishing them in the oven for incredible ease.

Makes 6 to 8 servings   Hands-On Time 10 min.
Total Time 2 hours, 30 min.

4   lb. unpeeled, large fresh shrimp
    or 6 lb. large shrimp with heads on
½   cup butter
½   cup olive oil
¼   cup chili sauce
¼   cup Worcestershire sauce
2   lemons, sliced
4   garlic cloves, chopped
2   Tbsp. Creole seasoning
2   Tbsp. lemon juice
1   Tbsp. chopped parsley
1   tsp. paprika
1   tsp. oregano
1   tsp. ground red pepper
½   tsp. hot sauce
French bread

1. Spread shrimp in a shallow, aluminum foil-lined broiler pan.

2. Combine butter and next 12 ingredients in a saucepan over low heat, stirring until butter melts, and pour over shrimp. Cover and chill 2 hours, turning shrimp every 30 minutes.

3. Preheat oven to 400°. Bake, uncovered, for 20 minutes; turn once. Serve with bread.

Chicken, Shrimp, and Ham Jambalaya

Rice is the main thing in jambalaya. After that, anything goes. This recipe, adapted from Eula Mae's Cajun Kitchen *by legendary Cajun cooks Eula Mae Doré and Marcelle R. Bienvenu, involves shrimp, chicken, and ham. But you can incorporate smoked sausage, pork, oysters, or whatever you have on hand. For more kick, add an extra dash of hot sauce to each serving.*

Makes 6 to 8 servings   Hands-On Time 45 min.
Total Time 1 hour, 50 min.

2 lb. unpeeled, medium-size raw shrimp	2 medium-size yellow onions, chopped (2 cups)
1 ½ lb. skinned and boned chicken thighs, cut into 1-inch cubes	2 celery ribs, chopped (1 cup)
1 tsp. table salt	1 medium-size green bell pepper, chopped (1 cup)
⅛ tsp. freshly ground black pepper	3 cups chicken broth
⅛ tsp. ground red pepper	1 (14.5-oz.) can diced tomatoes
2 Tbsp. vegetable oil	3 green onions, chopped (½ cup)
½ lb. cooked ham, cut into ½-inch cubes	2 Tbsp. chopped fresh parsley
	2 cups uncooked long-grain rice
4 garlic cloves, chopped	1 tsp. hot sauce

1. Peel shrimp; devein, if desired.

2. Sprinkle chicken evenly with salt, black pepper, and red pepper.

3. Heat oil in a Dutch oven over medium heat. Add chicken, and cook, stirring constantly, 8 to 10 minutes or until browned on all sides. Remove chicken using a slotted spoon.

4. Add ham to Dutch oven, and cook, stirring constantly, 5 minutes or until lightly browned. Remove ham using a slotted spoon.

5. Add garlic and next 3 ingredients to Dutch oven; stir to loosen particles from bottom. Stir in ham and chicken. Cover, reduce heat to low, and cook, stirring occasionally, 20 minutes.

6. Add chicken broth. Bring to a boil over medium-high heat; cover, reduce heat to low, and simmer 35 minutes. Add tomatoes and next 3 ingredients. Bring to a boil over medium-high heat; cover, reduce heat to medium-low, and simmer 20 minutes. Stir in shrimp and hot sauce; cook, covered, 10 more minutes or until liquid is absorbed and rice is tender.

Meet Actress
Angela Kinsey

The uptight, often-grumpy character whom Angela Kinsey plays on the American version of the popular British TV show *The Office* is known for her disagreeable, stuck-up attitude—and her love of cats.

This fictional Angela Martin is also so diminutive in size that Steve Carrell's character, Michael Scott, compares her to "a grain of rice."

In real life, however, Kinsey is upbeat and larger-than-life hilarious. She got her start in the acting world through her involvement in various improvisational and sketch comedy troupes, including The Groundlings and The Improv Olympic Theater.

Kinsey was born in Lafayette and into a family of good cooks. They moved to Indonesia for her father's job when she was a small child, came back to the States in her early teens, and settled in north Texas. Kinsey has a killer Texas-Louisiana accent to prove it, plus a trove of recipes from her mom, Bertie.

"I totally rely on my mom, Bertie, for recipes and inspiration. I'm learning to cook. It's hard to eat out with a 2-year-old, and I'm not going to be a takeout mom." —Angela Kinsey

Bertie's Corn Casserole

Makes 8 servings   Hands-On Time 15 min.   Total Time 40 min.

1	Tbsp. butter	1 ¾	cups (7 oz.) shredded sharp Cheddar cheese, divided
½	large onion, finely chopped		
½	green bell pepper, finely chopped	1 ½	tsp. table salt
4	cups cooked long-grain rice	½	tsp. freshly ground black pepper
2	cups drained canned whole kernel corn	¾	cup milk
		1	large egg

1. Preheat oven to 350°. Melt butter in a medium nonstick skillet over medium-high heat; add onion and bell pepper, and sauté 5 minutes or until tender. Transfer to a large bowl; add cooked rice and corn. Mix well. Add 1 ½ cups shredded cheese, salt, and pepper. Mix all together. Whisk together milk and egg; stir into rice mixture.

2. Spoon into a lightly greased 2-qt. baking dish, and sprinkle with remaining ¼ cup cheese. Bake at 350° for 25 minutes or until thoroughly heated.

Oak Alley Plantation
Vacherie, Louisiana

Cajun-Baked Catfish

Fried catfish is a favorite in and beyond Louisiana. This oven-fried version renders flavorful and crispy fish with no deep-frying and less mess.

Makes 4 servings   Hands-On Time 15 min.   Total Time 45 min.

2	cups cornmeal	2	Tbsp. Cajun seasoning
2	tsp. table salt	1	to 2 tsp. seasoned salt
1	Tbsp. black pepper	¼	cup butter, melted
8	(3- to 4-oz.) catfish fillets		Garnish: lemon wedges

1. Preheat oven to 400°. Combine first 3 ingredients. Dredge catfish fillets in cornmeal mixture; place fillets, skin sides down, on a greased baking sheet.

2. Combine Cajun seasoning and seasoned salt; sprinkle over fillets. Drizzle with butter.

3. Bake at 400° for 30 minutes or until golden and fish flakes with a fork.

~ A Recipe from a Local ~

Creole Potato Salad

**Makes 10 to 12 servings   Hands-On Time 35 min.
Total Time 1 hour, 10 min.**

5	lb. baby red potatoes	1½	cups finely chopped celery
¼	cup dry shrimp-and-crab boil seasoning	1	cup finely chopped green onions
12	hard-cooked eggs, peeled and chopped	1½	Tbsp. Creole seasoning
		2	cups mayonnaise
		⅓	cup Creole mustard

1. Bring potatoes, shrimp-and-crab boil seasoning, and 4 qt. water to a boil in a large stockpot over high heat. Boil 20 minutes or until tender; drain and cool 20 minutes.

2. Peel potatoes; cut into ¾-inch pieces. Toss together potatoes, eggs, and next 3 ingredients; stir in mayonnaise and mustard.

For Cajun Shrimp Potato Salad: Stir in 1 lb. peeled, medium-size cooked shrimp.

Sharon Cheadle
Slidell, Louisiana

Crawfish

Crawfish is what they're typically called in Louisiana, although "crayfish" is generally preferred almost everywhere else. Also known as "mudbugs" or "crawdads" down South, crawfish are freshwater crustaceans that look like miniature lobsters.

The diminutive creatures, which thrive at the bottom of muddy waters, are closely related to, and often referred to as a small freshwater version of, the much-lauded lobster. Their meat is delicate and sweet, the flesh meltingly tender, the flavor concentrated. Crawfish meat is "the candy of the salty world," the great Cajun chef Paul Prudhomme has said. "It has a very sweet, creamy, twice-as-rich-as-lobster taste."

The preparation and adoration of crawfish most likely began in France (where a European variety is raised), traveled to Nova Scotia, and then migrated to New Orleans right along with the French Canadians. Prime breeding ground for crawfish is in the nearly 1 million acres of wooded swampland known as the Atchafalaya Basin in south-central Louisiana. In the surrounding areas, locals discovered that they could raise crawfish in ponds, and that crawfish were an ideal crop to rotate with rice.

Although you can easily buy cooked crawfish tails frozen year-round, as many Cajun restaurants do, fresh crawfish do indeed have a season, from late January to early June. Their abundance in the area gave rise to the traditional spring crawfish boils in which great cauldrons of shellfish are boiled in spiced water and dumped onto newspaper-lined tables, along with sausages and sometimes new potatoes and sweet corn, for family and neighbors to feast upon. At boils, crawfish are eaten in the most traditional way: "Suck the head, and eat the tail," as the saying goes. The head is where delectable fatty meat is stored, and the tail is a nice little chunk of tender seafood.

Crawfish are sacred to the cooks of Cajun country in other ways, too. Probably the single most popular presentation is in a rich one-pot stew called étouffée. It literally means "smothered" and, like so many Cajun dishes, begins with a roux. Historians say it was created in the 1920s in the kitchens of the old Hebert Hotel in the town of Breaux Bridge, about 9 miles northeast of Lafayette in St. Martin Parish.

Today Breaux Bridge bills itself as the "crawfish capital of the world." The town hosts an annual crawfish festival the first weekend in May which, naturally, involves a crawfish étouffée cook-off.

How to Shell a Crawfish

1. Twist and snap head away from tail. Set aside.*
2. Peel shell away from widest part of tail.
3. Hold tip of tail; gently pull out tender meat.

Note: Suck flavorful juices from the head, if desired.

Crawfish Boil

Nothing is better on a spring or early summer night than a traditional Louisiana crawfish boil. Repeat as needed to feed a crowd. Serve with lemon wedges, hot sauce, rémoulade, French bread, and good Louisiana beer.

Makes 4 servings
Hands-On Time 1 hour
Total Time 2 hours, 25 min.

10	bay leaves
1	cup table salt
¾	cup ground red pepper
¼	cup whole allspice
2	Tbsp. mustard seeds
1	Tbsp. coriander seeds
1	Tbsp. dill seeds
1	Tbsp. dried crushed red pepper
1	Tbsp. black peppercorns
1	tsp. whole cloves
4	celery ribs, quartered
3	medium onions, halved
3	garlic bulbs, halved crosswise
2	lb. new potatoes
1	lb. andouille sausage
5	lb. crawfish

1. Bring 1½ gallons water to a boil in a 19-qt. stockpot over high heat. Add bay leaves and next 12 ingredients to water. Return to a rolling boil. Reduce heat to medium, and cook, uncovered, 15 minutes.

2. Add potatoes and sausage. Return to a rolling boil over high heat. Cook 10 min.

3. Add crawfish. Return to a rolling boil; cook 5 minutes. Remove stockpot from heat; let stand 30 minutes. (For spicier crawfish, let stand 45 minutes.) Drain. Serve crawfish, potatoes, and sausage on large platters or newspaper.

Jacques-Imo's Cafe
New Orleans, Louisiana

Crawfish Étouffée

You'll need 6 to 7 lb. cooked whole crawfish for 1 lb. of hard-earned crawfish tail meat. You can also substitute frozen, cooked, peeled crawfish tails.

Makes 4 to 6 servings   Hands-On Time 25 min.   Total Time 35 min.

- ¼ cup butter
- 1 medium onion, chopped
- 2 celery ribs, chopped
- 1 medium-size green bell pepper, chopped
- 4 garlic cloves, minced
- 1 large shallot, chopped
- ¼ cup all-purpose flour
- 1 tsp. table salt
- ½ tsp. to 1 tsp. ground red pepper
- 1 (14 ½-oz.) can chicken broth
- ¼ cup chopped fresh parsley
- ¼ cup chopped fresh chives
- 2 lb. cooked, peeled crawfish tails
- Hot cooked rice
- Garnishes: chopped fresh chives, ground red pepper

1. Melt butter in a large Dutch oven over medium-high heat. Add onion and next 4 ingredients; sauté 5 minutes or until tender. Add flour, salt, and red pepper; cook, stirring constantly, until caramel colored (about 10 minutes).

2. Add broth and next 2 ingredients; cook, stirring constantly, 5 minutes or until thick and bubbly. Stir in crawfish; cook 5 minutes or until thoroughly heated. Serve with rice.

Hot Crawfish Dip

In Louisiana, February means two things: Mardi Gras and crawfish. Two-thirds of all mudbugs are harvested in February. Most locals start with a boil. What's leftover goes into crawfish étouffée, crawfish pie, and luscious appetizer dips like this one.

Makes 8 to 10 servings   Hands-On Time 30 min.   Total Time 30 min.

- ½ cup butter
- 1 bunch green onions, sliced (about 1 cup)
- 1 small green bell pepper, diced
- 1 (1-lb.) package frozen cooked, peeled crawfish tails, thawed and undrained
- 2 garlic cloves, minced
- 1 (4-oz.) jar diced pimiento, drained
- 2 tsp. Creole seasoning
- 1 (8-oz.) package cream cheese, softened
- Toasted French bread slices
- Garnishes: sliced green onion, chopped flat-leaf parsley

1. Melt butter in a Dutch oven over medium heat; add green onions and bell pepper. Cook, stirring occasionally, 8 minutes or until bell pepper is tender. Stir in crawfish and next 3 ingredients; cook, stirring occasionally, 10 minutes. Reduce heat to low. Stir in cream cheese until mixture is smooth and bubbly. Serve with toasted French bread slices.

Meet Cajun Maven
Kay Robertson

Kay Robertson stars in A&E Network's smash hit *Duck Dynasty*, a reality show that chronicles the life and times of a Louisiana bayou family.

They make cedar duck calls and run a successful sport-hunting business. Miss Kay is the matriarch who brings the family together with her Cajun cooking.

Kay is fully aware of her power, wielding her kitchen skills to settle disputes and foster happy relations amongst her brood. Consequently, she usually ends up feeding all of the family and most of the neighborhood.

Her most famous dishes are banana pudding, fried deer steak, sticky frog legs, and this crawfish pie, which is essentially the Cajun version of a chicken pot pie.

"I was raised in my grandma's kitchen. My first memories are right there in that kitchen—learned how to do everything right there. I loved it from the very start. Food is the language, and I know how to speak it." —Kay Robertson

Crawfish Pies

These pies are perfect for a crowd. If you have fewer folks to feed, freeze one of the pies, unbaked, for later. You can thaw it in the refrigerator overnight and bake as directed when you're ready.

Makes 2 (9-inch) pies (8 servings each)
Hands-On Time 30 min.   Total Time 1 hour, 45 min.

2	Tbsp. butter	1	(10 ¾-oz.) can cream of
2	Tbsp. olive oil		mushroom soup
1 ¾	cups diced green bell pepper	1	Tbsp. Cajun seasoning
1	cup diced white onion	½	tsp. table salt
½	cup diced celery	1	tsp. black pepper
¼	cup chopped green onions		Pastry for 2 (9-inch) double-crust
8	garlic cloves, chopped		pies or 2 (14.1-oz.) packages
1 ½	Tbsp. cornstarch		refrigerated piecrusts
1	(5-oz.) can evaporated milk	1	large egg, lightly beaten
3	lb. peeled crawfish tails*		

1. Preheat oven to 350°. Melt butter with olive oil in a large cast-iron skillet over high heat. Add bell pepper and next 3 ingredients; cook, stirring occasionally, 8 minutes or until tender and starting to brown. Add garlic; cook 1 minute. Mix cornstarch with evaporated milk; add to skillet. Reduce heat to medium. Stir in crawfish and cream of mushroom soup; cook, stirring constantly, 3 minutes or until thickened. Remove from heat; stir in Cajun seasoning, salt, and pepper.

2. Fit 1 piecrust into each of 2 (9-inch) pie plates. Prick bottom and sides of piecrusts with a fork. Divide crawfish mixture between pies. Cover with remaining piecrusts; fold edges under, and crimp, sealing to bottom crust. Cut slits in top for steam to escape. Brush piecrusts with egg.

3. Bake at 350° for 45 minutes or until golden brown. Let stand 30 minutes before serving.

Note: You can use frozen pre-cooked crawfish tails or peeled shrimp for the crawfish.

Creole Bread Pudding with Bourbon Sauce

This bread pudding is from New Orleans chef Leah Chase, the "Queen of Creole Cuisine." And yes, it does call for 5 Tbsp. of vanilla extract!

Makes 10 to 12 servings   Hands-On Time 20 min.
Total Time 1 hour, 15 min.

2 (12-oz.) cans evaporated milk	1 ½ cups sugar
6 large eggs, lightly beaten	1 cup raisins
1 (16-oz.) day-old French bread loaf, cubed	5 Tbsp. vanilla extract
1 (8-oz.) can crushed pineapple, drained	¼ cup butter, cut into ½-inch cubes and softened
1 large Red Delicious apple, upeeled and grated	Bourbon Sauce
	Garnish: fresh currants

1. Preheat oven to 350°. Whisk together evaporated milk, eggs, and 1 cup water in a large bowl until well blended. Add bread cubes, stirring to coat thoroughly. Stir in pineapple and next 4 ingredients. Stir in butter, blending well. Pour into a greased 13- x 9-inch baking dish.

2. Bake at 350° for 35 to 45 minutes or until set and crust is golden. Remove from oven, and let stand 2 minutes. Serve with Bourbon Sauce.

Bourbon Sauce

Makes 1 ½ cups   Hands-On Time 20 min.   Total Time 20 min.

3 Tbsp. butter	2 Tbsp. bourbon
1 Tbsp. all-purpose flour	1 Tbsp. vanilla extract
1 cup whipping cream	1 tsp. ground nutmeg
½ cup sugar	

1. Melt butter in a small saucepan over medium-low heat; whisk in flour, and cook, whisking constantly, 5 minutes. Stir in cream and sugar; cook, whisking constantly, 3 minutes or until thickened. Stir in bourbon, vanilla, and nutmeg; cook, whisking constantly, 5 minutes or until thoroughly heated.

Chef Leah Chase, Dooky Chase's Restaurant
New Orleans, Louisiana

Bananas Foster Upside-Down Cake

The flaming wonder invented in New Orleans inspired this upside-down cake, which tumbles from the skillet, perfectly golden and party ready.

Makes 8 servings   Hands-On Time 20 min.   Total Time 1 hour, 20 min.

½	cup chopped pecans	¾	cup granulated sugar
½	cup butter, softened and divided	2	large eggs
		¾	cup milk
1	cup firmly packed light brown sugar	½	cup sour cream
2	Tbsp. rum	1	tsp. vanilla extract
2	ripe bananas	2	cups all-purpose baking mix
		¼	tsp. ground cinnamon

1. Preheat oven to 350°. Bake pecans in a single layer 8 to 10 minutes or until toasted and fragrant, stirring once.

2. Melt ¼ cup butter in a lightly greased 10-inch cast-iron skillet or 9-inch round cake pan (with sides that are at least 2 inches high) over low heat. Remove from heat; stir in brown sugar and rum.

3. Cut bananas diagonally into ¼-inch-thick slices; arrange in concentric circles over brown sugar mixture. Sprinkle pecans over bananas.

4. Beat granulated sugar and remaining ¼ cup butter at medium speed with an electric mixer until blended. Add eggs, 1 at a time, beating just until blended after each addition. Add milk and next 2 ingredients; beat just until blended. Beat in baking mix and cinnamon until blended (batter will be slightly lumpy). Pour batter over banana mixture in skillet. Place skillet on an aluminum foil-lined jelly-roll pan.

5. Bake at 350° for 40 to 45 minutes or until a wooden pick inserted in center comes out clean. Cool in skillet on a wire rack 10 minutes. Run a knife around edge to loosen. Invert onto a serving plate, spooning any topping in skillet over cake.

Traditional King Cake

If you like, hide a heat- and food-safe plastic baby (or a raisin or nut) in the dough of this Mardi Gras treat for one lucky (or unlucky) diner to find.

Makes 2 cakes (about 18 servings each)   Hands-On Time 30 min.
Total Time 2 hours, 30 min.

1. Cook first 4 ingredients in a medium saucepan over low heat, stirring often, until butter melts. Set aside; cool to 100° to 110°.

2. Stir together yeast, ½ cup warm water, and 1 Tbsp. sugar in a 1-cup glass measuring cup; let stand 5 minutes.

3. Beat sour cream mixture, yeast mixture, eggs, and 2 cups flour at medium speed with a heavy-duty electric stand mixer until smooth. Reduce speed to low, and gradually add enough remaining flour (4 to 4½ cups) until a soft dough forms. Turn dough out onto a lightly floured surface; knead until smooth and elastic (about 10 minutes). Place in a well-greased bowl, turning to grease top.

4. Cover and let rise in a warm place (85°), free from drafts, 1 hour or until dough is doubled in bulk.

5. Punch down dough, and divide in half. Roll each portion into a 22- x 12-inch rectangle. Spread ⅓ cup softened butter evenly on each rectangle, leaving a 1-inch border. Stir together ½ cup sugar and cinnamon, and sprinkle evenly over butter on each rectangle.

6. Roll up each dough rectangle, jelly-roll fashion, starting at 1 long side. Place 1 dough roll, seam side down, on a lightly greased baking sheet. Bring ends of roll together to form an oval ring, moistening and pinching edges together to seal. Repeat with second dough roll.

7. Cover and let rise in a warm place (85°), free from drafts, 20 to 30 minutes or until doubled in bulk.

8. Preheat oven to 375°. Bake for 14 to 16 minutes or until golden. Slightly cool cakes on pans on wire racks (about 10 minutes). Drizzle Creamy Glaze evenly over warm cakes; sprinkle with colored sugars, alternating colors and forming bands. Cool completely.

For Cream Cheese-Filled King Cake: Prepare each 22- x 12-inch dough rectangle as directed. Omit ⅓ cup softened butter and 1½ tsp. ground cinnamon. Increase ½ cup sugar to ¾ cup sugar. Beat ¾ cup sugar; 2 (8-oz.) packages cream cheese, softened; 1 large egg; and 2 tsp. vanilla extract at medium speed with an electric mixer until smooth. Spread cream cheese mixture evenly on each dough rectangle, leaving 1-inch borders. Proceed with recipe as directed.

1   (16-oz.) container sour cream
⅓   cup sugar
¼   cup butter
1   tsp. table salt
2   (¼-oz.) envelopes active dry yeast
½   cup warm water (100° to 110°)
1   Tbsp. sugar
2   large eggs, lightly beaten
6   to 6 ½ cups bread flour
⅓   cup butter, softened
½   cup sugar
1½   tsp. ground cinnamon
Creamy Glaze
Purple-, green-, and gold-tinted
    sparkling sugar sprinkles

Creamy Glaze

Makes 1½ cups   Hands-On Time 5 min.   Total Time 5 min.

3   cups powdered sugar
3   Tbsp. butter, melted
2   Tbsp. fresh lemon juice

¼   tsp. vanilla extract
2   to 4 Tbsp. milk

1. Stir together first 4 ingredients. Stir in 2 Tbsp. milk, adding additional milk, 1 tsp. at a time, until spreading consistency.

Welcome to
Bird Haven

Lake Martin, on the Cypress Island Preserve in the Cajun town of Breaux Bridge, is a birdwatcher's paradise.

It's one of the largest and most important wading-bird rookeries in the country. Scientists believe it was formed more than 6,000 years ago, the result of a Mississippi River flood. In 1953 the State of Louisiana encircled its 765 acres with a levee, and now it's a recreation area—and not just for people. Each spring until about July, some 20,000 herons, ibises, and other long-legged birds nest in the cypress trees and wade the swamps.

Any time of year is good for watching birds at Lake Martin, though. Swamp tour companies offer private tours to make it easy to spot the birds, most of which nest in the 250 acres at the southern end of the lake. We're talking little and great blue herons, cattle and snowy egrets, black-crowned and yellow-crowned night herons—plus songbirds such as warblers, vireos, grosbeaks, and buntings.

Plenty of gators live here, too. Just ask those swamp guides.

~ A Recipe from a Local ~

Coconut-Almond Cream Cake

If the tops of the layers are a little rounded, level them with a serrated knife. This is a tall cake, and it needs to be level if you want your friends to admire your work before they devour it, as they absolutely will.

Makes 12 servings   Hands-On Time 30 min.
Total Time 2 hours, 30 min.

2 cups sweetened flaked coconut	1 cup firmly packed light brown sugar
½ cup sliced almonds	
Parchment paper	5 large eggs
3 ½ cups all-purpose flour	1 cup whipping cream
1 Tbsp. baking powder	⅓ cup coconut milk
½ tsp. table salt	1 Tbsp. vanilla extract
1 ½ cups unsalted butter, at room temperature	1 Tbsp. almond extract
	Coconut-Almond Filling
1 ¼ cups granulated sugar	Coconut-Cream Cheese Frosting

1. Preheat oven to 325°. Bake coconut in a single layer in a shallow pan 6 minutes. Place almonds in a single layer in another shallow pan; bake, with coconut, 7 to 9 minutes or until almonds are fragrant and coconut is lightly browned, stirring occasionally.

2. Line 3 (9-inch) round cake pans with parchment paper. Grease and flour paper. Sift together flour, baking powder, and salt in a very large bowl.

3. Beat butter at medium speed with a heavy-duty electric stand mixer until creamy; gradually add sugars, beating until blended. Beat 8 minutes or until very fluffy, scraping bottom and sides of bowl as needed. Add eggs, 1 at a time, beating well after each addition (about 30 seconds per egg). Stir in whipping cream and next 3 ingredients.

4. Gently fold butter mixture into flour mixture, in batches, just until combined. Pour batter into prepared pans. Bake at 325° for 30 to 32 minutes or until a wooden pick inserted in center comes out clean. Cool in pans on wire racks 10 minutes; remove from pans to wire racks, and cool completely (about 1 hour).

5. Place 1 cake layer on a serving plate. Spread half of chilled Coconut-Almond Filling over cake layer. Top with 1 layer, pressing down gently. Repeat procedure with remaining half of Coconut-Almond Filling and remaining cake layer. Gently spread Coconut-Cream Cheese Frosting on top and sides of cake. Press toasted coconut onto sides of cake; sprinkle toasted almonds on top.

Coconut-Almond Filling

This filling is the glue that holds the layers together. It works best when chilled, so be sure not to skip that step.

Makes 3 cups   Hands-On Time 10 min.   Total Time 8 hours, 15 min.

1. Stir together cornstarch, almond extract, and 2 Tbsp. water in a small bowl.

2. Bring whipping cream, brown sugar, and butter to a boil in a saucepan over medium heat. Remove from heat, and immediately whisk in cornstarch mixture. Stir in coconut and sour cream. Cover and chill 8 hours.

2 Tbsp. cornstarch
1 tsp. almond extract
1¼ cups whipping cream
½ cup firmly packed light brown sugar
½ cup unsalted butter
2¼ cups loosely packed sweetened flaked coconut
¼ cup sour cream

Coconut-Cream Cheese Frosting

Makes about 3 cups   Hands-On Time 10 min.   Total Time 10 min.

2 (8-oz.) packages cream cheese, softened
½ cup unsalted butter, softened
2 cups powdered sugar
1 Tbsp. cream of coconut
1 tsp. vanilla extract

1. Beat cream cheese and butter at medium speed with an electric mixer until creamy. Gradually add powdered sugar, beating at low speed until blended. Increase speed to medium, and beat in cream of coconut and vanilla until smooth.

Brooks Hamaker
New Orleans, Louisiana

Café au Lait Pecan Pralines

Makes 2 dozen   Hands-On Time 35 min.   Total Time 1 hour, 20 min.

2	cups pecan halves and pieces	¼	cup butter
3	cups firmly packed light brown sugar	2	Tbsp. light corn syrup
2	Tbsp. instant coffee granules	1	tsp. vanilla extract
1	cup whipping cream		Wax paper

1. Preheat oven to 350°. Bake pecans in a single layer in a shallow pan 8 to 10 minutes or until toasted and fragrant, stirring halfway through. Cool completely (about 15 minutes).

2. Meanwhile, bring brown sugar and next 4 ingredients to a boil in a heavy Dutch oven over medium heat, stirring constantly. Boil, stirring occasionally, 6 to 8 minutes or until a candy thermometer registers 236° (soft ball stage). Remove sugar mixture from heat.

3. Let sugar mixture stand until candy thermometer reaches 150° (20 to 25 minutes). Stir in vanilla and pecans using a wooden spoon; stir constantly 1 to 2 minutes or just until mixture begins to lose its gloss. Quickly drop by heaping tablespoonfuls onto wax paper; let stand until firm (10 to 15 minutes).

Vieux Carré

Offer this classic 1930s cocktail after dinner. Vieux Carré (voo cah–RAY) means "old square," a reference to the French Quarter.

Makes 1 serving   Hands-On Time 5 min.   Total Time 5 min.

	Crushed ice	1	tsp. Bénédictine liqueur
2	Tbsp. (1 oz.) rye whiskey	2	dashes Peychaud's bitters
2	Tbsp. (1 oz.) cognac	2	dashes Angostura bitters
2	Tbsp. (1 oz.) sweet vermouth		Lemon twist or lemon peel strip

1. Fill 1 (8-oz.) glass with crushed ice. Pour rye whiskey and remaining ingredients into glass; stir. Top with a lemon twist or lemon peel strip. Serve immediately.

The Praline Connection
New Orleans, Louisiana

Say 'Praline' Like a Local

The candy of New Orleans is the praline, an old-fashioned confection made with pecans, milk, butter, and lots of teeth-sticking sugar.

It's a freeform candy, meaning that instead of being poured into a mold, it's poured onto a baking sheet while hot and allowed to harden in any old shape. Pralines are sold on the street, in drugstores, and in candy shops in the French Quarter and far beyond.

Legend has it that Ursuline nuns from France brought a recipe for almond candy when they came to New Orleans in 1727, but finding no almonds, they improvised with local pecans.

You'll find similar confections today in France and Belgium and Luxembourg, but nowhere else in the world are they pronounced the way that they are in New Orleans: "prah-lean."

Café au Lait Pecan Pralines

Rough Creek Lodge and Resort
Glen Rose, Texas

Four Sixes Ranch
Guthrie, Texas

Big, Bold Texas

In his sweeping historical novel *Texas*, Pulitzer Prize-winning author James Michener writes: "Texas is so big that you can live your life within its limits and never give a damn about what anyone in Boston or San Francisco thinks." Indeed, the bigness of Texas cannot be overstated.

With more than 267,000 square miles, Texas makes up 7.4 percent of the nation's total land mass. It's the largest state in the Lower 48. More land is farmed, more sheep are raised, and more wool is produced in Texas than in any other state. More species of bats live here, too, including 1.5 million of the Mexican free-tailed species that congregate under the Congress Avenue Bridge in Austin each summer.

But it's not just the grand physical size—it's the big attitude. You can find lots of big hair and big talkin' in Texas. And no one is more proud of this image than Texans themselves. They're a varied and diverse crowd, united only by a notion that theirs is the best state. The legendary pride of Texans probably comes in no

small part from the state's origins. If you were paying attention in history class, you'll know Texas fought for its independence from Mexico and was its own sovereign nation from 1836 to 1845.

It's also big ideas. The Lone Star State is home to one of America's first suspension bridges (the Waco Bridge built in 1870), the country's first domed stadium (the Astrodome built in Houston in 1965), and the world's first rodeo (held in Pecos on July 4, 1883, although other states also claim this "first"). Dr Pepper was invented in Waco, and in Texas, it is illegal to graffiti someone else's cow.

Fueling a lot of the big aspirations, independence, and swagger is big money. AT&T, Exxon, Southwest Airlines, J.C. Penney, Kimberly-Clark,

Dell, and Marathon Oil: These Fortune 500 companies are all headquartered in Texas. What brought the money in the first place was the oil. And what followed in Texas's biggest cities, especially Dallas and Houston, was a proliferation of got-rich-quick people trying to figure out how to class up the place.

Thanks in no small part to oil monies, Texas now offers citizens and visitors some serious fine arts.

Take Dallas, for example: I.M. Pei, the great modernist Chinese-American architect, designed its sharp-angled, impressively windowed Meyerson Symphony Center. (It was funded in large part by H. Ross Perot, the Texarkana native, former two-time presidential candidate, and founder of Electronic Data Systems

Fort Worth, Texas

Alpine, Texas

Everything's bigger in Texas: the hair, the talk, the attitude. From cowboys to musicians to artists, Texans are a proud bunch, united by the notion that theirs is the best state.

who made a mint when he sold the company to General Motors in 1984 and again when he sold his second company, Perot Systems, to Dell for $3.9 billion.)

The beloved Dallas Symphony Orchestra has played Carnegie Hall, the Kennedy Center, and the great halls of Europe. And the Nasher Sculpture Center, opened in 2003, features expansive indoor and out-door garden spaces in which you can view works by Joan Miró, Alexander Calder, and Isamu Noguchi.

San Antonio boasts the Nelson A. Rockefeller Center for Latin American Art at the San Antonio Museum of Art. Its centerpiece: a staggering collection of Mexican folk art that provides an artistic connection to the state's Mexican heritage that no other museum in the world can rival.

Austin claims the annual South by Southwest Music and Media

Conference, a massive showcase for up-and-coming and established bands, record labels, independent filmmakers, and the techie set. It's a pop-culture fiesta like no other, a kind of modern Woodstock for a new breed of hippies, ambitious performers, and media enthusiasts with money and stamina.

Football is a big deal all over the South, but it's something else entirely in Texas, as anyone who has ever been there knows. Whether it's a kids' team playing or the pros, Texans' devotion to the pigskin is unmatched. "Sectional football games have the glory and despair of war," John Steinbeck wrote, "and when a Texas team takes the field against a foreign state, it is an army with banners."

The pinnacle, of course, is the Dallas Cowboys, a franchise founded in 1960 and coached for 29 years by football legend Tom Landry. The

cheerleading squad, which debuted in earnest in the 1972-1973 season, is no small part of the attraction. Incidentally, while basketball is generally not a big deal in Texas, the San Antonio Spurs are hometown hoopster heroes—especially the "Twin Towers" of (now retired, ever beloved) David "The Admiral" Robinson and Tim Duncan. The team hasn't missed the NBA playoffs since 1997.

To discuss Texas properly, at a certain point you've got to break it down into manageable chunks, the first and most obvious being the **Dallas-Fort Worth** area. What do most Americans know about Dallas? They know about J.R. Ewing and his family's Southfork ranch, they know that this is where Neiman Marcus was founded, and they know that President John Fitzgerald Kennedy was shot here in November 1963 (more about JFK on page 118).

Nearby Fort Worth is much less discussed but no less full of wealth and bluster. "Where the West Begins" is its motto, after all.

Once the terminus of the Chisholm Trail, the well-worn route cowboys used when they drove cattle from Texas ranches to Kansas railheads, Fort Worth today is less honky-tonk than it is Bassville, a nod to oil baron Sid Bass and his father and brothers, who all number among the world's billionaires. The Bass family has given the city the Nancy Lee and Perry R. Bass Performance Hall. Inspired by the old limestone European opera houses, it's a major Fort Worth landmark and a big part of the revitalized downtown.

Founded in 1836, **Houston** is always mentioned in terms of its sprawl, its miles of commercial and residential development, its relentless capitalism buoyed by its history as a city built by oil. Since that first gusher of petroleum spurted on January 10, 1901, the spoils that came rolling in with it have driven the city.

Houston's infrastructure could never quite keep up with its rapid expansion. Because of this, today it is a thriving, vibrant, busy-feeling city but not an especially beautiful one. It does, however, have real pockets of gorgeousness.

Take the lushly landscaped River Oaks neighborhood, one of the wealthiest neighborhoods in America. It's got its own country club and chamber orchestra, and its notable residents have included oil baron Oscar Wyatt, professional basketball player Clyde Drexler, and the tough-talking Texas journalist Molly Ivins.

Main Street
Dallas, Texas

Mission Espada Church
San Antonio, Texas

And the Bayou Bend Collection and Gardens, which offers free general admission one day a week, has an honest-to-goodness lazy river flowing through its 14 acres of statues, fountains, and magnificent azalea gardens.

Oil money built Houston and sustained it for a long, long time, but the city wasn't immune to modern economic struggles. The Enron scandal, revealed in 2001, hit the city hard. What was once the nation's seventh largest company was busted for major fraud, costing its shareholders billions and leaving a hole in the fine arts community. Enron had been a major backer of the city's arts programs and institutions.

Today, Houston is a thriving multicultural port with some excellent culture, renowned institutions, and some incredibly serious shopping.

Start with The Galleria, the largest shopping center in Texas and the fourth largest in the country. It's home to Saks Fifth Avenue, Nordstrom, Houston's branch of Neiman Marcus, and not one but two Macy's department stores—plus boutique outposts of Fendi, Gucci, Louis Vuitton, Chanel, Prada, and Valentino—not to mention 12 beauty salons, an ice-skating rink, a video game arcade, a post office, and 30 restaurants.

But wait—there's culture, too! The Alley Theatre, running since 1947 and one of the country's oldest theaters with stage actors in residence, has hosted world premieres for Tony Award-winning plays that went straight from there to Broadway.

Houston also has Rice University, "the Ivy League of Texas" (some student chat boards boast: "You almost forget what state you're in!"), and Texas Medical Center, not only

the largest but also one of the finest in the country.

San Antonio lays claim to the most enduring symbol of the "us-versus-them" mentality in Texas: the Alamo, the Spanish mission site where Texas defenders fell to the Mexican general Santa Anna in March 1836 in the battle for Texas independence. After a dramatic 13-day standoff in which they were vastly outnumbered, the band of almost 200 men eventually was conquered; all of them died, including Davy Crockett.

The defeat became a rallying cry ("Remember the Alamo!"), inciting Texans led by Sam Houston to take down Santa Anna a couple of weeks later and win independence. The event, according to many historians, served as inspiration for Americans to forge ahead with the Mexican-American War a decade later.

Unlike Dallas and Houston, San Antonio had a rich culture well before foreign arrivals or oil. It's an *old* Texas city—and the one with the closest ties to its Mexican roots.

Mi Tierra Cafe
San Antonio, Texas

King William District
San Antonio, Texas

Long a prime stop between Mexico City and Louisiana, San Antonio is the birthplace of Tex-Mex food.

Money is less a factor in San Antonio's collective mentality than it is in many other Texas cities. By and large, San Antonio's a lot poorer than other Texas top dogs. It's also a lot older. Founded by Native Americans who made camps along its riverbanks, San Antonio became a Spanish mission settlement in 1718. It's a rare Texas city with a history that doesn't depend on foreign arrivals or oil, and it's the one with the closest ties to its Mexican roots.

In its earliest years, San Antonio was a prime stop on the *Camino Real*, the "royal road" linking Mexico City to Louisiana. Nowhere is this more evident than in its food scene; San Antonio is the birthplace of Tex-Mex food.

The hybrid cuisine sprang up in the days when Texas was part of Mexico's outer reaches and the folks who moved there from central Mexico had to make do with what they could find there, giving rise to crisp-shelled tacos, chile con queso, and chips and salsa. Award-winning food writer and *Saveur* co-founder Colman Andrews described Tex-Mex food as "the working-class fare of Mexico (especially northern Mexico), but cooled down and Americanized and expressed through ingredients like ground meat, garlic powder, chili powder, and processed cheese."

The combination plate is the defining symbol of Tex-Mex and, according to Andrews, should include enchiladas (cheese or ground beef, preferably) with refried beans and seasoned Spanish rice on the side—and maybe a taco or tamale to boot. Andrews contends that Tex-Mex food is no less authentic than the regional Mexican varieties to be found south of the border.

Food and music are equally beloved in **Austin,** whose burgeoning culinary, college, and music scenes make it hard not to love. The city resonates with a distinctive and lively college town vibe, one of the nation's most beloved. The University of Texas at Austin campus spans more than 350 acres, houses more than 50,000 students, and is home to the Texas Memorial Stadium, where the Longhorns play football.

Austin is also the state capital, the most southerly in the continental United States, and has a huge domed pink granite Capitol to show for it. The mixture of collegiate counterculture, margaritas, and local politics does a lot to give Austin its flavor.

A major tech boom in the 1990s also did much to put Austin on the map, infusing the town with dough, which helped feed its fine arts scene. During that era, Austin's work force grew by a full two-thirds.

The big boom was followed by a bust, but through it entrepreneur Michael Dell remained front and center in Austin's tech revolution. Once America's youngest Fortune

500 company chief executive and routinely among its richest, richer than the Basses or Perot, Dell made his money not in software but in hardware. He sold computers directly to the public and created a whole bunch of "Dellionaires"—folks who were among the company's first employees—in the process.

Viewed through its food markets, Austin is both the Berkeley and the Hong Kong of the South. Opened in 1994 and modeled on the old-fashioned European food hall, the flagship Central Market Grocery Store is one of Austin's most popular tourist destinations, claiming more than 2 million visitors a year.

It's an enormous place with an enormous selection: 700 kinds of cheese; more than 100 varieties of saltwater and freshwater fish and seafood flown in daily from Hawaii, Ecuador, and Maine; 150 varieties of organic produce. It's not just for locavores, for in Texas people love things from Texas and can easily find them all over. Instead, it's a kind of food lover's museum where it's OK to taste and smell what's on offer.

Whole Foods Market also began in Austin. Its flagship store opened in 1980 as a tribute to what was then called the natural foods movement (and what today we just call healthy eating). It was such a mom-and-pop organization in those days that cofounder and co-CEO John Mackey, today a powerful force in food legislation in the United States, lived in the store and reportedly bathed in its Hobart dishwasher.

Nowadays Whole Foods is most Americans' first experience with organic food and a powerful symbol of food's importance in our collective national culture.

Even though Austin has more dollars in circulation today than it used to, it retains a distinctively hippie feeling. Bumper stickers, T-shirts, and graffiti proclaim "Keep Austin Weird." Austinites love their reputation as laid-back, music-and-beer-loving, barbecue-eating, bicycle-riding folks who just like a little peace (and some organic kale on the side.)

Excellent examples include singer Willie Nelson and actor Matthew McConaughey, who both live here, as do tennis ace Andy Roddick and his *Sports Illustrated* model wife, Brooklyn Decker, and noted filmmakers Robert Rodriguez and Richard Linklater. Billy Bob Thornton has a house here, and so does Led Zeppelin's lead singer, Robert Plant. And celebrities from Bill Murray to Drew Barrymore drop in during the annual music, tech, and cultural happening that is South by Southwest.

Austin is a big-in-its-own-right, bold-in-its-own-way draw for a state that has more than its share of big, bold enticements.

Austin has more dollars in local circulation today than it used to, but it retains a distinctively hippie feeling.

Room Service Vintage
Austin, Texas

South Congress Avenue
Austin, Texas

Welcome to
Dallas

Even if they've never been near Dallas, most Americans associate it with one big happening and three capital letters: JFK.

Dallas, of course, was where President John F. Kennedy was assassinated on November 22, 1963. A somber X painted on Elm Street marks the spot where at least one bullet struck the president as his motorcade rolled by. Conspiracy theorists still take up residence and talk up visitors on the grassy knoll near the Texas School Book Depository, now the Dallas County Administration Building. The top two floors house The Sixth Floor Museum, which features historical exhibits and public programming.

And the Texas Theatre, where convicted assassin Lee Harvey Oswald was arrested, still stands on West Jefferson Boulevard. The venue's life before and after the tragedy mirrors that of Dallas itself.

The Texas Theatre was a big deal when it opened in 1931. The largest in Dallas and the first in the state to have air-conditioning, the theater was fitted with state-of-the-art sound and projection equipment for its time and had all kinds of architectural flourishes: towers and campaniles, *trompe l'oeil* stars and clouds on the ceilings, and, outside, an enormous neon sign spelling out T-E-X-A-S.

The depression that the city sank into after the Kennedy assassination affected the theater: The facade and many of the interior details were covered up with Spanish-style stucco. It closed due to poor ticket sales in 1989. Director Oliver Stone restored the exterior to its former appearance for his movie *JFK*. The interior was renovated in early 2005.

Today it's a bar, a theater showing mostly independent movies, and a must-visit for students of American history.

Margaret Hunt Hill Bridge
Dallas, Texas

Bloody Mary Punch

Instead of stirring all the ingredients together, you can serve optional shots of vodka on the side and let guests add it or not, depending on their preference.

Makes 1½ qt.   Hands-On Time 5 min.   Total Time 5 min.

1   (46-oz.) container low-sodium vegetable juice, chilled*
1   Tbsp. freshly ground black pepper
3   Tbsp. fresh lime juice
1   Tbsp. hot sauce
1   Tbsp. Worcestershire sauce
½   tsp. Old Bay seasoning
½   cup vodka (optional), chilled
Celery sticks (optional)
Garnishes: pickled okra, lemon slices

1. Combine vegetable juice, next 5 ingredients, and, if desired, vodka in a punch bowl or a pitcher. Serve over ice in glasses with celery sticks, if desired.

Note: We tested with V8 Low Sodium 100% Vegetable Juice.

Meet Choreographer Judy Trammell

Dancing is both a passion and a way of life for Judy Trammell, choreographer of the Dallas Cowboys Cheerleaders.

A former squad member herself, Trammell is a Texas native who studied jazz, tap, drill team, and pom-pom routines as a child and worked her way up to running the routines for the international phenomenon the squad is today. If you've watched a Cowboys game in the past few decades, chances are that Trammell choreographed the halftime show, plus the sideline routines and pregame dances. She has been involved, in one way or another, with the squad since 1980.

She also appears on the CMT network show *Dallas Cowboys Cheerleaders: Making the Team*, now in its eighth season. Viewers see an ever-poised Trammell as she judges potential cheerleaders on their grace, style, dance, and performance abilities.

Though the cheerleading uniform is famously unforgiving, Trammell is known among her family and friends for her delicious down-home cooking. (Don't worry, Judy. We won't tell 'em it's healthy.)

"I use this to top my favorite pasta. And sometimes I like it with a little grilled tilapia, too. I put a fillet with chunky sauce inside a foil pouch, place it on a preheated medium-high grill, cook it until the fish is flaky, and finish it with a squeeze of lemon." —Judy Trammell

Chunky Tomato and Veggie Sauce

Makes 7 to 8 cups   Hands-On Time 15 min.   Total Time 45 min.

3	(10-oz.) package sweet red grape tomatoes	1	bunch green onions, chopped with some of the greens
2	tsp. minced garlic	1	yellow bell pepper, chopped
¼	cup extra virgin olive oil	1	red bell pepper, chopped
¼	cup butter (optional: you can omit if you're really trying to be healthy)	1	orange bell pepper, chopped
		½	tsp. table salt
1	white onion, chopped	1	tsp. black pepper

1. Cut tomatoes in quarters, and cook over medium heat in a large sauté pan with the garlic, olive oil, and butter about 5 minutes. Add remaining ingredients, and sauté to your liking. (I like mine crunchy with the vegetables almost raw, which takes the sauce about 5 more minutes. If you like yours softer, cover and simmer the sauce for about 30 minutes.)

Peppery Texas Freezer Pickles

This easy pickle starts in the microwave, moves to the fridge, and finishes in the freezer so there's no heating up your kitchen—especially nice in Texas.

Makes 3 qt.   Hands-On Time 15 min.
Total Time 20 min., plus 2½ days for chilling and freezing

1. Place first 5 ingredients in a large glass or plastic bowl.

2. Combine vinegar, 1 cup water, sugar, and next 2 ingredients in a large glass measuring cup. Microwave at HIGH 3 minutes; remove from microwave, and stir until sugar dissolves. Pour hot mixture evenly over cucumber mixture. Cover and chill 48 hours.

3. Spoon evenly into 1-qt. canning jars or freezer containers, leaving ½ inch of room at the top; seal, label, and freeze 8 hours or up to 6 months. Thaw in refrigerator before serving; use thawed pickles within 1 week.

2	lb. pickling cucumbers, sliced
1	cup chopped fresh cilantro
6	small dried red chile peppers
4	garlic cloves, thinly sliced
1	large sweet onion, sliced
3	cups white vinegar (5% acidity)
⅓	cup sugar
2	Tbsp. canning-and-pickling salt
1	Tbsp. pickling spices

Lime-Cornmeal Cookies

Meet Country Star Miranda Lambert

She grew up in the small East Texas town of Lindale, 88 miles southeast of Dallas and once the blackberry capital of the world.

And Miranda Lambert is something else: A gorgeous blonde babe with a tough-talkin', pistol-packin', take-no-prisoners persona. Her first three albums went platinum, she's been the Country Music Association's female vocalist of the year, and she is a tireless tour performer around the country. She got her start as a runner-up on the TV show *Nashville Star* and, with her trademark feisty determination, made it onto the country music scene.

Along the way, she acquired an equally charismatic performer for a husband, one Mr. Blake Shelton, who has turned her into an Oklahoma girl. "I'm from Texas," Lambert says, "Just as much as I love Texas, I now love Oklahoma."

"My mom, Bev, and I have cooked together as far back as she could bring a stool to the kitchen counter, and her meatloaf has always been my favorite recipe. It's been the choice 'birthday dish' for me and my brother since we were little."

—Miranda Lambert

Bev's Famous Meatloaf

Makes 10 servings   Hands-On Time 25 min.   Total Time 2 hours

2 lb. lean ground beef	1 Tbsp. Worcestershire sauce
1 lb. ground pork sausage	1 tsp. yellow mustard
18 saltine crackers, crushed	½ cup firmly packed brown sugar, divided
½ green bell pepper, diced	
½ onion, finely chopped	½ cup ketchup
2 large eggs, lightly beaten	

1. Preheat oven to 350°. Combine first 8 ingredients and ¼ cup brown sugar in a medium bowl just until blended. Place mixture in a lightly greased 11- x 7-inch baking dish, and shape into a 10- x 5-inch loaf.

2. Bake at 350° for 1 hour. Remove from oven, and drain. Stir together ketchup and remaining ¼ cup brown sugar; pour over meatloaf. Bake 15 more minutes or until a meat thermometer inserted into thickest portion registers 160°. Remove from oven; let stand 20 minutes. Remove from baking dish before slicing.

Numbers are not always the best way to take a city's pulse. But few cities boast numbers as impressive as Houston's.

Start with land area: Houston's 634 square miles are big enough to contain the entire New York City metropolitan area.

America's fourth-most-populous city also has one of its largest museum districts: 18 venues within walking distance of one another. These include the Children's Museum of Houston, the country's most-visited youth museum; the Rothko Chapel, a cathedral as well as a museum that *GQ* calls one of the "most mind-blowing, energizing, unorthodox and flat-out-cool places to experience art in America"; and the Health Museum, an educational institution with a giant human body exhibit that includes a 22-foot-long backbone and ceiling-to-floor ribs.

Fourteen major institutions of higher education call Houston home, including Rice University, Baylor University, and the University of Houston (and its prestigious Thurgood Marshall School of Law). Its Texas Medical Center is the site of the most heart transplants each year in the world (and also the first successful human heart transplant in 1968).

There are more than 8,000 restaurants, 50,632 acres of park space, and 90 languages spoken in Houston. And "Houston" was the first word spoken in space, when astronaut Neil Armstrong uttered the words, "Houston, Tranquility Base here. The Eagle has landed."

No fewer than five major fashion brands have launched here, including the high-end cosmetics giant Laura Mercier and the Jackie O-favorite footwear brand Bernardo. At least a dozen block-buster movies have been filmed here, including *Terms of Endearment* and the indie favorite *Rushmore*.

Mojo Chicken with Mandarin-Black Bean Salad

Mix up the Mandarin–Black Bean Salad and take a siesta while the chicken marinates.

Makes 4 servings   Hands-On Time 10 min.   Total Time 45 min.

¼ cup fresh orange juice
¼ cup fresh lime juice
2 garlic cloves, minced
1 tsp. ground cumin
½ tsp. dried oregano, crushed
½ tsp. paprika

½ tsp. table salt
4 (5-oz.) boneless, skinless chicken breasts
Mandarin-Black Bean Salad
Garnish: fresh mint sprigs

1. Combine first 7 ingredients in a zip-top freezer bag or shallow dish; add chicken. Cover or seal, and let stand 20 minutes. Remove chicken from marinade, reserving marinade. Pat chicken dry with paper towels.

2. Lightly grease a large nonstick skillet; heat skillet over medium-high heat. Add chicken, and cook 4 to 5 minutes on each side or until desired degree of doneness. Remove chicken from skillet, and keep warm.

3. Wipe skillet clean. Add reserved marinade, and bring to a boil. Boil 2 minutes, stirring often.

4. Cut chicken diagonally into ½-inch-thick slices. Spoon Mandarin-Black Bean Salad in center of 4 serving plates. Arrange chicken slices around salad, and drizzle chicken evenly with warm marinade.

Mandarin-Black Bean Salad

Makes about 4 cups   Hands-On Time 10 min.   Total Time 10 min.

2 cups mandarin orange segments, well drained
1 cup canned black beans, rinsed and drained
¾ cup diced jicama

2 Tbsp. chopped red onion
2 Tbsp. seeded, minced jalapeño
2 Tbsp. shredded fresh mint leaves
¼ tsp. table salt

1. Stir together all ingredients in a large bowl. Let stand until ready to serve, tossing occasionally.

Gloria Duke
Tomball, Texas

Houston Vietnamese Food

There is serious Vietnamese food to be eaten in Texas, both "authentic" and hybrid versions (no less authentic, but more amalgamated), and both delicious. Houston has a sizable population of Vietnamese immigrants, who came to the United States after the fall of Saigon in the 1970s. Almost immediately they gravitated to the warm weather on Houston's Gulf Coast, and a lot of them found work in the seafood business.

The inevitable happened from there: The Vietnamese set up shrimp shacks on the port and began making their way into area food markets and restaurants. Along with them came some of their signature dishes—a few of which Texans have adopted and enjoyed enough to make staples. In Texas, you'll find good pho, the Vietnamese beef noodle soup, not to mention the spicy, crunchy, cilantro-topped banh mi sandwiches that are now part of the national zeitgeist (pork, pickles, peppers, and pâté on a French baguette—thank you, colonization).

The single most popular dish, though, has to be bo luc lac, beef tenderloin chunks "shaken" in a hot wok until medium-rare (and thus sometimes referred to on restaurant menus as "shaken beef" or "rock'n'roll beef") and served over salad greens dressed with a rice vinegar and shallot vinaigrette.

At its best, the dish is tangy, sweet, and toothsome—simultaneously elegant enough for ladies who lunch and unique enough for college students who love ethnic food.

Vietnamese Dipping Sauce

Serve this versatile sauce with Vietnamese Barbecue Tacos or rice rolls, or use it as a salad dressing.

Makes 1 cup   Hands-On Time 5 min.   Total Time 5 min.

¼ cup fish sauce
¼ cup white vinegar
3 Tbsp. sugar
2 Tbsp. fresh lime juice

2 garlic cloves, minced
1 serrano pepper or Thai chile pepper, sliced and seeded

1. Stir together ½ cup water, fish sauce, vinegar, sugar, lime juice, garlic, and serrano pepper in a medium bowl. Refrigerate in an airtight container up to 1 week.

Vietnamese Barbecue Tacos

Vibrant Vietnamese and Tex-Mex flavors meet in these Houston-inspired tacos.

Makes 8 servings
Hands-On Time 30 min.
Total Time 8 hours, 50 min.

3   beef strip steaks (about 2 ½ lb.)
¼   cup fish sauce
¼   cup rice wine vinegar
2   Tbsp. grated fresh ginger
3   garlic cloves, minced
2   Tbsp. sugar
2   Tbsp. honey
1   Tbsp. sesame oil
1   tsp. freshly ground black pepper
½   medium-size red onion, sliced
8   (8-inch) soft taco-size flour
     tortillas, warmed
Vietnamese Dipping Sauce
Toppings: thinly sliced red cabbage,
     matchstick carrots, thinly sliced red
     onion, chopped fresh cilantro,
     chopped fresh mint, cucumber slices

1. Place steaks in a large zip-top plastic freezer bag. Whisk together fish sauce and next 7 ingredients. Stir in red onion, and pour mixture over steaks in freezer bag. Seal and chill 8 to 24 hours, turning once.

2. Preheat grill to 350° to 400° (medium-high) heat. Remove steaks from marinade, discarding marinade.

3. Grill steaks 7 to 8 minutes on each side or to desired degree of doneness, turning every 3 to 5 minutes. Cover loosely with aluminum foil, and let stand 10 minutes.

4. Cut steaks diagonally across the grain into thin strips, and serve in warm flour tortillas with Vietnamese Dipping Sauce and desired toppings.

Granite Ranch
Roosevelt, Texas

Welcome to
San Antonio

Tourism is big in San Antonio. More than 26 million people visit each year. That it's right smack in the middle of the lower United States, equidistant from the East and West coasts, surely helps.

But a key part of its allure is that it's a walkable city with generally awesome weather. San Antonio has an annual average of 300 days of sunshine and an average daily temperature of 70 degrees. It's got 68 miles of urban hiking and biking trails, and it's home to B-Cycle, Texas's first bike-share program. The crown jewel in all of this walking around has got to be the River Walk, which hugs the San Antonio River one story below street level and is often described as an urban sanctuary. Galleries, shops, and public art installations line some sections of it, while others feature tranquil waterfalls.

Also good for a walking tour—and just a short walk away—is The Alamo, a 4.2-acre complex that includes the original Spanish mission where a small band of Texans held out for 13 days against the mighty army of Centralist Mexican General Santa Anna. A group called the Daughters of the Republic of Texas, Inc. manages what remains of the mission: three buildings with Texas Revolution exhibits, plus gardens and a gift shop. Exhibits include an original Bowie knife, Davy Crockett's buckskin vest, and a flintlock rifle used in the battle.

For thrill-seekers there's Six Flags Fiesta Texas, a gigantic slice of Americana known as an amusement park. No less fun but definitely more unique is the Schlitterbahn, about 30 miles away in New Braunfels. Routinely listed among the best destinations for kids, it boasts the world's longest waterpark ride, an attraction that lets you float on inner tubes over rapids, down waterfalls, and atop tall waves.

Museum Reach segment of the River Walk
San Antonio, Texas

Guacamole

Fuel a San Antonio stroll with crisp chips and cool, creamy guacamole.

Makes 3 ½ cups   Hands-On Time 10 min.   Total Time 40 min.

5 ripe avocados	1 garlic clove, pressed
2 Tbsp. finely chopped red onion	¾ tsp. table salt
2 Tbsp. fresh lime juice	Tortilla chips
½ medium jalapeño pepper, seeded and chopped	

1. Cut avocados in half. Scoop pulp into a bowl, and mash with a potato masher or fork until slightly chunky. Stir in chopped red onion and next 4 ingredients.

2. Cover with plastic wrap, allowing wrap to touch mixture, and let stand at room temperature 30 minutes. Serve guacamole with tortilla chips.

For Cilantro Guacamole: Stir in 3 Tbsp. chopped fresh cilantro and an additional 1 Tbsp. lime juice.

Big, Bold Texas

139

Meet Actress
Eva Longoria

This tiny San Antonio-dwelling dynamo—you might call her "The Little Latina Who Could"—is one hugely motivated Texan.

You probably know Eva Longoria from her role on the hit TV show *Desperate Housewives*. You may even know she was Miss Corpus Christi before landing a gig on *The Young and the Restless*. What you may not know is that she's one of the country's 100 most influential Hispanics. So says *People*, and not for nothing.

She's profoundly philanthropic, tirelessly promoting causes. Inspired by her sister with Down syndrome, she co-founded Eva's Heroes, a San Antonio nonprofit that benefits developmentally disabled children. She also produces documentaries such as *Harvest*, a film exploring the plight of child farm workers.

And then there's her love of food: She co-owns Latin steakhouses in Las Vegas and Hollywood. Her late Aunt Elsa taught her the joys of preparing food and was, she says, the inspiration for her 2011 cookbook, *Eva's Kitchen*.

"We had lemon trees and mint all over our ranch when I was a kid. I don't remember when I tasted the two together for the first time, but since then I've never liked lemonade any other way." —Eva Longoria

Mint Lemonade

For kids or anyone not drinking alcohol, this is a fabulously festive and beautiful nonalcoholic treat. Or add a shot of rum or vodka to each glass, and make a cocktail out of it!

Makes 4 servings   Hands-On Time 7 min.   Total Time 7 min.

½   cup sugar
¼   cup hot water
½   cup fresh lemon juice (about 3 large lemons)

3   cups ice cubes (about 24 large cubes)
12   sprigs of fresh mint, plus 4 more for garnish

1. Place the sugar and hot water in a 2-qt. container with a lid. Close tightly, and shake until the sugar dissolves. Add lemon juice and enough cold water to make 3 cups lemonade total. Shake until well combined.

2. Place half of ice in a blender. Pour in half of lemonade. Pull the leaves off 6 mint sprigs and add to the blender. Blend until well combined and slushy. If too liquid, add more ice, and blend; if too slushy, add a little more water, and blend. Pour into pitcher, and repeat procedure with remaining ice, lemonade, and 6 mint sprigs.

3. Pour into 4 (12-oz.) glasses. Serve immediately.

Watermelon Agua Frescas

Makes about 5 cups   **Hands-On Time 10 min.**   **Total Time 10 min.**

1. Process watermelon, cantaloupe, or honeydew melon and sugar in a blender until smooth, stopping to scrape down sides as needed. Pour mixture through a fine wire-mesh strainer into a pitcher, discarding solids. Stir in 2 cups cold water. Cover and chill until ready to serve. Serve over ice.

4   cups cubed seedless watermelon, cantaloupe, or honeydew melon

¼   cup sugar

2   cups cold water

Owner Maria Corbalan, Taco Xpress
Austin, Texas

Big, Bold Texas

Avocado Soup

Cool down with this cold, creamy soup.

Makes 8 cups
Hands-On Time 15 min.
Total Time 1 hour, 15 min.

4   avocados, peeled and quartered
1   tsp. table salt
1   tsp. green hot sauce
1   (14.5-oz.) can chicken broth
1½ cups half-and-half
1   (8-oz.) container sour cream
¼   cup Johannisberg Riesling
3   Tbsp. lime juice
Garnish: thinly sliced green onions

1. Process avocados and next 3 ingredients in a blender or food processor until smooth, stopping to scrape down sides.

2. Pour mixture into a large bowl; stir in half-and-half and next 3 ingredients until smooth. Place plastic wrap directly over soup; chill 1 hour.

Note: Off-dry white wines such as Gewürztraminer or Chenin Blanc may be substituted.

Susan Auler
Austin, Texas

Southwest Watermelon Salad

Use reserved watermelon from the Pickled Watermelon Rind for this recipe.

Makes 8 to 10 servings   Hands-On Time 30 min.
Total Time 2 hours, 5 min., plus 2 days for chilling the rind

4	cups seeded and cubed red watermelon	¼	cup coarsely chopped fresh basil
4	cups seeded and cubed yellow watermelon	1	Tbsp. chopped fresh chives
2	Tbsp. sugar	1	Tbsp. seeded and thinly sliced jalapeño pepper
1	Tbsp. lime zest	1	Tbsp. thinly sliced shallots
2	Tbsp. fresh lime juice	1	tsp. minced garlic
½	cup Pickled Watermelon Rind	2	Tbsp. olive oil
¼	cup coarsely chopped fresh cilantro	½	cup crumbled Cotija or feta cheese

1. Combine first 5 ingredients in a large glass bowl. Stir in Pickled Watermelon Rind and next 6 ingredients. Drizzle with oil; sprinkle with cheese. Serve immediately, or cover and chill up to 2 hours.

Pickled Watermelon Rind

Makes 1 qt.   Hands-On Time 30 min.
Total Time 1 hour, 35 min., plus 2 days for chilling

½	small watermelon (about 5 lb.)	¾	cup vinegar
3	Tbsp. table salt	2	star anise
¾	cup sugar		

1. Remove rind from watermelon, leaving a small amount of red flesh attached to rind. Reserve watermelon flesh for another use. Peel rind, and cut into 1-inch cubes (about 5 cups cubed). Place in a large bowl.

2. Stir together salt and 3 cups water. Pour over rind. Cover and chill 24 hours. Drain; rinse well.

3. Combine rind, sugar, next 2 ingredients, and ¾ cup water in a large Dutch oven. Bring to a boil; remove from heat. C[ ]
completely (about 1 hour), stirring occasionally. Cover and ch[ ]
24 hours before serving. Refrigerate in an airtight container up to 1 week.

Chef Shawn Cirkiel, Parkside
Austin, Texas

~ You've Gotta Try ~
King Ranch Chicken Casserole

The story of Texas's King Ranch, one of the largest ranches in the world, begins with Richard King and an only-in-America rags-to-riches story.

King, sold as a child by his destitute family into servitude to a New York City jeweler, ran away and made his way by steamboat to Texas in search of fortune. He found it as a steamship captain running Union blockades under a Mexican flag during the Civil War. He bought a whole lot of land with some partners after that, with the dream of combining the best of Southern plantation culture and the best of Mexican hacienda life.

The ranch, situated between Corpus Christi and Brownsville, was known for its epic cattle drives and expansive way of life. In 1933, oil was discovered there as well. Thoroughbred horses still are raised on the ranch, now a national historic landmark that you can tour.

The extremely popular and beloved casserole that bears its name, known to Texas cooks everywhere, is an institution of its own.

Though it's obviously named for the ranch and clearly embodies the mixture of Mexican and Southern flavor that King built there, historians say it's unclear if the dish actually originated on the ranch. And some King descendants claim the ranch was more associated with meat and game dishes than with poultry dishes like this one. It's a rich and easy Tex-Mex delight either way.

King Ranch Chicken Casserole.

Makes 8 to 10 servings   Hands-On Time 30 min.
Total Time 3 hours, 30 min.

1   (4 ½- to 5-lb.) whole chicken
2   celery ribs, cut into 3 pieces each
2   carrots, cut into 3 pieces each
2 ½ to 3 tsp. table salt
2   Tbsp. butter
1   medium onion, chopped
1   medium-size green bell pepper, chopped
1   garlic clove, pressed
1   (10 ¾-oz.) can cream of mushroom soup
1   (10 ¾-oz.) can cream of chicken soup
2   (10-oz.) cans diced tomatoes and green chiles, drained
1   tsp. dried oregano
1   tsp. ground cumin
1   tsp. Mexican-style chili powder*
3   cups (12 oz.) shredded sharp Cheddar cheese
12 (6-inch) fajita-size corn tortillas, cut into ½-inch strips

1. If applicable, remove giblets from chicken, and reserve for another use. Rinse chicken.

2. Place chicken, celery, carrots, and salt in a large Dutch oven with water to cover. Bring to a boil over medium-high heat; reduce heat to low. Cover and simmer 50 minutes to 1 hour or until chicken reaches desired degree of doneness. Remove from heat. Remove chicken from broth; cool 30 minutes. Remove and reserve ¾ cup cooking liquid. Strain any remaining cooking liquid, and reserve for another use.

3. Preheat oven to 350°. Melt butter in a large skillet over medium-high heat. Add onion, and sauté 6 to 7 minutes or until tender. Add bell pepper and garlic, and sauté 3 to 4 minutes. Stir in reserved ¾ cup cooking liquid, cream of mushroom soup, and next 5 ingredients. Cook, stirring occasionally, for 8 minutes.

4. Skin and bone chicken; shred meat into bite-size pieces. Layer half of chicken in a lightly greased 13- x 9-inch baking dish. Top with half of soup mixture and 1 cup Cheddar cheese. Cover with half of corn tortilla strips. Repeat layers once. Top with remaining 1 cup cheese.

5. Bake at 350° for 55 minutes to 1 hour or until bubbly. Let stand 10 minutes before serving.

Note: You can substitute 1 tsp. chili powder and ⅛ tsp. ground red pepper for the Mexican-style chili powder.

For Quick-and-Easy King Ranch Chicken Casserole (pictured): Substitute 1 (2-lb.) skinned, boned, and shredded deli-roasted chicken for whole chicken, 3 cups coarsely crumbled lime-flavored white corn tortilla chips for corn tortillas, and ¾ cup chicken broth for cooking liquid. Omit celery, carrots, and salt. Prepare recipe as directed, beginning with Step 3.

Shop at Boggy Creek Farm Like a Local

For 18 years, Larry Butler and Carol Ann Sayle of Austin's Boggy Creek Farm have turned their 5 certified organic acres into a farmers' market twice a week.

When that happens, on Wednesdays and Saturdays, you want to be there.

Butler and Sayle sit on their front porch, welcoming visitors and selling their farm-fresh sunflowers, herbs, veggies (okra, eggplants, radishes), and fruit (figs, peaches, pears)—more than 100 crops total, including pecans from the giant trees lining the property.

These crops have been grown on their land since the late 1830s, long before "urban farming" and "locavore" became buzzwords. Boggy Creek is a marvelous place to linger awhile in the fields and get in touch with where your food comes from. The farm also supplies Whole Foods, but it's a whole lot more fun to buy it here.

Bonus: At the farm, you get to see what "eating a rainbow" means. Sayle, a former artist, assembles gorgeous piled-high displays, tables, and baskets of produce and flowers.

Big, Bold Texas

Grilled Tri-Tip with Citrus-Chile Butter

The tri-tip cut of beef is a thick and flavorful cut of lean bottom sirloin that is tender enough to serve medium–rare.

Makes 8 to 10 servings   Hands-On Time 30 min.   Total Time 40 min.

1. Preheat grill to 350° to 400° (medium-high) heat. Sprinkle steaks with 1½ tsp. salt and 1 tsp. pepper. Grill steaks, covered with grill lid, 9 to 12 minutes on each side or to desired degree of doneness.

2. Remove from grill, and rub 3 Tbsp. Citrus-Chile Butter onto steaks. Cover steaks with aluminum foil; let stand 5 minutes.

3. Meanwhile, toss onions with olive oil; season with remaining ½ tsp. salt and ¼ tsp. pepper. Grill onions, without grill lid, 2 minutes; turn and grill 1 more minute.

4. Uncover steaks, and cut diagonally across the grain into thin slices. Serve with grilled onions and remaining Citrus-Chile Butter.

- 2   (2-lb.) tri-tip steaks or 2 lb. (2-inch-thick) strip steaks
- 2   tsp. table salt, divided
- 1¼ tsp. black pepper, divided
- Citrus-Chile Butter
- 3   bunches baby Vidalia or green onions, trimmed
- 3   Tbsp. olive oil

Citrus-Chile Butter

Makes 1 cup   Hands-On Time 10 min.   Total Time 10 min.

- 1   cup butter, softened
- 2   Tbsp. lime zest
- 2   Tbsp. lemon zest
- 3   garlic cloves, minced
- 1   Tbsp. seeded and minced jalapeño pepper
- 1   tsp. chopped fresh thyme

1. Stir together all ingredients. Season with table salt and freshly ground black pepper to taste. Cover and chill until ready to serve, or shape into a log with plastic wrap, and freeze up to 1 month.

Chef Shawn Cirkiel, Parkside
Austin, Texas

Beer 'Garitas

For fast measuring and one less dirtied measuring cup, use the empty limeade can to measure the tequila. One 12-ounce can is equivalent to 1½ cups.

Makes 6 cups   Hands-On Time 5 min.   Total Time 5 min.

- 1   (12-oz.) container frozen limeade concentrate, thawed
- 1½ cups tequila
- 2   (12-oz.) bottles beer
- Crushed ice

1. Stir together first 3 ingredients in a large pitcher until blended. Serve immediately over crushed ice in salt-rimmed glasses, if desired.

Remember
LBJ and Lady Bird
Like a Local

Dedicated in 1971 on the campus of the University of Texas at Austin, the LBJ Presidential Library and Museum houses all of the records and memorabilia of President Lyndon Baines Johnson's incredible public career.

The highlight of Johnson's personal life, however, was probably his 1934 marriage to Claudia "Lady Bird" Taylor, who acquired her nickname from a baby nurse who said that she was "purty as a ladybird." Johnson met her when he was a congressional secretary visiting Austin on official business, and legend had it that he applied his charms to courting her so intensely that she had little choice but to marry him—after only seven weeks.

Lady Bird was a tireless campaigner: In 1960, she covered 35,000 miles for the Kennedy and Johnson ticket, and in 1964, she campaigned independently on a whistle-stop train throughout the South for the Johnson and Humphrey ticket. When LBJ was in the Navy in World War II, she managed his congressional office in his stead. And when, as Senate Majority Leader, he had a massive heart attack in 1955, Lady Bird managed his staff until he recovered.

Her personal passion, though, was nature and the environment. An avid gardener, she co-authored the book *Wildflowers Across America* and led the charge to get Congress to enact the Highway Beautification Act of 1965, which spruced up roadsides all over the country. At the age of 70, she co-founded the National Wildflower Research Center. Later renamed the Lady Bird Johnson Wildflower Center, it's dedicated to preserving and re-establishing native plants. She died in 2007 at the age of 94, one of the most beloved First Ladies of all time.

Duke University
Durham, North Carolina

Monticello
Charlottesville, Virginia

The Piedmont & the Mountains

A piedmont is a geological phenomenon that, in and of itself, is not all that phenomenal. In the simplest sense, it is the land at the base of a mountain or hill. The term comes from *ai piede della montagne*, Italian for "at the foot of the mountains," and it is most often associated with Italy.

The Italian Piedmont region, *Piemonte*, is special—phenomenal, even—thanks in part to a cuisine built upon indigenous ingredients including truffles, porcini mushrooms, veal, and Nebbiolo grapes, the source of some especially incredible wine.

Equally special, though, is the American Piedmont—the gorgeous plateau and foothills region between the Atlantic Coastal plains and the Blue Ridge Mountains, the easternmost range of the great Appalachian Mountains. Although this region technically stretches all the way from New Jersey to Alabama, its widest point is in North Carolina.

And the isosceles-shaped heart of North Carolina's considerable stretch of the Piedmont is the Research Triangle (the Triangle for short). This 13-county region-within-a-region, the Triangle encompasses the cities of Durham, Raleigh, and Chapel Hill, and it is perennially ranked among the country's best places to live. Why? The answer is in the name.

Since the 1950s, "Research Triangle" has referred to the nexus of renowned research universities in the area: Duke University in Durham, North Carolina State University in Raleigh, and the main campus of the University of North Carolina in Chapel Hill.

Combined, the three draw more than 150,000 college students, supply world-class medical facilities, and offer unparalleled educational opportunities in the world's largest university-related research park. Research Triangle Park, as it is known, is a hub for international health-care and technology businesses and the corporate headquarters of more than 170 major research and development companies, including Bayer, IBM, Underwriters Laboratories, and GlaxoSmithKline.

Each company maintains its own campus of buildings, and the park also includes multiuse and cooperative spaces. Business interests in the park cluster around the biotechnology (both agricultural and pharmaceutical) industry that gave the Triangle its start, as well as newer fields such as nanotechnology, advanced gaming, e-learning, and microelectronics. By its own count,

159

Mateo Bar de Tapas
Durham, North Carolina

Durham is the Brooklyn of North Carolina's ResearchTriangle, complete with a hipster-urban downtown and good homemade preserves, bakeries, record companies, authentic pizza parlors, and tapas bars.

the park has produced at least 3,539 patents and 1,854 trademarks.

Does the area attract science's top minds because it's an attractive place to live? Or is it so attractive because of the people it attracts? Either way, it's clear the Triangle enjoys a high quality of life. In recent years, *Business Week* named Raleigh "America's Best City," *The Daily Beast* named Durham one of "America's Brainiest Cities," *Kiplinger's* included the Triangle on a list of "Great Cities for Raising Families," and *Bon Appétit* named Chapel Hill-Durham "America's Foodiest Small Town."

Durham, North Carolina, is best known as the hometown of Duke University, which was built with tobacco money. Some born-and-raised Durhamites swear that at night you can still smell the tobacco drying

in the warehouses—never mind that most of those warehouses haven't processed tobacco for years and are now antiques shops, art studios, radio stations, restaurants, and jewelry stores. The legacy is still important.

Washington Duke, who grew up on his family's farm near present-day Durham, later grew a family fortune by manufacturing tobacco products. His post-Civil War tobacco company all but bankrolled the town into industrialization, and many of his philanthropic-related decisions, including helping fund moving what was once Trinity College (now Duke University) from its original site in Randolph County to Durham and encouraging the school to admit women, are still felt today.

Since the early part of the 21st century, Durham has experienced a

renaissance, yet at heart it remains an old Southern city with a past that stretches to the Native Americans who settled it first, the Eno and Occaneechi tribes, relatives of the Sioux.

The gristmills came, courtesy of early Scottish, Irish, and English settlers, in the mid-1700s. Between the Revolutionary and Civil Wars, large plantations sprouted up in Durham, including some relatively famous ones such as Hardscrabble, Cameron, Leigh, and Stagville, which primarily grew tobacco, wheat, cotton, and corn. And by 1860 slaves had been shipped into the area to work them.

North Carolina was the last state to secede from the Union, and when the Civil War ended a lot of celebrations featured Washington Duke's hand-harvested "bright leaf" tobacco. The charcoal-cured bright yellow

Tobacco District
Durham, North Carolina

dried tobacco product, first discovered by a slave named Stephen Slade, would give rise to an international tobacco dynasty that at its height included American Tobacco, Liggett & Meyers, R.J. Reynolds, and P. Lorillard.

Durham's domination of the tobacco market didn't last forever, though. The American Tobacco Company began to acquire a wide range of non-tobacco products during the 1970s and 1980s, changed its name to American Brands in 1986 (and later to Fortune Brands), and sold off all of its tobacco brands to competitors the following decade.

Even without tobacco, Durham was an industrial center, at one time home to the world's largest hosiery maker and the country's first denim mill. Today it's the Brooklyn of the Triangle, complete with a hipster-urban downtown surrounding Duke University and good homemade preserves, bakeries, record companies, authentic pizza parlors, and tapas bars to go with it. Durham's suburbs are diverse— some with manicured lawns and country clubs, others with Latino barbershops, taquerias, and bodegas.

Raleigh, North Carolina, has an entirely different vibe. Think Atlanta. Think Houston. Think of those fast-growing Southern cities where the pace is hectic and the money is important. Its charms may be mostly unsung, paling in the light of nearby Atlanta and, even closer, the banking center that is Charlotte. But Raleigh is an honest-to-goodness big city—and proud of it.

It bears the name of the 16th-century visionary who helped pave the way for the New World and shares that name with an earlier Raleigh that was lost to history. It's a fascinating story: After exploring the coast of what would become North Carolina in the 1580s, Sir Walter Raleigh directed colonist John White to establish the "Cittie of Raleigh"

The Piedmont & the Mountains

161

State Farmers Market
Raleigh, North Carolina

Downtown
Raleigh, North Carolina

Its charms may pale in the light of Atlanta
and the banking center that is Charlotte, but Raleigh is
an honest-to-goodness big city—and proud of it.

on Roanoke Island, about 190 miles east of present-day Raleigh. Virginia Dare, the first child born to English colonists in the New World, was born there in August 1587.

That same year, White took a ship to England for what was to be a quick supply run. But his ship was needed to fend off the Spanish armada. When he finally returned to the newly founded settlement in 1590, it had inexplicably disappeared. It's now known as the "Lost Colony of Roanoke." Today's Raleigh, the capital of North Carolina, was named in honor of the famous explorer in 1792, more than two centuries later.

Raleigh wasn't a bustling metropolis when it was declared the capital, so taverns, inns, dry goods stores, and other businesses grew up right around the statehouse. And although Raleigh's citizenry was hit hard by the Civil War—North Carolina lost more men than any other state—

the city itself was spared the kind of destruction visited upon so many of its neighbors.

After the war came the railroad, good news for the young city, and a flourishing retail scene followed. Fayetteville Street became the place where folks from all around the state went to see the moving pictures and operas, shop for clothes, and enjoy vaudeville performances. East Hargett Street became a similar kind of Main Street for the area's African-American community.

A huge housing boom hit the city after World War II, and Raleigh saw the development of the Southeast's first "shopping center" (don't call it a strip mall) at Cameron Village in 1949. Shortly thereafter came the two biggest factors in modern Raleigh's development and workforce: the creation of the Research Triangle and the culmination of the Civil Rights movement when black students took

to the streets and staged sit-ins to oppose the Jim Crow laws.

Since the 1970s, the twin forces of suburban sprawl and downtown revitalization have shaped Raleigh, and the transformation is ongoing. Take, for example, the downtown Glenwood South neighborhood, a half-dozen or so blocks northwest of the Capitol. In 2000, it consisted almost entirely of abandoned factories and mills and was deserted after the nine-to-fivers clocked out. Today it's lined with restaurants and music venues. Aficionados call it GloSo, and *The New York Times* has accurately described it as "a hive" where hipsters throng.

Chapel Hill, North Carolina, is the quintessential Southern college town. Yes, folks do say that about Oxford, Mississippi, and about Athens, Georgia. And those are idyllic places, for sure—but Chapel Hill is special.

It's a bit more liberal, a little more relaxed, and a lot more intellectual than its peers. Perhaps that's because Chapel Hill was built to house the university.

When the University of North Carolina board of trustees selected the site for the university in 1793, they established a committee to create a town adjacent to the school. Town lots were auctioned when the ground was broken for the university.

The quiet winding streets, wooded lawns, stone walls, and little shops surrounding the university were designed to foster the charming mystique of small-town Southern life.

Franklin Street, which was named for Benjamin Franklin, is the main drag in Chapel Hill. Running the length of the university, it's bordered on one side by the school and on the other by grand historic homes and numerous coffee shops, museums, restaurants, salons, bookstores, a retro movie theater, and more of precisely what you'd expect to find in a college town.

"Mayberry meets M.I.T." is how *The New York Times* aptly described it. What Chapel Hill has that Mayberry didn't is a white-hot restaurant scene complete with nationally award-winning venues, a beloved biweekly farmers' market, and bars that range from typical sports-watching venues to the kind that age the bourbon on the premises.

For all its grown-up attractions and big-city pleasures, the North Carolina Piedmont is also an incredibly rustic pocket of the United States, rife with tradition, blessed with stunning natural resources, and rich with a vibrant culture.

You'll discover significant literary heritage, baseball history, folklore, and folk art in these foothills. You can explore woods, hiking trails, and wilderness habitats. You can float and fish a fine collection of rivers and rapids, and you'll ooh and aah at spectacular waterfalls. And yes, oh yes, you can eat barbecue.

North Carolina barbecue is a beloved style of cooking hog with a vinegar-based sauce. A source of much regional pride, it's often served with sides of distinction: flavorful beans, greens like chard and cress, red

The quiet winding streets, wooded lawns, stone walls, and little shops surrounding the university in Chapel Hill epitomize the allure of small-town Southern life.

West Franklin Street
Chapel Hill, North Carolina

Just a wee bit different

Highland Brewing Company
Asheville, North Carolina

Monticello
Charlottesville, Virginia

Wing Haven Gardens and Bird Sanctuary
Charlotte, North Carolina

Charlottesville is about two hours from Washington, D.C., and a world away in attitude, geography, and almost every other measure—except perhaps reverence for Thomas Jefferson.

and green tomatoes, peppers of every hue, squash, corn, and fennel. It's tempting to call these unadulterated flavors "simple," but the truth is more like "straightforwardly delicious." You can find these flavors in Raleigh's hipper-than-thou restaurants—and also due north across the North Carolina border and into Virginia.

In the northern part of the Piedmont, where the Blue Ridge Mountains meet rolling hills and lush farmland, you'll find **Charlottesville, Virginia.** This small city is about two hours from Washington, D.C., and a world away in attitude, geography, and almost every other measure—except perhaps reverence for Thomas Jefferson.

Because Charlottesville sits between Richmond and the Blue Ridge Mountains, Native Americans and new settlers alike wore a back-

and-forth path right through it, mainly for hunting purposes, in the country's earliest days.

Charlottesville's formation as a city got more serious in 1735 when Nicholas Meriwether II (the great-great-grandfather of the great, great territorial explorer Meriwether Lewis) obtained patents from the King of England for land along the Southwest Mountains, including about 1,200 acres west of the Rivanna River. That land, a clearing in an otherwise virgin forest, comprises a good deal of modern Charlottesville, including its Locust Grove and Belmont neighborhoods.

Charlottesville acquired its name in honor of Princess Charlotte, who became queen of England in 1761 when she married King George III. The town officially became a city in 1888.

Though Confederate uniforms were manufactured in Charlottesville,

the city remained physically relatively unscathed by the Civil War. That's a blessing because the Charlottesville area is home to two UNESCO (United Nations Educational, Scientific, and Cultural Organization) World Heritage Sites: Thomas Jefferson's home, Monticello, and the rotunda and grounds of the University of Virginia.

It's fascinating to consider how Jefferson connected the neoclassical architecture of these places to the intellect he hoped they would imbue. For instance, he designed the rotunda and adjoining pavilions that comprise the University of Virginia Lawn as a "bulwark of the human mind in this hemisphere."

Between the Blue Ridges and the Smoky Mountains, about two hours northwest of Charlotte, lies **Asheville, North Carolina.** This mountain resort town along the French Broad River has been the subject of national attention and curiosity since the late 1800s when Manhattan aristocrat George Vanderbilt built himself a castle there.

Reportedly modeled on a 16th-century European-style château, the historic Biltmore Mansion is one of the world's largest private residences. It's particularly beloved by horticultural types, who revel in the Frederick Law Olmsted-designed gardens.

The construction brought hundreds of artisans to town, giving rise to a local tradition of decorative arts and architecture that visitors can still experience at the mansion and in the lovingly preserved 1920s-era Art Deco buildings downtown.

"You can't go home again," wrote American novelist and Asheville native Thomas Wolfe. But Wolfe did just that in his fiction, returning again and again to his hometown for inspiration—especially obvious in his classic novel *Look Homeward, Angel.*

Set in a thinly veiled Asheville called Altamont, it fictionalizes many of the stories Wolfe first observed in real life in his mother's boarding-house. Literary-minded visitors can tour the boardinghouse at 48 Spruce Street, which stands as a museum to this day.

Asheville also sits along the national treasure that is the Blue Ridge Parkway. The incredible stretch of road near Asheville is especially beloved because it's where the parkway begins to approach its highest elevation—6,047 feet, in the Nantahala National Forest. Many of the mileposts around Asheville offer spectacular hiking trails and views. If you have to choose just one spot to see, make it Looking Glass Rock—a striking, sheer-faced granite landmark in the Pisgah National Forest that is sacred to rock climbers and photographers alike.

Nearby are gorgeous waterfalls and the tiny village of Hot Springs, a spa destination in the oldest sense of the word, where hikers rest their bones in warm and allegedly healing mineral waters.

You can "take the waters," as the locals still say, and refresh yourself in the way weary travelers have done for hundreds of years—and will probably do for hundreds of years more—enjoying a natural phenomenon in a region that has become, well, phenomenal.

For all its grown-up attractions and big-city pleasures, North Carolina's Piedmont remains an incredibly rustic pocket of the United States, rife with tradition, blessed with stunning natural resources, and rich with a vibrant culture.

Welcome to the Triangle

Two remarkable and remarkably different men help shape the collective voice of the Triangle, and the place wouldn't be the same without them.

"In my mind, I'm going to Carolina." So begins James Taylor's quiet, loving elegy to the state. The classic sing-along appeared on his self-titled 1968 debut album and has since taken on a life of its own. The Boston-born Taylor grew up in the Chapel Hill area, where his dad was a professor at the University of North Carolina School of Medicine. Taylor has said that he wrote the piece, "Carolina In My Mind," when homesick while overseas.

This unofficial anthem of North Carolina is especially sacred in Chapel Hill, where it is played at pep rallies, graduation ceremonies, and athletic events far and wide. "Chapel Hill, the Piedmont, the out-lying hills were tranquil, rural, beautiful, but quiet," Taylor has said. "I feel as though my experience of coming of age there was more a matter of landscape and climate than people."

If Taylor is the soft, gentle voice of the Triangle, Michael William Krzyzewski is his booming counterpoint. The Duke University men's basketball coach since 1980, Krzyzewski is one of the most successful coaches of any team in American history. In fact he was named "America's Best Coach" by *Time* magazine in 2001.

A Chicago-born West Point graduate often seen yelling at the refs and, sometimes, his players, Coach K has also been known to bring pizzas to the students who camp out for basketball tickets. And despite NBA courting, he has remained steadfast to the Triangle and the team. "Turning down the Lakers was tough," he has said. "But it is always good to renew your vows to the loves of your life."

University of North Carolina
Chapel Hill, North Carolina

~ A Recipe from a Local ~

Asparagus-New Potato Hash

Makes 8 servings   Hands-On Time 20 min.   Total Time 1 hour

1	lb. small red potatoes	½	tsp. black pepper
1	lb. fresh asparagus	2	tsp. fresh lemon juice
2	shallots, minced	⅓	cup crumbled farmer's cheese or
2	Tbsp. olive oil		queso fresco (fresh Mexican
1	tsp. chopped fresh thyme		cheese)
1	tsp. table salt		Garnish: lemon slices

1. Bring potatoes and salted water to cover to a boil in a Dutch oven over medium-high heat. Cook 15 minutes or just until tender; drain well. Cool 15 minutes; cut into quarters.

2. Snap off and discard tough ends of asparagus. Cut asparagus into ½-inch pieces.

3. Sauté shallots in hot oil in a large nonstick skillet 1 minute. Add asparagus, thyme, salt, pepper, and lemon juice; sauté 2 to 3 minutes or until asparagus is crisp-tender. Add potatoes, and sauté 3 minutes or until mixture is thoroughly heated. Remove from heat, and sprinkle with cheese.

Note: We tested with Chapel Hill Creamery farmer's cheese.

**Chef-Owner Amy Tornquist, Watts Grocery
Durham, North Carolina**

The Piedmont & the Mountains

167

Watts Grocery-Style Spoon Bread

Makes 8 servings   **Hands-On Time 20 min.**   **Total Time 1 hour, 15 min.**

1. Preheat oven to 375°. Grease a 2½-qt. soufflé dish with 1 Tbsp. butter. Dust with 2 Tbsp. cornmeal (tap dish lightly to remove excess cornmeal).

2. Combine 1¼ cups cornmeal and next 3 ingredients in a large bowl; make a well in center of mixture.

3. Bring 3 cups water to a boil in a saucepan over medium-high heat. Remove from heat, and whisk into cornmeal mixture, whisking until smooth. Add 2 Tbsp. butter, whisking until butter melts. Cool 5 minutes.

4. Whisk together eggs and next 5 ingredients; whisk into cornmeal mixture. Pour cornmeal mixture into prepared baking dish.

5. Bake at 375° for 45 to 50 minutes or until golden brown and center is almost set. Serve immediately.

1	Tbsp. butter, softened
2	Tbsp. plain white cornmeal
1¼	cups plain white cornmeal
¾	cup all-purpose flour
2	Tbsp. sugar
2	tsp. table salt
2	Tbsp. butter
4	large eggs
1	cup buttermilk
1	cup whipping cream
2	tsp. baking soda
1	tsp. chopped fresh thyme
⅛	to ¼ tsp. ground red pepper

Chef-Owner Amy Tornquist, Watts Grocery
Durham, North Carolina

Brown Butter Cauliflower Mash

Makes about 6 servings (3½ cups)   **Hands-On Time 15 min.**
Total Time 30 min.

1. Fill a large Dutch oven with water to depth of ¼ inch. Arrange cauliflower in Dutch oven. Cook, covered, over medium-high heat 7 to 10 minutes or until tender. Drain.

2. Process cauliflower, sour cream, salt, and pepper in a food processor 30 seconds to 1 minute or until smooth, stopping to scrape down sides as needed. Stir in Parmesan cheese and chives. Place in a bowl.

3. If desired, microwave mixture at HIGH 1 to 2 minutes or until thoroughly heated, stirring at 1-minute intervals.

4. Cook butter in a small heavy saucepan over medium heat, stirring constantly, 4 to 5 minutes or until butter begins to turn golden brown. Remove from heat, and immediately drizzle butter over cauliflower mixture. Serve immediately.

1	medium head cauliflower (about 2 lb.), chopped
½	cup sour cream
¾	tsp. table salt
½	tsp. black pepper
¼	cup grated Parmesan cheese
1	Tbsp. chopped fresh chives
2	Tbsp. butter

Jennifer Pinna
Raleigh, North Carolina

Meet Chef
Andrea Reusing

Don't call it fusion. What chef-owner Andrea Reusing creates at her Chapel Hill restaurant Lantern are Asian flavors with local, seasonal ingredients.

Lantern's use of North Carolina's bounty in traditional Asian dishes from Korean kimchi to Vietnamese shaking beef is the hottest game in town.

The eclectic menu combined with the minimalist dining room and its black-ceilinged, tiny back bar helped land it on *Gourmet* magazine's list of America's top 50 restaurants. It also helped propel Reusing to a James Beard Foundation Award for Best Chef: Southeast in 2011.

Reusing is passionate not only about her brand of fine dining but also about the environment. She serves on the boards of the Center for Environmental Farming Systems and the Chefs Collaborative. She is also the author of a collection of recipes devoted to seasonal eating, *Cooking in the Moment*.

"This dish is all about timing: Poach the eggs first, and keep them in a warm spot." —Andrea Reusing

Asparagus with Butter, Soy, and Egg

Makes 2 servings   Hands-On Time 15 min.   Total Time 35 min.

1 tsp. white vinegar	2 Tbsp. lite soy sauce
2 large eggs, at room temperature	5 Tbsp. unsalted butter, softened
½ lb. slender fresh asparagus spears	Flaky sea salt, such as Maldon
2 tsp. vegetable oil	Freshly ground black pepper
	Garnish: fresh chives

1. Pour water to a depth of 3 inches in a large saucepan. Bring to a boil; reduce heat, and maintain at a light simmer. Add white vinegar. Break eggs, and slip into water, 1 at a time, as close as possible to surface. Simmer 3 to 5 minutes or to desired degree of doneness. Remove with a slotted spoon; trim edges, if desired. Keep warm.

2. Snap off and discard tough ends of asparagus. Fill a large pot with water, and bring to a boil over high heat. Meanwhile heat a large skillet over medium-high heat. When the skillet is very hot, drop the asparagus into the boiling water in the saucepan, and cook for 1 minute. Drain the asparagus, and gently shake to dry.

3. Add the oil to the hot skillet, and gently swirl. Immediately add the asparagus, and toss constantly for 1 minute or until slightly blistered in spots. Do not lower the heat; add the soy sauce, and shake the pan to coat the asparagus. As soon as the soy sauce almost evaporates, remove the pan from the heat; add 1 Tbsp. water, and immediately add the butter. Continue to toss the asparagus until the butter melts, creating a dark golden brown emulsified sauce. If the sauce breaks, add up to 1 Tbsp. more water, and continue to toss until it comes back together.

4. Divide the asparagus and the sauce between two plates, and top each serving with a warm poached egg. Sprinkle the eggs with a little sea salt and pepper.

~ You've Gotta Try ~
Carolina Barbecue

North Carolina barbecue is all about the hog, but it can taste different depending on where you are in the state. The dividing line between Eastern and Western Carolina barbecue country cuts through the Triangle, where you can find both styles.

If you head east toward the Atlantic Coast, pork shoulder (also known as Boston butt) is slow-cooked over hardwood coals, drenched in a spicy-tangy sauce of vinegar and red pepper flakes, chopped or sliced depending on preference, tucked into a soft white bun, and topped with a cool, sweet, mayonnaise-based coleslaw. If you head west to where the Piedmont's sand gives way to clay, the barbecue is as red as the soil. Western Carolina barbecue, also known as Lexington-style barbecue after the small North Carolina town where it was popularized, involves slow-cooked pork shoulder seasoned with a vinegar and pepper sauce that is sweetened by ketchup (which is what makes it so richly red in comparison to the Eastern style).

The difference between Eastern and Western styles of Carolina barbecue may seem slight, but it's the cause of deep division: As veteran news reporter William E. Schmidt wrote in *The New York Times*, Southern barbecue is "a cultural ritual, practiced with a kind of religious fervor among various barbecue sects, each of whom believes their particular concoction of smoke and sauce and spices is the only true way to culinary salvation."

Lexington-Style Cider Vinegar Barbecue Sauce

This sauce, beloved in Western North Carolina, has many variations. Most folks can't resist adding their own touch.

Makes 2 cups
Hands-On Time 10 min.
Total Time 10 min.

1 ½   cups cider vinegar
⅓   cup firmly packed brown sugar
¼   cup ketchup
1   Tbsp. hot sauce
1   tsp. browning and seasoning sauce
½   tsp. table salt
½   tsp. onion powder
½   tsp. black pepper
½   tsp. Worcestershire sauce

1. Stir together all ingredients in a medium saucepan; cook over medium heat, stirring constantly, 7 minutes or until sugar dissolves. Cover and chill sauce until ready to serve. Serve with Smoked Pork Butt.

Note: We tested with Texas Pete Hot Sauce and Kitchen Bouquet Browning & Seasoning Sauce.

Smoked Pork Butt

**Makes 6 to 8 servings   Hands-On Time 30 min.
Total Time 8 hours, 30 min.**

Serve on buns with slaw or relish and Lexington Style Cider Vinegar Sauce.

1	(4- to 5-lb.) bone-in Boston butt pork roast	¼	cup Smoky-Sweet BBQ Rub

1. Trim pork roast. Rinse and pat dry. Sprinkle with Smoky-Sweet BBQ Rub; let stand at room temperature 30 minutes.

2. Bring internal temperature of smoker to 225° to 250° according to manufacturer's directions, and maintain temperature 15 to 20 minutes. Place pork, fattier side up, on cooking grate directly over coals in center of smoker.

3. Cover with lid, and adjust ventilation to maintain temperature between 225° and 250°. Smoke, covered with lid and maintaining temperature, 5 hours; turn pork, fattier side down, and smoke 2 to 3 more hours or until a meat thermometer inserted into thickest portion registers 195°.

4. Transfer to a cutting board; cool 15 minutes. Shred pork.

Smoky-Sweet BBQ Rub

Makes 1 cup   Hands-On Time 5 min.   Total Time 5 min.

¼	cup kosher salt	2	tsp. garlic powder
¼	cup firmly packed dark brown sugar	2	tsp. freshly ground black pepper
2	Tbsp. plus 2 tsp. smoked paprika	1	tsp. dry mustard
2	Tbsp. granulated sugar	1	tsp. ground cumin
		1	tsp. ground ginger

1. Stir together all ingredients. Store in an airtight container up to a month.

Cheer On the Durham Bulls Like a Local

"This is a very simple game. You throw the ball, you catch the ball, you hit the ball. Sometimes you win, sometimes you lose, some-times it rains."

So says Ebby Calvin LaLoosh, the meat-headed pitching prodigy played by Tim Robbins in *Bull Durham*. The minor league team the 1988 baseball movie was based on has had a similarly up-and-down history.

The club that began in 1902 as the Durham Tobacconists has evolved through three leagues, four ballparks, owners' disputes, shutdowns during World War I and the Great Depression, a Triple-A affiliation with the Tampa Bay Rays, 12 league championships, one national title, and a host of Major League players who started out wearing its jerseys.

The Durham Bulls' latest stadium opened in 1995, was expanded in 1998, and got a makeover for the 2012 season. This modern take on an old-fashioned ballpark, designed by the team behind Baltimore's Camden Yards offers the quintessential American baseball experi-ence: seats close to the field; postgame fireworks; and hot dogs, ice cream, and cotton candy almost as good as they are in your best baseball memories.

Meet Reality Star
Emily Maynard

America's favorite *Bachelorette* from the smash reality TV show doesn't technically live in the Triangle.

Emily Maynard lives in Charlotte, about 140 miles west. But she loves the home cooking of North Carolina so much that we let her share her favorite recipe anyway.

She won her way into our hearts in the first place because of her unique life story. Engaged in 2004 to Ricky Hendrick, the promising young NASCAR driver and scion of the Hendrick family racing team, her heart was broken when Hendrick was killed in a tragic plane crash. A week after the crash, Maynard discovered she was pregnant with his baby.

Today Maynard lives in Charlotte near the Hendrick family with her young daughter, and she is a passionate volunteer for various children's causes.

"This is my favorite picnic, cookout, and barbecue side dish. It's incredible!" —Emily Maynard

Cornbread Salad

This salad is as sweet as the cornbread you start with. (And Jiffy mix is pretty sweet; if you prefer a less-sweet version, substitute a less-sweet cornbread.)

**Makes 8 to 10 servings   Hands-On Time 25 min.
Total Time 3 hours, 25 min.**

1 green bell pepper, chopped	2 (8.5-oz.) boxes Jiffy corn
1 firm tomato, seeded and chopped	muffin mix, prepared according to package
¾ cup finely chopped red onion	directions for cornbread,
1 cup mayonnaise	cooled, and crumbled
2 Tbsp. chopped bread-and-butter pickles	(8 cups crumbles)
1 tsp. bread-and-butter pickle juice	9 cooked bacon slices, chopped
	¼ cup chopped green onions

1. Stir together the vegetables in a medium bowl. Stir together the mayonnaise, pickles, and pickle juice in a small bowl.

2. Layer half the crumbled cornbread, half the vegetables, and half the mayonnaise mixture in a large salad bowl. Repeat layers with remaining cornbread, vegetables, and mayonnaise mixture. Sprinkle with bacon and green onions. Cover and chill 3 hours. Toss before serving.

Crook's Corner Shrimp and Grits

This classic dish was first served at Crook's Corner by the late chef Bill Neal, who has influenced young chefs all across the South. Executive chef Bill Smith has added some creative touches to the menu, but diners still enjoy Neal's recipes at the landmark restaurant—and this dish is still a mainstay.

Makes 4 servings   Hands-On Time 30 min.   Total Time 35 min.

1 (14-oz.) can chicken broth	¼ tsp. black pepper
¾ cup half-and-half	⅛ tsp. table salt
¾ tsp. table salt	¼ cup all-purpose flour
1 cup regular grits	1 cup sliced mushrooms
¾ cup (3 oz.) shredded Cheddar cheese	½ cup chopped green onions
¼ cup grated Parmesan cheese	2 garlic cloves, minced
2 Tbsp. butter	½ cup reduced-sodium, fat-free chicken broth
½ tsp. hot sauce	2 Tbsp. fresh lemon juice
¼ tsp. white pepper	¼ tsp. hot sauce
3 bacon slices	Lemon wedges
1 lb. medium-size raw shrimp, peeled and deveined	

1. Bring first 3 ingredients and 2 cups water to a boil in a medium saucepan; gradually whisk in grits.

2. Reduce heat, and simmer, stirring occasionally, 10 minutes or until thickened.

3. Add Cheddar cheese and next 4 ingredients. Keep warm.

4. Cook bacon in a large skillet until crisp; remove bacon, and drain on paper towels, reserving 1 Tbsp. drippings in skillet. Crumble bacon, and set aside. Sprinkle shrimp with pepper and salt; dredge in flour.

5. Sauté mushrooms in hot drippings in skillet 5 minutes or until tender. Add green onions, and sauté 2 minutes. Add shrimp and garlic, and sauté 2 minutes or until shrimp are lightly brown. Stir in chicken broth, lemon juice, and hot sauce, and cook 2 more minutes, stirring to loosen particles from bottom of skillet.

6. Serve shrimp mixture over hot cheese grits. Top with crumbled bacon; serve with lemon wedges.

Executive Chef Bill Smith, Crook's Corner
Chapel Hill, North Carolina

The Piedmont & the Mountains

Meet Chef Ashley Christensen

No chef in Raleigh is hotter than Ashley Christensen, a sentiment that Christensen herself—a real behind-the-scenes type of person—finds surprising.

Christensen has been cooking in this town since she was a 21-year-old college student. What folks love about her is not just her food but also her love of the city itself. She spearheaded a downtown restaurant revitalization when she opened Poole's Diner in 2007. The restaurant takes its name and industrial-chic speakeasy decor from the building's original tenant.

It's a place where Christensen re-imagines comfort-food classics with local ingredients and French technique. In addition to Poole's, she has opened three other Raleigh establishments, in a building once occupied by a Piggly Wiggly. Beasley's Chicken + Honey is her ode to fried chicken and Southern sides; Chuck's is a gourmet burger joint; and Fox Liquor Bar, in the building's basement, is a craft cocktail bar.

At each, she puts a modern twist on traditional Southern dishes.

"This recipe celebrates some of my favorite parts of great banana pudding. The roasted banana gives it a fruit-forward flavor (without making it too sweet), and the barely set gelatin adds a rich creaminess that's not too heavy."

—Ashley Christensen

Roasted Banana Panna Cotta with Bourbon Caramel

Makes 6 servings   Hands-On Time 40 min.
Total Time 3 hours, 35 min.

PANNA COTTA
1	medium banana
1 ½	cups heavy cream
¼	cup firmly packed brown sugar
Pinch of sea salt	
1	envelope unflavored gelatin
¼	cup cold water
¾	cup milk

BOURBON CARAMEL
2	cups sugar
1	Tbsp. light corn syrup
6	Tbsp. bourbon or whiskey
¾	cup unsalted butter, cut up
1	cup heavy cream, heated to just below a simmer
1	tsp. sea salt

GARNISH
1	banana, thinly sliced (if desired, sprinkled with 2 tsp. sugar and brûléed with a kitchen torch)

1. Prepare Panna Cotta: Preheat oven to 350°. Place unpeeled banana on a baking sheet, and roast at 350° for 15 minutes or until skin is black. Cool 10 minutes, and peel. Mix together banana, heavy cream, brown sugar, and pinch of sea salt in a saucepan; simmer 5 minutes, allowing fruit to infuse the cream. Remove from heat, and puree in a blender.

2. Sprinkle gelatin over cold water in a medium bowl; let stand 3 minutes. Add warm pureed cream mixture; stir until gelatin dissolves. Stir in milk. Divide mixture among 6 (4-oz.) ramekins or custard cups. Place plastic wrap directly on warm mixture (to prevent a film from forming), and chill 2 hours or until set.

3. Prepare Bourbon Caramel: Stir together sugar, corn syrup, ¼ cup water, and ¼ cup bourbon in a medium saucepan; cook over medium heat 18 minutes or until mixture is amber color and a candy thermometer registers 320°, swirling pan as mixture begins to turn amber. Remove from heat. Whisk in butter, heavy cream, and sea salt. Cool 30 minutes, and stir in remaining 2 Tbsp. bourbon.

4. Once the custards are chilled and set, uncover and invert each on a plate; remove the custard cup. Drizzle with desired amount of Bourbon Caramel; refrigerate any remaining caramel in an airtight container.

Welcome to Charlottesville

You can't talk about this city without mentioning Thomas Jefferson or the University of Virginia, which he founded.

A former President and by most accounts one of the greatest Americans to have lived, Jefferson gets credit for doubling the land area of the country with the Louisiana Purchase and writing much of the language of the Declaration of Independence.

Old T.J. also loved wine, a taste for which he acquired living in Europe as the associate U.S. ambassador to France in the late 1780s. He kept lists of the wines he loved and planned to import to this country—among them Yquem, Meursault, and Margaux, all familiar to modern connoisseurs.

Sadly he never succeeded in growing grapes and producing wine at Monticello, his magnificent home in Charlottesville. But things have come a long way in the world of Virginia wine. You can judge for yourself at Tastings, a local wine shop and restaurant with a convivial, educational environment.

Jefferson isn't Charlottesville's only famous dude. The city also produced the incredibly successful rock 'n' roll act, the Dave Matthews Band.

A native of South Africa, Matthews became a professional musician while he was a young adult tending bar at the Charlottesville club Miller's. First recording around 1991, Matthews and his jam band went on to make history. From 2000 to 2010, the Dave Matthews Band sold more concert tickets and earned more revenue than any other musical act in the country.

Today Matthews divides his time between Seattle, that indie-rock haven, and a farm outside of Charlottesville.

Monticello
Charlottesville, Virginia

Peanut Soup

The peanut has been farmed commercially in the Piedmont and other parts of the Southeast since the early 1800s. Its popularity as a food spread during the Civil War, when soldiers from both North and South relied on the humble legume, which grows underground, as a source of nutrition. It became an important rotation crop in cotton-growing regions in the early 1900s after the boll weevil destroyed cotton crops and farming technology made planting and harvesting peanuts easier. This rich, creamy soup uses two of the most popular products made from the peanut plant, peanut butter and roasted peanuts.

Makes 4 cups   Hands-On Time 15 min.   Total Time 45 min.

2	Tbsp. butter or margarine	½	cup creamy peanut butter
2	Tbsp. grated onion	½	cup half-and-half
1	celery rib, minced	2	Tbsp. chopped roasted peanuts
2	Tbsp. all-purpose flour		Garnish: cilantro sprigs
3	cups chicken broth		

1. Melt butter in a large saucepan over medium heat; add onion and celery, and sauté 5 minutes. Stir in flour, and cook, stirring constantly, 1 minute.

2. Add broth; bring to a boil, stirring constantly. Reduce heat; simmer 30 minutes.

3. Stir in peanut butter and half-and-half. Cook over low heat, stirring constantly, 3 to 4 minutes or until heated. Sprinkle with peanuts.

"Jefferson" Virginia Ham Pasta

Wild mushrooms and sheep's milk cheese lend earthy notes to this dish, a nod to the Virginia wine country and Thomas Jefferson's love of wine and pasta.

Makes 6 to 8 servings   Hands-On Time 30 min.   Total Time 30 min.

2 (8.8-oz.) packages strozzapreti pasta or penne pasta	1 cup Viognier or dry white wine*
¼ lb. country ham, cut into ⅛-inch-thick strips (about ¾ cup)	½ cup frozen sweet peas
2 Tbsp. olive oil	⅓ cup coarsely chopped fresh flat-leaf parsley
3 shallots, thinly sliced	¼ cup heavy cream
8 oz. assorted wild mushrooms, sliced	3 Tbsp. butter
1 garlic clove, thinly sliced	¼ tsp. black pepper
	1 cup freshly grated Pecorino Romano cheese

1. Prepare pasta according to package directions.

2. Meanwhile, sauté ham in hot oil in a large skillet over medium heat 2 minutes or until lightly browned and crisp. Add shallots; sauté 1 minute. Add mushrooms and garlic, and cook, stirring often, 2 minutes or until mushrooms are tender. Stir in wine; cook 5 minutes or until reduced by half.

3. Add peas, next 4 ingredients, and ½ cup cheese, stirring until cheese begins to melt and cream begins to thicken. Stir in hot cooked pasta, and toss until coated. Serve immediately with remaining ½ cup cheese.

Note: We tested with Jefferson Vineyards Viognier.

Enjoy Virginia Wine Like a Local

Hailing from upstate New York, Bill Curtis came to Charlottesville in 1968 for the usual reason: graduate school.

And he did what a lot of graduate students do to support themselves: worked in local restaurants. But Curtis was a lot better at it than most, taking over the management at top places in what was then a tiny dining scene.

He had already bought and sold the Wine Club of Charlottesville by 1990, when he turned an old sandwich shop into Tastings. A combined restaurant, wine shop, and wine-tasting room, Tastings is a local institution beloved for its rustic, French-accented down-home food (regulars love the homemade chicken liver pâté, crabmeat casserole, and beef tenderloin with Marchand de Vin sauce), as well as its incredible wine selection—more than 120 varieties on offer by the half-glass, glass, or flight.

Curtis knows a lot about a lot of wine, but he happens to be a true expert on the wines of Virginia, which many oenophiles believe are finally getting to be pretty good—a few hundred years later than Thomas Jefferson hoped.

Orange-Sweet Potato Pie with Rosemary-Cornmeal Crust

The simple addition of fresh chopped rosemary in the crust complements the flavors of the citrusy sweet potatoes in the filling.

Makes 8 servings **Hands-On Time 35 min.**
Total Time 4 hours, 35 min.

1. Prepare Crust: Whisk together first 5 ingredients in a medium bowl until well blended. Cut butter into flour mixture with a pastry blender or fork until mixture resembles small peas and is crumbly.

2. Sprinkle cold water, 1 Tbsp. at a time, over surface of mixture in bowl; stir with a fork until dry ingredients are moistened. Place dough on a plastic wrap-lined flat surface, and shape into a disc. Wrap in plastic wrap, and chill 30 minutes.

3. Unwrap dough, and roll between 2 new sheets of lightly floured plastic wrap into a 12-inch circle. Fit into a 9-inch pie plate. Fold edges under, and crimp. Chill 30 minutes.

4. Preheat oven to 400°. Bake crust 20 minutes, shielding edges with aluminum foil to prevent excessive browning. Cool completely on a wire rack (about 1 hour).

5. Meanwhile, prepare Filling: Bake sweet potatoes at 400° on a baking sheet 50 to 55 minutes or until tender. Let stand 5 minutes. Cut potatoes in half lengthwise; scoop out pulp into a bowl. Mash pulp. Discard skins.

6. Whisk together eggs and granulated sugar until well blended. Add milk, next 6 ingredients, and sweet potato pulp, stirring until blended. Pour mixture into Rosemary-Cornmeal Crust.

7. Bake at 400° for 20 minutes. Reduce heat to 325°, and bake 20 to 25 minutes or until center is set. Cool completely on a wire rack (about 1 hour).

Note: You can substitute ½ (15-oz.) package refrigerated piecrusts for cornmeal crust ingredients. Unroll on a lightly floured surface. Sprinkle with 1 Tbsp. plain white cornmeal and 2 tsp. chopped fresh rosemary. Lightly roll cornmeal and rosemary into crust. Fit into a 9-inch pie plate according to package directions. Fold edges under; crimp. Proceed as directed, beginning with Step 5.

Crystal Detamore Rodman
Charlottesville, Virginia

CRUST
- ¾ cup all-purpose flour
- ½ cup plain white cornmeal
- ¼ cup powdered sugar
- 2 tsp. chopped fresh rosemary
- ¼ tsp. table salt
- ½ cup cold butter, cut into pieces
- ¼ cup very cold water

FILLING
- 1 ½ lb. sweet potatoes
- 3 large eggs
- ¾ cup granulated sugar
- 1 cup evaporated milk
- 3 Tbsp. butter, melted
- 2 tsp. orange zest
- 1 Tbsp. fresh orange juice
- ½ tsp. ground cinnamon
- ¼ tsp. ground nutmeg
- 1 ½ tsp. vanilla extract

Bourbon-Glazed Ham

Bourbon, brown sugar, and mustard make a sweet and smoky glaze.

Makes 12 servings   Hands-On Time 20 min.   Total Time 3 hours

1   (10-lb.) smoked fully cooked ham
¾   cup whole cloves
¾   cup bourbon or apple juice
2   cups dark brown sugar
1   Tbsp. dry mustard
2   navel oranges, sliced

1. Preheat oven to 325°. Wrap ham in aluminum foil, and place in a lightly greased 13- x 9-inch pan; bake for 2 hours.

2. Remove ham from oven, and increase oven temperature to 450°. Unwrap ham; discard foil. Remove skin from ham, and trim fat to ¼-inch thickness. Make shallow cuts in fat ¾ inch apart in a diamond pattern. Insert cloves in centers of diamonds.

3. Stir together ¼ cup bourbon, sugar, and mustard in a small bowl; set aside. Brush ham with remaining ½ cup bourbon. Pat sugar mixture evenly over ham; arrange orange slices over sugar, and secure with wooden picks. Lightly baste with drippings; bake at 450° for 15 to 20 minutes or until sugar melts and forms a glaze.

Clairiece Gilbert Humphrey
Charlottesville, Virginia

Home-style Green Bean Casserole

Fresh veggies and a lightened sauce enliven this essential Southern casserole.

Makes 8 servings   Hands-On Time 25 min.   Total Time 55 min.

1 ½   lb. fresh green beans, trimmed
2   Tbsp. butter
¼   cup all-purpose flour
1 ½   cups 2% reduced-fat milk
½   cup nonfat buttermilk
1   Tbsp. Ranch dressing mix
2   tsp. chopped fresh thyme
¼   tsp. table salt
¼   tsp. black pepper
1   tsp. butter
1   (8-oz.) package sliced fresh mushrooms
Vegetable cooking spray
1   cup French-fried onions, crushed
½   cup panko (Japanese breadcrumbs)
2   plum tomatoes, seeded and chopped

1. Preheat oven to 350°. Cook green beans in boiling salted water to cover in a Dutch oven 4 to 6 minutes or to desired degree of doneness; drain. Plunge into ice water to stop the cooking process; drain and pat dry.

2. Melt 2 Tbsp. butter in Dutch oven over medium heat; whisk in flour until smooth. Cook, whisking constantly, 1 minute. Gradually whisk in milk; cook, whisking constantly, 3 to 4 minutes or until sauce is thickened and bubbly. Remove from heat, and whisk in buttermilk and next 4 ingredients.

3. Melt 1 tsp. butter in a medium skillet over medium-high heat; add mushrooms, and sauté 6 to 8 minutes or until lightly browned. Remove from heat; let stand 5 minutes. Gently toss mushrooms and green beans in buttermilk sauce. Place in a 13- x 9-inch or 3-qt. baking dish coated with cooking spray.

4. Combine French-fried onions and next 2 ingredients; sprinkle over green bean mixture. Bake at 350° for 25 to 30 minutes or until golden brown and bubbly. Serve immediately.

Refrigerator Yeast Rolls

Makes about 7 dozen   Hands-On Time 45 min.
Total Time 9 hours, 45 min.

1. Stir together yeast and warm water in a medium bowl; let mixture stand 5 minutes. Stir together flour, sugar, and salt in a large bowl. Cut shortening into flour mixture with a pastry blender until crumbly; stir in yeast mixture and eggs just until blended (do not overmix). Cover and chill 8 hours.

2. Roll dough to ¼-inch thickness on a well-floured surface (dough will be soft); cut with a 1½-inch round cutter, rerolling dough scraps as needed.

3. Brush rounds with melted butter. Make a crease across each round with a knife, and fold rounds in half, gently pressing edges together to seal. Place in a 15- x 10-inch jelly-roll pan and a 9-inch round cake pan (edges of rounds should touch). Cover and let rise in a warm place (85°), free from drafts, 45 minutes or until doubled in bulk.

4. Preheat oven to 400°. Bake rolls for 8 to 10 minutes or until golden brown.

1	(¼-oz.) envelope active dry yeast
2	cups warm water (105° to 115°)
6	cups bread flour
½	cup sugar
½	tsp. table salt
½	cup shortening
2	large eggs
½	cup butter, melted

Meet Chefs Dean and Erin Maupin

Growing up in Charlottesville's Albemarle County, Dean Maupin spent summers working at his grandfather's fruit stand.

When he grew up and found a serious passion for cooking, he moved to West Virginia to work at the venerable Greenbrier Hotel, cooking for visiting food-world dignitaries. But it was when Maupin began running the locally famed kitchen at Keswick Hall, a property near Monticello, that he came into his own as a chef.

It's also where he met his wife, Erin, an executive pastry chef who graduated from the Culinary Institute of America and worked at the Manhattan outpost of the utterly glamorous Fouchon bakery in Paris (think the world's most beautiful macarons and éclairs) before coming to the Piedmont.

While Erin has put her pastry ambitions on pause to raise the couple's three small kids ("hopefully," she says, she'll get back to turning out gorgeous sweets soon), Dean lately has taken over at C&O, a Charlottesville institution since 1976 where the kitchen is devoted to serving the bounty produced by local cheese makers, vintners, and ranchers. C&O is known for its warm, inviting ambience and its six distinct dining areas. Maupin is thrilled to helm what *The Washington Post* has called "the least prepossessing fine dining restaurant in America."

"This recipe takes a bit of effort, but the payoff is a priceless family memory and a huge sweet grin. It's also fabulous when made with sliced ripe summer peaches or any combination of fruits." —Dean Maupin

Strawberry-Rhubarb Cobbler Pie

This rustic hybrid of cobbler and pie, which dates back more than 80 years in Erin's family, has an unusual method and hard-to-describe texture. A sugar-flour-butter mixture is placed both beneath and on top of the fruit, and then the top of the pie is drizzled with thinned beaten egg. Rather than staying in distinct top and bottom layers, the sugary mixture sinks into and bobs out of the filling during baking, creating soft custardy pockets below the surface and sugar-cookie-like bits on top.

Makes 8 servings   Hands-On Time 20 min.   Total Time 5 hours, 20 min.

PIECRUST
1 ¼ cups all-purpose flour
½ cup cold unsalted butter, diced
½ tsp. table salt
½ tsp. sugar
4 to 6 Tbsp. ice water

CRUMB MIXTURE
¾ cup sugar
⅓ cup all-purpose flour
¼ cup cold unsalted butter, diced
¼ tsp. table salt

FRUIT FILLING
1 (16-oz.) package fresh strawberries, quartered
1 ½ cups (½-inch-thick) sliced fresh (not frozen) rhubarb
½ cup sugar
3 Tbsp. cornstarch
2 tsp. orange zest
3 Tbsp. fresh orange juice

ADDITIONAL INGREDIENTS
1 large egg
Sweetened whipped cream

1. Prepare Piecrust: In a food processor, pulse the flour, butter, salt, and sugar until it resembles cornmeal with random chunks of butter. Transfer to a bowl, and add ice water, mixing the dough with your hands. It should look crumbly and not wet, but if you press it together, it should hold. Wrap tightly in plastic wrap, and chill at least 1 hour.

2. On a floured work surface, roll dough to a 13-inch circle. Carefully place into a 9-inch pie plate; fold edges under, and use your fingers to create a decorative edge. Chill until crumb mixture and filling are ready.

3. Preheat oven to 400°. **Prepare Crumb Mixture:** Pulse all ingredients in a food processor until very crumbly.

4. Prepare Fruit Filling: Mix together all ingredients in a bowl.

5. Put half of the crumb mixture on the bottom of the piecrust. Put all the fruit on top of the crumb mixture. Top with remaining crumb mixture. Whisk together egg and 1 Tbsp. water; drizzle over pie.

6. Bake at 400° for 50 minutes to 1 hour or until juices are bubbly and crumb bits are lightly browned and form a crust, shielding with aluminum foil to prevent excessive browning, if necessary. Cool completely on a wire rack (about 3 hours). Serve with whipped cream.

Welcome to
Asheville

Before the arrival of the railroads in the 1880s, Asheville was a crossroads of Native American trails and trading routes. It became the rustic, vacation-oriented mountain resort town it's known as only after attracting some genuine patrons.

The one with the deepest pockets by far was George W. Vanderbilt, a descendant of a family of Dutch immigrants to New York who became railroad barons. According to his obituary in the March 7, 1914, *New York Times*, Vanderbilt was a dilettante—a man educated entirely by private tutors, who spoke eight languages and whose chief occupation was "world traveler."

What he wanted to create in Asheville was a magnificent European-style country estate, and he stopped at nothing to do it. According to Vanderbilt's obituary, "It was begun in 1890 and finished five years later at a cost of more than $3,000,000." The largest private home in America, the Biltmore has 250 rooms (34 bedrooms and 43 bathrooms—just think of the cleaning!), and it sits on 125,000 acres. Vanderbilt considered it to be the perfect place to pursue his attendant interests in birds, gardening, and forestry. He became a farmer, raising prize hogs, and a serious horticulturalist before his untimely death of "weak heart."

Still owned by George Vanderbilt's heirs, the Biltmore is now a massive tourist attraction where visitors can spend the night (if they can afford it); dine in one of six restaurants or have a more casual meal or snack in one of the six shops on the estate; tour the gardens; and canoe, bike, horseback ride, or Segway around the grounds. The Biltmore offers a chance to live like a king on vacation in the North Carolina mountains.

Apple-Pear Salad with Maple-Pecan Bacon

Makes 8 servings   Hands-On Time 20 min.
Total Time 1 hour

8	thick bacon slices
¼	cup maple syrup
1 ½	cups finely chopped pecans
2	(5-oz.) packages gourmet salad greens
1	large Bartlett pear
1	large Gala apple
1	cup halved seedless red grapes
4	oz. Gorgonzola cheese, crumbled

Cranberry Vinaigrette

1. Preheat oven to 400°. Place a lightly greased wire rack in an aluminum foil-lined 15- x 10-inch jelly-roll pan. Dip bacon slices in syrup, allowing excess to drip off; press pecans onto both sides of bacon. Arrange bacon slices in a single layer on rack, and bake at 400° for 20 minutes; turn bacon slices, and bake 5 to 10 more minutes or until browned and crisp. Remove from oven, and let stand 5 minutes. Cut bacon crosswise into 1-inch pieces.

2. Place salad greens on a serving platter. Cut pear and apple into thin slices; toss with salad greens. Top with grapes, cheese, and bacon.

3. Serve salad with Cranberry Vinaigrette.

Cranberry Vinaigrette

Makes 2 cups   Hands-On Time 10 min.
Total Time 10 min.

1	cup canned whole-berry cranberry sauce
1	tsp. orange zest
½	cup fresh orange juice
¼	cup balsamic vinegar
¼	cup olive oil
1	Tbsp. light brown sugar
2	tsp. grated fresh ginger
½	tsp. table salt

1. Whisk together all ingredients in a medium bowl until blended and smooth.

Meet Chef
Katie Button

It takes guts to jump from a safe, prestigious career track into the great unknown, but that's exactly what Asheville chef Katie Button did in 2007 when she left a PhD program in neuroscience to pursue a life in food.

Button was in Washington, D.C., for a position with the National Institutes of Health, but she couldn't stay out of the kitchen. She finagled a job with José Andrés, the Spanish chef and owner of a slew of D.C. hotspots. That was when the real change took place: Button fell in love with the flavors of regional Spanish food and has devoted her life to re-creating them.

Along the way she had an internship at El Bulli, the experimental and extremely famous restaurant in the mountains of Rosas, Spain, owned by the chef Ferran Adrià.

When Button returned to the States, she moved to Asheville with her mother (a professional caterer), her fiancé (a former El Bulli service manager), and her dad. Their goal: to open an authentic Spanish restaurant in the North Carolina mountain town they love. And so they have: Cúrate Bar de Tapas. *Cúrate* means "cure yourself" in Spanish.

"I spent three months working as a server at El Bulli (Ferran Adrià's famous restaurant in Spain), and it was there that I made the decision that I really wanted to be on the other side, with my hands in the dishes, creating."

—Katie Button

Gambas al Ajillo
(Shrimp Sautéed in Garlic)

This simple dish is the most popular appetizer at Cúrate.

Makes 4 servings   Hands-On Time 15 min.   Total Time 15 min.

16 unpeeled large raw shrimp	½ tsp. table salt, plus more to taste
¼ cup light olive oil or olive oil blend	2 dried arbol chiles
4 garlic cloves (2 whole, with skin on; 2 peeled and thinly sliced)	1 bay leaf
	¼ cup dry sherry

1. Peel shrimp, leaving tails on. Butterfly shrimp by making a deep slit down back of each from large end to tail, cutting to but not through inside curve of shrimp; devein.

2. Heat oil in a sauté pan over medium heat; add whole garlic cloves. Meanwhile, sprinkle the shrimp with ½ tsp. salt. When the skin of the whole garlic cloves has just begun to brown, add the sliced garlic; As soon as the sliced garlic just barely begins to brown, add the arbol chiles, bay leaf, and salted shrimp.

3. Toss everything together in the pan, and sauté about 1 minute or until the shrimp are halfway cooked (still raw in the center). Remove from the heat, stir in the sherry, and return to the stove over medium heat.

4. As soon as the shrimp are just cooked through (1 to 2 minutes), remove them from the pan with tongs, and place on the serving dish. Return the sauce to the stove, and reduce a little bit, tasting and adjusting the seasoning for amount of salt. Remove chiles, bay leaf, and whole garlic cloves.

5. Pour the hot sauce over the shrimp, and serve immediately.

Blue Ridge Mountains
near Asheville, North Carolina

Grilled Rainbow Trout with Mushroom Stuffing

Rainbow, brown and brook trout abound in the streams and creeks of western North Carolina and are favorites of fly fishermen and those lucky enough to share their tables.

Makes 6 servings   Hands-On Time 15 min.   Total Time 30 min

6	(1 ½-lb.) dressed rainbow trout		1	Tbsp. fresh thyme leaves
¼	cup olive oil		½	tsp. table salt
2	shallots, minced		½	tsp. black pepper
½	lb. fresh mushrooms, chopped		2	lemons, thinly sliced
¼	cup fine dry breadcrumbs		12	fresh thyme sprigs

1. Preheat grill to 350° to 400° (medium-high) heat.

2. Brush inside of trout with oil. Combine shallots and next 5 ingredients; spoon evenly into trout. Place lemon slices and thyme sprigs on stuffing and outside of fish; tie trout with kitchen string. Brush outside of trout with oil.

3. Cook, covered with grill lid, about 8 minutes per side or until fish flakes easily with a fork.

Meet Author
Charles Frazier

"What we have lost will never be returned to us. The land will not heal—too much blood. All we can do is learn from the past and make peace with it."

So says Ada, the heroine of Charles Frazier's epic Civil War novel, *Cold Mountain*. Frazier himself is no deserter. A native of Asheville and a graduate of the University of North Carolina, the University of South Carolina, and Appalachian State University, Frazier went from English professor to super-star author with the 1997 publication of *Cold Mountain*.

The meticulously researched love-and-war story—based loosely on the life of one of Frazier's forebears, a many-times-great uncle who deserted the Confederacy—captured the minds and hearts of its readers. The 2003 movie version won supporting actress Renée Zellweger an Academy Award.

Frazier makes his home in North Carolina, and he is beyond passionate about his method for making soup beans, so much so that calling it a recipe doesn't do it justice. It's more a love story, and we print it here in its unabridged glory.

Soup Beans, a Love Story

By Charles Frazier

This dish—an adaptation of an old-time Southern Appalachian staple usually called soup beans rather than bean soup—is the food I remember loving first. Its most traditional form was very simple: just pintos cooked with a hunk of fatback in water and served with chopped raw onion, maybe a dollop of sweet-hot pepper relish, and a wedge of cornbread. But the version I first loved was made by our neighbor, Mrs. Fuller. By about age three, I began keeping track of when she was cooking soup beans and would wander over. I remember her kitchen, the fragrance of cooking as I came in the back door, and bowls of white beans still whole but buttery soft in a thick broth rich with cooked onions and smoky pork.

I've been chasing that flavor for decades, tinkering pot by pot with composition and proportion. What I make these days has more vegetables, less pork. I don't have a written recipe, and I don't measure anything, this being neither baking nor a science project, so I'll just estimate based on a pound of dried navy beans. I usually don't presoak them, but just allow extra cooking time. Besides, when you change the soaking water, a bit of flavor goes down the drain. A latterday bean-related improvement I've made is the addition of yellow split peas—a scant handful for a pound of beans. During the long slow cooking, the peas completely fall apart, thickening and enriching the broth, and adding a slight butter color as well.

As for pork, at various times I've used ham hock, ham, kielbasa, and thick-cut bacon. All good, so take your pick. I dice ham or sausage into pieces no bigger than the bean I'm using, and I cut the bacon into lardons. For my tastes, I use no more than a half pound of pork to a pound of dried beans; otherwise the flavor of the vegetables becomes overwhelmed by hog. Unless you're using hock, you will need to brown the pork lightly. The vegetables are the basic mirepoix—at least one large onion, four to six carrots depending on size, and three or four celery ribs. I dice the vegetables fairly small and sauté them slowly in the fat left in the pan from browning the pork, perhaps enhanced with a little olive oil. Near the end of the sauté, add a couple of cloves of minced garlic.

At that point, combine the beans, peas, pork, and vegetables in the pot and add liquid to cover by at least a couple of inches. I use a roughly half-and-half mixture of water and either chicken or vegetable broth. Add two or three teaspoons of summer savory and a bay leaf or two, salt and pepper. After bringing to a boil, cook low and slow. Allow a minimum of four hours, though cook time on dried beans varies by the size and freshness of the beans and your altitude. Check the pot at least every hour to adjust spices and add more liquid as needed. My goal is a point of doneness where the split peas are entirely dissolved and the navy beans are still whole but completely soft. Al dente has no place in soup beans. Some mountain cooks like this dish thick enough to serve on a plate and eat with a fork. I go for a stew texture, bowl food but not thin soup. Serve soup beans the traditional way, with raw onion, relish, and cornbread. Or, substitute my favorite nontraditional finishing touch, a drizzle of high quality olive oil and a grind of coarse pepper.

Please turn the page for the *Southern Living* take on the recipe.

The Piedmont & the Mountains

Soup Beans

Here's how we prepared the dish, based on Charles Frazier's ode (page 198). Ours was delicious and just as he described: "bowl food but not thin soup."

Makes 8 cups Hands-On Time 20 min. Total Time 3 hours, 50 min.

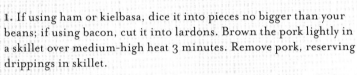

8	oz. cured pork (ham, kielbasa, or thick-cut bacon) or 1½ lb. ham hocks
1	large onion
4	carrots
4	celery ribs
	Olive oil, as needed
2	garlic cloves, minced
1	lb. dried navy beans
	Scant handful (¼ cup) yellow split peas
4	cups chicken or vegetable broth
3	tsp. dried savory
1	bay leaf
	Table salt
	Freshly ground black pepper
	Chopped raw onion, sweet-hot pepper relish, and wedges of cornbread or good olive oil and coarse black pepper

1. If using ham or kielbasa, dice it into pieces no bigger than your beans; if using bacon, cut it into lardons. Brown the pork lightly in a skillet over medium-high heat 3 minutes. Remove pork, reserving drippings in skillet.

2. Dice the vegetables fairly small, and cook them gently in the hot drippings (or in 2 Tbsp. olive oil, if using ham hocks) over medium-low heat 5 minutes. Enhance with a little olive oil if desired or if you don't have enough drippings. When vegetables are fragrant and translucent but not browned, add minced garlic, and cook 1 to 2 more minutes.

3. Combine navy beans, split peas, pork or ham hocks, and vegetables in a large Dutch oven. Cover by at least 2 inches with equal parts water and broth (about 4 cups each). Add savory, bay leaf, and ¼ tsp. each salt and pepper. Bring to a boil; cover, reduce heat, and simmer 2 hours. Uncover and cook 1½ hours more or until split peas are entirely dissolved and navy beans are still whole but completely soft, stirring occasionally and adding liquid if needed to keep the beans submerged. (Cook time will vary depending on the size and freshness of the beans and your altitude.) Season with additional salt and pepper to taste.

4. Serve with chopped raw onion, sweet-hot pepper relish, and wedges of cornbread, or substitute a nontraditional finishing touch: a drizzle of good olive oil and a grind of coarse pepper.

Ginger Ale-Brown Sugar Smoked Ham

Grab a bottle of your favorite spicy or "hot" ginger ale (such as Blenheim from South Carolina or Buffalo Rock from Alabama) to use in this recipe.

**Makes 16 to 18 appetizer servings   Hands-On Time 15 min.
Total Time 4 hours, 50 min.**

1 (8- to 9-lb.) smoked, ready-to-cook, bone-in ham	2 tsp. coarsely ground black pepper
2 (12-oz.) bottles or cans spicy ginger ale	½ tsp. kosher salt
½ cup bourbon	½ tsp. dry mustard
¼ cup firmly packed dark brown sugar	¼ tsp. ground red pepper
	Garnish: flat-leaf parsley sprigs

1. Preheat oven to 325°. Remove skin from ham, and trim fat to ¼-inch thickness. Make shallow cuts in fat 1 inch apart in a diamond pattern. Place ham, fat side up, in a roasting pan; add ginger ale and bourbon to pan. Cover loosely with aluminum foil.

2. Bake, covered, at 325° for 4 to 4½ hours or until a meat thermometer inserted into ham registers 140°, basting with pan juices every 30 minutes.

3. Stir together brown sugar and next 4 ingredients. Remove ham from oven; uncover and sprinkle sugar mixture over ham, lightly pressing mixture into fat.

4. Bake, uncovered, at 325° for an additional 20 to 25 minutes or until crust is browned and a meat thermometer registers 145°. Transfer ham to a cutting board, and let stand 15 minutes before carving.

Warm Lentil-and-Potato Salad

French green lentils remain firm after cooking, adding flavor, color, and texture to this warm bacon-imbued potato salad.

Makes 8 servings   Hands-On Time 25 min.   Total Time 50 min.

1. Bring lentils and 4 cups salted water to a boil in a heavy 2-qt. saucepan over medium-high heat. Reduce heat to low; simmer 20 to 25 minutes or just until tender.

2. Meanwhile, cook potatoes in boiling salted water to cover 15 minutes or just until tender. Drain lentils and potatoes.

3. Cook bacon in a large, deep nonstick skillet over medium heat 6 to 7 minutes or until crisp; remove bacon, and drain on paper towels, reserving 2 Tbsp. drippings in skillet. Crumble bacon.

4. Add olive oil to hot drippings in skillet, and heat over medium heat. Sauté shallots, celery, and garlic in hot olive oil mixture 3 minutes. Remove from heat, and stir in vinegar and mustard. Season with salt and pepper to taste. Gently stir in lentils, potatoes, bacon, and parsley.

½ cup dried French green lentils
1 (28-oz.) package small red potatoes, halved
5 bacon slices
3 Tbsp. olive oil
2 large shallots, finely chopped
1 celery rib, sliced
2 garlic cloves
2 to 3 Tbsp. red wine vinegar
2 tsp. whole grain Dijon mustard
1 ½ cups loosely packed fresh flat-leaf parsley leaves

Meet Actress Andie MacDowell

Rosalie Anderson "Andie" MacDowell–the model, actress, philanthropist, and mother of three–has long lived in Asheville, North Carolina, when she wasn't working in Los Angeles.

Originally from Gaffney, South Carolina, MacDowell got her start modeling, dropping out of college to pursue it, and made the transition to acting—breaking out as the love interest of Emilio Estevez in the 1985 film *St. Elmo's Fire*. From there MacDowell was in a string of hits, including lauded performances in *Sex, Lies, & Videotape* (1989), *Groundhog Day* (1993), and *Four Weddings and a Funeral* (1994).

MacDowell chose to live in North Carolina because when she was a child her family owned a summer home in the town of Arden, just south of Asheville. The home has since become a bed-and-breakfast called Blake House Inn.

Here MacDowell shares a recipe for a favorite salad, which happens to be both vegetarian and gluten free.

"My favorite way to cook is to trust my instincts—to follow a recipe but with the freedom to make it my own. That is what Southern cooking and this salad are all about."

—Andie MacDowell

Anything-Goes Salad with Lemon-Mustard Dressing

You can switch the recipe around each night and make it a little different depending on your choice of vegetables. It also goes well with fish.

Makes 4 servings   Hands-On Time 10 min.   Total Time 10 min.

DRESSING (makes about ½ cup)
¼ cup delicious extra virgin olive oil
2 Tbsp. freshly squeezed lemon juice
½ tsp. Dijon mustard
¼ tsp. fine sea salt

SALAD
1 (5-oz.) package baby spinach and arugula

4 cups chopped fresh vegetables of your choosing (I prefer cauliflower, broccoli, beets, carrots, cucumber, celery, and tomatoes)
½ cup grapefruit segments
4 oz. goat cheese, at room temperature

1. Prepare the Dressing: Combine all ingredients in a small jar with a tight-fitting lid. Shake vigorously for 30 seconds until emulsified. Taste and adjust salt, lemon juice, and olive oil as needed to achieve a pleasing balance.

2. Prepare the Salad: Toss greens with vegetables, grapefruit, and dressing. Add additional salt and pepper to taste. Add dollops of goat cheese. Enjoy.

Buttermilk Biscuits

This versatile biscuit recipe, beloved across the South, only requires three ingredients. The keys are Southern staples: self-rising soft wheat flour (such as White Lily or Martha White brands), good butter and good buttermilk. For a flavor kick, try one of the four recipe variations.

Makes 2 dozen   Hands-On Time 22 min.   Total Time 45 min.

½   cup cold butter
2 ¼ cups self-rising soft wheat flour
1 ¼ cups buttermilk

Self-rising soft wheat flour
2   Tbsp. melted butter

1. Cut cold butter with a sharp knife or pastry blender into ¼-inch-thick slices. Sprinkle butter slices over flour in a large bowl. Toss butter with flour, and then cut butter into flour with a pastry blender until crumbly and mixture resembles small peas. Cover and chill 10 minutes. Add buttermilk, stirring just until dry ingredients are moistened.

2. Preheat oven to 450°. Turn dough out onto a lightly floured surface; knead 3 or 4 times, gradually adding additional flour as needed. With floured hands, press or pat dough into a ¾-inch-thick rectangle (about 9 x 5 inches). Sprinkle top of dough with additional flour. Fold dough over onto itself in 3 sections, starting with 1 short end; fold dough rectangle as if folding a letter-size piece of paper). Repeat entire process 2 more times, beginning with pressing into a ¾-inch-thick dough rectangle (about 9 x 5 inches).

3. Press or pat dough to ½-inch thickness on a lightly floured surface; cut with a 2-inch round cutter. Place biscuits, side by side, on a parchment paper-lined or lightly greased jelly-roll pan (biscuits should touch).

4. Bake at 450° for 13 to 15 minutes or until lightly browned. Remove from oven; brush with 2 Tbsp. melted butter.

For Cinnamon-Raisin Biscuits: Omit 2 Tbsp. melted butter. Combine ½ cup golden raisins, ½ tsp. ground cinnamon, and ⅓ cup chopped pecans with flour in a large bowl. Proceed with recipe as directed. Stir together ½ cup powdered sugar and 2 Tbsp. buttermilk until smooth. Drizzle over warm biscuits. Makes 2½ dozen.

For Black Pepper-Bacon Biscuits: Combine ⅓ cup cooked and crumbled bacon slices (about 5 slices) and 1 tsp. black pepper with flour in a large bowl. Proceed with recipe as directed. Makes 2½ dozen.

For Feta-Oregano Biscuits: Combine 1 (4-oz.) package crumbled feta cheese and ½ tsp. dried oregano with flour in a large bowl. Proceed with recipe as directed. Makes 2½ dozen.

For Pimiento Cheese Biscuits: Combine 1 cup (4 oz.) shredded sharp Cheddar cheese with flour in a large bowl. Reduce buttermilk to 1 cup. Stir together buttermilk and 1 (4-oz.) jar diced pimiento, undrained. Proceed with recipe as directed. Makes 2½ dozen.

Visit Malaprop's Like a Local

People who champion the underdog and rally around independent bookstores would do well to adopt Malaprop's as their emblem.

This Asheville institution is so much more than a place to buy a book.

Since opening in 1982, when downtown Asheville was blighted and rents were super cheap, Malaprop's Bookstore has been a gathering place for the sharing of ideas, gossip, poetry—all the essentials for a literary life.

It's named for a female character in Richard Brinsley Sheridan's 1775 play *The Rivals*—best known for her colorful (mis)use of language. And it's chock-full of personality.

Owner Emöke Zsuzsanna B'Racz—a native of Budapest, Hungary, and an established poet—brings a decidedly European sensibility to the place. She wraps each purchase with craft paper and a red bow, encourages a strong selection of women's writing and poetry in the store, and makes sure her newsletter to customers is witty and engaging.

The Bluegrass, Bourbon & Barbecue Trail

Singer, modern poet, and rhinestone cowboy Neil Diamond immortalized a woman from Kentucky when he crooned, "Well, she ain't the kind makes heads turn at the drop of her name. But something inside that she's got turns you on just the same." He penned the 1967 classic "Kentucky Woman" in a limo on his way to a gig in Paducah. He might as well have been singing about the state itself.

You might not get excited at the mention of Kentucky or, for that matter, neighboring state Tennessee—at least not at first. But who doesn't love the strummy twang of bluegrass, the addictive sting of bourbon, and the smoky flavor of blues and barbecue. Kentucky and Tennessee are unsung heroes of the South, places with a distinct sweet-hot vibe that comes from the perfect fusion of good music and good food.

Start with **Louisville, Kentucky**. Although nearly three-quarters of a century have passed since *Kentucky: A Guide to the Bluegrass State* was first published, many of its sentiments still ring true.

The slender 1939 travelogue rightly describes Louisville as a great American city featuring "fine whisky, beautiful women, and the Kentucky Derby." Written as a project of the federal Work Projects Administration, it pegs the city's work-hard-play-hard character: "Louisville is too busy making and selling things to have the languor of a town in the Deep South, but it does have its special graces. Its people are friendly and hospitable. Bourbon and water or a cocktail after work is popular; amusement and relaxation are as important as work."

Louisville is where the mighty Ohio River, on its way to merge with the Mississippi, is interrupted by rapids known as the Falls of the Ohio. In its early territorial days, it was a place where trappers, traders and explorers crossed paths.

England won the land of the Ohio Valley from the French in 1763, but it wasn't until 1778 that frontier explorer George Rogers Clark (brother of Meriwether Lewis's partner William Clark) founded the first real settlement, indeed the first city west of the Allegheny Mountains. It was named a few years later for Louis XVI, the French king who aided the colonists

Woodford Reserve Distillery
Versailles, Kentucky

in their fight for independence.

Louisville (pronounced LOU-uh-vull by locals) quickly became a thriving steamboat center, a place where settlers came from Virginia and the Carolinas to try their luck and connect with the rivers of commerce.

As a border city situated in a border state, Louisville has a lot of competing concerns to balance. The Civil War years were particularly hard. Louisville had many plantations, and those places employed plenty of slaves, but Kentucky stayed in the Union during the War. It was only *after* Appomattox that it became inhabited by Confederate veterans and seceded.

Louisville established railroad connections around the South—to Memphis, New Orleans, Mobile, and Atlanta—and tobacco trading and manufacturing were its big moneymakers.

Nothing is bigger in Louisville, though, than the thing we most know it for: the Kentucky Derby, often described as "the most exciting two minutes in sports." Horseracing has been going on in Louisville since 1783, when races were held on Market Street; the first racetracks were actually built to get the sport *out* of the streets.

The Louisville Jockey Club racetrack was the brainchild of "Colonel" Meriwether Lewis Clark, Jr., the grandson of Louisville's founding father. His mother had come from a prominent Louisville family who invested in Thorough-bred horses.

During a visit to Paris in the mid-1800s, he was inspired by the pari-mutuel betting machines he saw at the French racetracks and the way these machines eliminated bookies. Upon his return, he

Wild Turkey Distillery
Lawrenceburg, Kentucky

Soul Fish Cafe
Memphis, Tennessee

Sun Studio
Memphis, Tennessee

Kentucky and Tennessee are unsung heroes of the
South, places with a distinct sweet-hot vibe that comes
from the perfect fusion of good music and good food.

convinced some of his mother's relatives to back him in a new racetrack that would make use of this new betting system and also showcase the family's Thoroughbreds.

The Kentucky Derby was held at that racetrack—later known as Churchill Downs (Clark's mother's maiden name was "Churchill")—when it opened on May 17, 1875, and on the first Saturday in May ever since (more about the Derby on page 218).

Louisville also has been a bourbon town since (and before) the Brown-Forman Distillery opened in 1870. Its Old Forester Kentucky Straight Bourbon Whiskey was the first commercially produced bottled bourbon in the country.

Today Kentucky's 255-mile Bourbon Trail of local distilleries includes such familiar brands as Jim Beam, Maker's Mark, Woodford Reserve, and Wild Turkey as well

as museums and exhibits devoted to Kentucky's history as a bourbon capital.

It's quite a history. Since the 1700s Kentuckians have been converting corn and other grains into whiskey, which made it easier to transport on narrow trails and over mountains on the way to market. The bourbon name traces to 1785 and Bourbon County, one of three Kentucky counties in existence since Kentucky territory was part of Virginia. In those days, farmers shipped their whiskey in oak barrels stamped "Bourbon County."

As it traveled down the Ohio and Mississippi Rivers on its way to New Orleans and other markets, it aged and acquired the distinctive oaky notes we associate with it today. The Kentucky Distillers' Association has trademarked the phrase "America's Official Native Spirit" for its product, and it's a real point of pride.

Pride is a feeling that most folks in **Memphis, Tennessee,** can relate to thanks in part to the beloved music of B.B. King and Isaac Hayes, both natives, and Elvis Presley, who made his impressive home there.

Historians say the blues were born in the North Mississippi Delta after the Civil War. Highway 61, which stretches from Mississippi to Memphis, along with parts of Highway 49, which intersects it near Clarksdale, Mississippi, have come to be known as the Blues Trail because they cross the region where so many legendary musicians were born.

Memphians will tell you that the Delta begins in the lobby of the Peabody Hotel (more about the hotel on page 238). And it's true that the city loves its music—especially blues, rockabilly, soul, and gospel.

A lot of people say rock 'n' roll was born in Memphis, too, on approximately July 5, 1954. That's

Beale Street Brass Note
Walk of Fame
Memphis, Tennessee

JERRY LEE LEWIS
"THE KILLER"

Sun Studio
Memphis, Tennessee

B.B. King

Music just may have saved Memphis. Most of the great
musicians we associate with the city came there to make a
living because Memphis supported the music.

the day a 19-year-old Presley walked into Sun Studio and sang the old blues song "That's All Right." Even Paul Simon sings about the magical musical powers of Memphis: "The Mississippi Delta was shining/Like a National guitar/I am following the river/Down the highway/Through the cradle of the Civil War/I'm going to Graceland" (more about Elvis and Graceland on page 230).

Long before the music, there were the bluffs, the little hills where the Spanish explorer Hernando de Soto happened upon the Mississippi River at Memphis. The site was variously a Native American village, a French fort, and a Spanish fort.

All of western Tennessee was part of the Chickasaw Indian Territory—although this distinction didn't stop Europeans from laying claim to it—until about 1820.

That's when investors, including General Andrew Jackson and Nashville lawyer John Overton, sent surveyors to lay out a town and sell lots on it; they named it "Memphis" after a city in ancient Egypt.

The town initially competed with the nearby city of Randolph, Tennessee, for money and resources. But when the railroad came to Memphis and the city began shipping cotton out, Memphis won the battle.

Things in Memphis progressed swimmingly until the late 1870s, when the city was hit with one of the worst yellow fever epidemics in American history. Within days of the August 1878 outbreak, more than half of the city's citizens fled.

The majority of those who remained were African-Americans who could not afford to leave. The city declared bankruptcy, churches became makeshift hospitals, and officials quarantined not only the city but also anyone from there. When the fever lifted in October, Memphis was crippled—and it would be a long time before it got back on its feet.

Music just may have saved the city. Most of the great musicians we associate with Memphis weren't actually born there; rather they came there to make a living because Memphis supported the music, offering places to perform on Beale Street and radio stations to play the songs.

The tradition came into sharper focus in 1909 when W.C. Handy came to town. A former bandleader for Alabama A&M University in Huntsville, Handy was a minister's son who found his own spirituality in music. He moved to Memphis and began leading Beale Street's bands, writing music, and starting a music revolution. His seminal "Memphis Blues" originally began its life as a campaign song for "Boss" Ed Crump, a onetime Memphis mayor and major Tennessee political operative.

Handy paved the way for B.B. King, who was born on a Mississippi plantation and began playing music on street corners for dimes as a little boy. Young Riley King hitchhiked to Memphis in 1947, which was by then a hub for African-American musicians. When he got there, he picked up the nickname "Blues Boy," later shortened to "B.B."

He went on to become one of the hardest-working blues musicians in the business—playing up to four shows a night in small-town cafes (the so-called "chitlin' circuit") when he started out and 250 gigs a year even in his mid-70s.

Memphis has seen its share of trauma. In April 1968, Dr. Martin Luther King, Jr., was in town to support the city's sanitation workers, who had been striking for months. The National Guard had occupied the city, and there were riots.

"Let us rise up tonight with a greater readiness. Let us stand with a greater determination. And let us move on in these powerful days, these days of challenge to make

America what it ought to be," King said at Mason Temple on April 3.

The next day King, standing on the balcony of the Lorraine Motel, was shot and killed by James Earl Ray. One of the few locations in the South that served African-Americans during the segregation that preceded the race riots of the 1960s, the motel is now the site of the National Civil Rights Museum. Its "Exploring the Legacy" exhibit addresses key aspects of King's assassination, such as the future of the Civil Rights movement and various conspiracy theories surrounding Ray.

Memphis is also synonymous with barbecue. That's in no small part because of the Memphis Barbecue Network. Now one of the largest and most prestigious barbecue sanctioning organizations in the world, it was formed by a loose coalition of barbecue contest organizers devoted to preserving Memphis-style barbecue.

The tradition involves competitions for cooking the best whole smoked hog, pork shoulder, and

pork ribs. It also means cooking "low and slow" (at 250 degrees or less) and using no gas or electric cookers. Since 1976, it has culminated during the annual Memphis in May International Festival. The monthlong extravaganza includes the Beale Street Music Festival, an entire week devoted to exploring exotic cultures, and the World Championship Barbecue Cooking Contest—the largest pork barbecue competition in the world.

It's something to see: throngs of folks bellying up to smoker rigs, tasting the pride of the South and what's arguably the very best regional American cooking.

Like Memphis, **Nashville, Tennessee,** counts music as its cornerstone. The city's economy rises (and falls) with the popularity of the twang and drawl of it all. And fortunately for Nashville residents and country music fans, there has long been much to sing about: Music City is one of the South's big boomtowns.

Legend has it that Nashville's early settlers, who hiked from

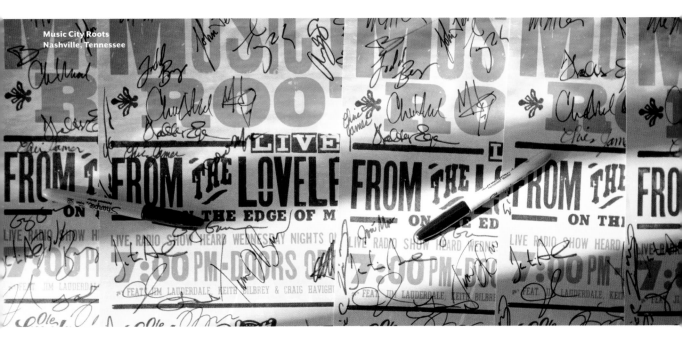

Music City Roots
Nashville, Tennessee

The Ryman Auditorium
Nashville, Tennessee

The Bluebird Cafe
Nashville, Tennessee

No matter what kind of music you like, from indie rock to classic country honky-tonk, you can wander into any old joint in Nashville and get the feeling that you're listening to a star in the making.

Virginia through the Cumberland Gap (near the point where the states of Virginia, Tennessee, and Kentucky meet) in the 1700s, celebrated their new home along the Cumberland River with fiddle playing and jig dancing. The Music City moniker didn't catch on until the 1870s, when the Jubilee Singers from Fisk University, a historically African-American college founded in Nashville after the Civil War, toured the globe. As the story goes, when they performed for Queen Victoria in 1873, she remarked that they were so talented "they must come from the Music City."

History was made in 1897 when a band of former Confederate soldiers staged a reunion in the Union Gospel Tabernacle built by Nashville businessman and steamboat captain Thomas G. Ryman. After his death in 1904, the venue was known as the Ryman Auditorium and hosted community gatherings as well as musical

and theatrical performances. In 1943 it became known around the world as the home of the *Grand Ole Opry,* "the oldest continuously running radio show in America." (Think old-time songs, dancing in sparkly costumes, and jokes—corny, good-humored, and performed for better or worse, without irony, since it hit the airwaves in 1925.) Until 1974, that is, when the Opry moved to its own riverside site on the edge of town.

The Ryman is still in operation, a locally beloved venue that has seen a plethora of world-class acts, including Enrico Caruso, John Phillip Sousa, and the Vienna Orchestra, and continues to host performers ranging from Alan Jackson to the Indigo Girls and Gotye.

You can tour the historic site during off hours, too, and see Minnie Pearl and Hank Williams memorabilia plus collectibles from other artists who've walked its halls, from James

Brown to Bruce Springsteen.

No matter what kind of music you like, from indie rock to classic country honky-tonk, you can wander into any old joint in Nashville and get the feeling that you're listening to a star in the making. There's the sense that the player on the stage is a song and a prayer away from the big time and that the little girl in the corner tapping her foot is the next Taylor Swift. Nashville has stars in its eyes that way, and it's hard not to feel it when you visit.

Even if you set its music aside, Nashville is interesting culturally and politically. As *New York Times* reporter Kim Severson aptly put it, Nashville is "the place where conservative Christians and hipsters overlap."

West of downtown is a jewel in the crown of Southern education and privilege, Vanderbilt University. The private school perennially ranks among the country's wealthiest

institutions. That's just continuing its tradition of being well endowed; the steamship and railroad magnate Cornelius Vanderbilt founded the school in 1873.

The "Commodore" was 79 when he bestowed $1 million to Holland N. McTyeire, the Methodist bishop of Nashville and cousin of Vanderbilt's young second wife, to build what they both hoped would become a prestigious place for serious scholarship. It is indeed, and it has retained certain vestiges of the Old Southern college experience, including coeds who dress up and wear pearls to Commodores football games.

The state of Tennessee has produced *almost* two presidents: former President Andrew "Old Hickory" Jackson, who was one of the founding fathers of both Nashville and Memphis, and former Vice President Al Gore, who hails from the town of Carthage in the Nashville area. Jackson revolutionized Washington when he got there in early 1829, the consummate outsider riding into town with a big gust of bravado. A self-made man and a war hero, he opposed the Electoral College system, and he took on the monopoly that was the Second Bank of the United States (making more than a few enemies along the way).

Gore, a senator's son and a collegiate football star at Harvard, memorably won the popular vote in the presidential election of 2000 but not the Electoral College tally (Old Hickory must've been rolling over) before turning over a new leaf as an environmentalist and winning the Nobel Prize for his efforts.

Tennessee also produced physician-turned-politician Bill Frist, the former Senate Majority Leader and onetime presidential hopeful.

Frist's father founded Hospital Corporation of America (HCA), the country's largest hospital management company. It's still headquartered in Nashville, along with a string of top hospitals including Vanderbilt Medical Center and Saint Thomas Hospital.

Any place that's home to so many well-educated folks is bound to have a thriving local food scene, and in this Nashville does not disappoint. Before getting all fancy, there are two things you should try when you visit: A traditional meat-and-three joint and the famous "hot chicken."

The latter is a concoction of fried chicken that's been assaulted by cayenne pepper—marinated in cayenne-spiked buttermilk, dredged in cayenne-laced flour, and fried in cayenne-infused oil that gets spicier as the night progresses, and sometimes even finished with yet more pepper. It is "hot" in every way. Traditional accompaniments of pickles and white bread help ease the exquisite pain.

The former is a kind of cafeteria that serves a big protein—a roast, some "regular" fried chicken, a stew—with a choice of Southern side dishes, like long-cooked collards, okra stewed or fried, and macaroni and cheese. If they're feeling retro, that's where the hipsters go.

If they're feeling more virtuous and, well, hip, they head to Margot McCormack's restaurants, Margot Café and Marché Artisan Foods. Both places specialize in farm-to-table, French-inflected specialties like roasted local chicken, artisanal cheese plates, and omelets with good frites. There's not a sparerib in sight but plenty of the turn-ons this region is famous for—pleasures that are earthy, sweet-hot, and sometimes unsung.

Welcome to
Louisville

You know about the horses and the whiskey, of course. But those aren't the only swingin' things in Louisville.

Louisville is the birthplace of the Slugger, made by the Hillerich & Bradsby bat company. It all began in 1884 at a Louisville Eclipse baseball game when young Bud Hillerich, the son of woodworker J.F. Hillerich, noticed that his favorite hitter, Pete Browning, had broken his bat. Hillerich offered to make him a new one. The new one, as it happened, was made from a billet of high-quality ash wood on a special lathe.

Browning, who'd been in a slump, got three hits. Baseball being that most superstitious of sports, other hitters went to the Hillerich shop looking for similar bats.

By 1894, the term "Louisville Slugger" was registered with the U.S. Patent Office. The Hillerich company has sold more than 100 million Louisville Sluggers. Fans can visit the Louisville Slugger Museum and see the factory produce the bats and such relics as the bat from Babe Ruth's historic 60-home run 1927 season.

Also swinging in Louisville was Muhammad Ali. Born in Louisville in 1942 as Cassius Marcellus Clay, Jr., Ali learned to box at the age of 12 after his bicycle was stolen. As an amateur he won the National Golden Gloves Tournament of Champions, a spot on the U.S. Olympic boxing team, and the gold medal for the United States in Rome. After he turned pro, he became the heavyweight champion of the world.

He's known as much for his bold public pronouncements—"float like a butterfly, sting like a bee"—as for his truly indomitable spirit. Admirers can learn all about it at the Muhammad Ali Center in downtown Louisville, which offers "a journey into the heart of a champion."

Louisville Slugger Field
Louisville, Kentucky

A Mint Julep

Although historians say it was made with cognac in the days before Kentucky's booming bourbon industry, the mint julep is a bourbon drink. Its origins, like those of many cocktails, are disputed.

"Kentucky's julep heritage reaches at least as far back as the early years of the 19th century, when Henry Clay was a young congressman," says food historian John Egerton, "and virtually every Kentucky politician of note since that time has waxed eloquent on the subject."

It's always served in a silver cup and always with fresh mint leaves and lots of crushed ice.

Blackberry Mint Julep

Blackberries, mint, and bourbon make this the Triple Crown of juleps. It's a sweet, refreshing cocktail that's powerful yet approachable. The muddled mint and fruit nestle comfortably under the ice for added flavor and color.

Makes 1 serving   Hands-On Time 5 min.   Total Time 5 min.

1. Place mint leaves in a 12-oz. julep cup. Add sugar, blackberries, and lemon pieces. Muddle well to dissolve sugar and release flavors.

2. Fill cup three-fourths full with ice; add bourbon. Stir well with an iced-tea spoon until blended, dispersing all ingredients throughout the drink.

3. Top with seltzer water, and stir. Add more sugar to taste, if desired.

¼   cup firmly packed fresh mint leaves
1   Tbsp. sugar
4   large blackberries
1   lemon wedge, seeded and cut
    into pieces
¼   cup (2 oz.) fine Kentucky bourbon
¼   cup (2 oz.) seltzer water or club soda
Garnishes: blackberries, lemon
    wedge, fresh mint sprig

Kentucky Bibb Lettuce Salad with Bourbon Vinaigrette

Tender Bibb lettuce comes from Kentucky. Dress it up with bourbon-infused vinaigrette, and serve it with Country Ham Corn Cakes.

Makes 8 servings   Hands-On Time 30 min.   Total Time 1 hour, 20 min.

1 ½ cups pecan halves and pieces
2   Tbsp. butter, melted
3   Tbsp. light brown sugar
⅛   tsp. ground red pepper
6   bacon slices, cooked and crumbled
8   cups torn Bibb lettuce (2 to 3 medium heads)

4   cups trimmed watercress
4   large peaches, sliced
1   small red onion, halved and thinly sliced
4   oz. Gorgonzola cheese, crumbled
Bourbon Vinaigrette
Country Ham Corn Cakes

1. Preheat oven to 350°. Toss pecans in butter. Stir together brown sugar and red pepper in a bowl; add pecans, tossing to coat. Spread pecans in a single layer in a lightly greased aluminum foil-lined shallow pan. Bake at 350° for 10 to 12 minutes or until lightly browned, toasted, and fragrant. Remove from oven, and toss pecans with crumbled bacon. Cool in pan on a wire rack 20 minutes; separate pecans with a fork.

2. Combine Bibb lettuce, next 3 ingredients, and pecan mixture in a large bowl. Top with crumbled cheese. Serve with Bourbon Vinaigrette and Country Ham Corn Cakes.

Bourbon Vinaigrette

Makes 1¼ cups   Hands-On Time 5 min.   Total Time 5 min.

⅓ cup apple cider vinegar
1   Tbsp. light brown sugar
3   Tbsp. bourbon
2   tsp. Dijon mustard

¾ tsp. table salt
½ tsp. freshly ground black pepper
⅔ cup canola oil

1. Whisk together vinegar, brown sugar, bourbon, Dijon mustard, salt, and pepper in a medium bowl. Add canola oil in a slow, steady stream, whisking constantly until smooth.

Country Ham Corn Cakes

Makes 8 servings   Hands-On Time 15 min.   Total Time 15 min.

1   (6-oz.) package buttermilk cornbread mix

¾ cup fresh corn kernels
⅓ cup finely chopped country ham

1. Stir together cornbread mix and ⅔ cup water in a small bowl until smooth. Stir in corn kernels and ham. Pour about ¼ cup batter for each cake onto a hot, lightly greased griddle or large nonstick skillet. Cook over medium heat 3 to 4 minutes or until tops are covered with bubbles and edges look dry and cooked; turn and cook other side.

Bourbon Mushrooms

Makes 8 to 10 servings   Hands-On Time 20 min.   Total Time 20 min.

¼	cup butter	¼	tsp. black pepper
¼	cup olive oil	½	cup bourbon or chicken broth
2	lb. assorted fresh mushrooms, sliced	3	garlic cloves, minced
¾	tsp. table salt	2	Tbsp. chopped fresh parsley
		1	Tbsp. chopped fresh thyme

1. Melt butter with olive oil in a large skillet over medium heat; add mushrooms, salt, and pepper. Cook, stirring occasionally, 12 to 15 minutes or until tender and almost all liquid has evaporated. Remove from heat. Stir in bourbon or chicken broth; return to heat, and cook 2 to 3 minutes or until slightly thickened. Reduce heat to low; stir in garlic, parsley, and thyme. Cook 1 more minute.

Do the Kentucky Derby Like a Local

A Thoroughbred horse race is something everyone should experience at least once. And the mac daddy of them all is the Kentucky Derby.

It is "decadent and depraved," as the late great gonzo journalist, Louisville native Hunter S. Thompson, once put it. But that's not a bad thing. It's also called the "Run for the Roses," a reference to the Derby tradition of draping the winner with a blanket of 554 red roses. (The Dan Fogelberg song of that name is the race's semiofficial anthem.)

For seven days leading up to the event, Derby Week, there are parties, concerts, and steamboat races. And the Louisville Visitors Bureau maintains a list of hotel rooms still available up until the last minute. On race day, there are really good cocktails, tradition, pageantry, and two completely thrilling, adrenaline-spiked minutes of full-on athleticism.

Churchill Downs is arranged in tiers, and the highest and most exclusive place to sit is "Millionaires Row." The most egalitarian is the infield, a 40-acre grassy patch inside the track with room for 80,000. Wherever you sit, the ladies wear big hats, and the crowd drinks the official Derby drink, the mint julep.

Bourbon-Marinated Pork Tenderloin

An overnight dip in a mixture of bourbon, soy sauce, Worcestershire sauce, and spices makes for exceptionally juicy and deceivingly easy grilled pork.

Makes 6 servings   Hands-On Time 15 min.
Total Time 12 hours, 45 min.

1. Rinse pork, and pat dry.

2. Combine soy sauce, bourbon, ¼ cup water, Worcestershire sauce, and next 6 ingredients in a large zip-top plastic freezer bag or shallow dish; seal or cover, and chill at least 12 hours. Preheat grill to 400° to 500° (high) heat. Remove pork from marinade, discarding marinade. Sprinkle evenly with salt.

3. Grill, covered with grill lid, for 30 minutes or until a meat thermometer inserted into thickest portion registers 145°, turning occasionally. Remove from heat; cover with aluminum foil, and let stand 10 minutes.

Note: We tested with Maker's Mark Kentucky Straight Bourbon Whisky.

2 ½ lb. pork tenderloin
¾ cup soy sauce
½ cup bourbon
¼ cup Worcestershire sauce
¼ cup canola oil
4 garlic cloves, minced
3 Tbsp. brown sugar
2 Tbsp. ground black pepper
1 tsp. white pepper
½ tsp. ground ginger
1 tsp. table salt
Garnish: fresh parsley sprigs

~ You've Gotta Try ~
A Kentucky Hot Brown

"Sandwich" doesn't really do this savory knife-and-fork entrée justice. The Kentucky Hot Brown is an open-faced affair of turkey laid on toast, ladled with creamy Mornay sauce, broiled, and garnished with bacon and tomato. Chef Fred K. Schmidt created this decadent comfort food classic in the Roaring Twenties as a unique midnight snack to serve to the throngs who came for the weekly dinner dances at the Brown Hotel.

A downtown Louisville landmark since 1922, the Brown is an English Renaissance-style building that's near both the University of Louisville and Churchill Downs. It's fancy in an old-fashioned, English manor sort of way: ornate chandeliers, Italian marble floors, and elaborate gilded plasterwork. It's got a fancy restaurant and a less formal affair, J. Graham's Café, where the Hot Brown was first served.

The sandwich is beloved not only by locals but also by pretty much anyone who tastes it. It's served in many places around town nowadays. The original recipe, used at the Brown Hotel today, is still the gold standard. Use fresh, thick-sliced, unseasoned Texas toast from the bread aisle as the base for this sandwich. It's best with homemade roast turkey (and a great use for Thanksgiving leftovers), but deli-roasted will do. The Mornay sauce is divine and seriously rich, making each serving shareable, if you're in a giving mood.

Kentucky Hot Brown Sandwiches

Makes 2 servings
Hands-On Time 15 min.
Total Time 20 min.

¼ cup butter
¼ cup all-purpose flour
2 cups heavy cream
½ cup freshly grated Pecorino Romano cheese
½ tsp. table salt
¼ tsp. freshly ground black pepper
2 Texas toast bread slices
1 lb. thinly sliced roasted turkey breast
2 plum tomatoes, halved
1 Tbsp. freshly grated Pecorino Romano cheese
4 crisply cooked bacon slices
Paprika and chopped fresh parsley

1. In a 2-qt. saucepan, melt butter. Slowly whisk in flour until combined and mixture forms a thick paste; cook 2 more minutes over medium-low heat, stirring frequently. Whisk in heavy cream, and cook over medium heat, stirring often, 3 to 4 minutes or until thickened. Remove from heat, and slowly whisk in ½ cup Pecorino Romano cheese until the sauce is smooth. Stir in salt and pepper.

2. Preheat broiler with oven rack 5½ inches from heat. Cut crusts from bread slices. For each sandwich, place 1 slice of bread in a shallow, rimmed, ovenproof serving dish, and cover with 8 oz. of turkey. Nestle 2 tomato halves, cut sides up, alongside the turkey and bread slice. Pour half of the sauce over the top, completely covering the sandwich. Sprinkle with 1½ tsp. Pecorino Romano cheese. Broil 4 minutes or until cheese begins to brown and bubble. Remove from broiler, and cross 2 pieces of bacon on top. Sprinkle with paprika and parsley, and serve immediately.

Kentucky Burgoo

Burgoo (ber-GOO) is a thick, hearty, mixed-meat stew native to Kentucky. Like the Brunswick stews of Virginia and Georgia, burgoos have many variations. Most involve a variety of meats (ranging from rabbit and poultry to pork, beef, and mutton) cooked slowly in a big pot with vegetables and a tomato-based sauce. Most also make enough to feed a crowd.

Makes 3 qt. (6 qt. if using rabbit)   Hands-On Time 20 min.
Total Time 5 hours, 10 min.

1	(3- to 4-lb.) whole chicken	1	cup frozen baby lima beans
1	(2-lb.) beef chuck roast	1	cup frozen English peas
2	lb. pork loin chops, trimmed	3	garlic cloves, minced
1	dressed rabbit (optional)	2	qt. beef broth
1	lb. tomatoes	1	(32-oz.) bottle ketchup
5	potatoes	2	cups dry red wine
5	celery ribs	1	(10-oz.) bottle Worcestershire
4	carrots		sauce
2	onions	¼	cup white vinegar
2	green bell peppers	1	Tbsp. table salt
1	small cabbage	1	Tbsp. black pepper
2	cups frozen whole kernel corn	1	Tbsp. dried thyme

1. Bring first 3 ingredients, 5 qt. water, and, if desired, rabbit to a boil in a large heavy stockpot. Cover, reduce heat, and simmer 1 hour or until tender. Remove meats, reserving liquid in stockpot; skin, bone, and shred meats, and return to pot.

2. Chop tomatoes and next 5 ingredients; shred cabbage. Add chopped vegetables, corn, and next 11 ingredients to meats; cook over low heat, stirring often, 4 hours.

Tee's Corn Pudding

This classic recipe has a rich, soufflé-like texture without the hassle. The result is an impressive side dish the entire family will love.

Makes 8 servings   Hands-On Time 25 min.   Total Time 1 hour, 10 min.

12	to 13 ears fresh corn, husks removed	1 ½	tsp. table salt
¼	cup sugar	6	large eggs
3	Tbsp. all-purpose flour	2	cups whipping cream
2	tsp. baking powder	½	cup butter, melted

1. Preheat oven to 350°. Cut corn kernels from cobs into a large bowl (about 6 cups). Scrape milk and remaining pulp from cobs with a spoon or back of a knife; discard cobs.

2. Combine sugar and next 3 ingredients in a small bowl. Whisk together eggs, whipping cream, and butter in a large bowl. Gradually add sugar mixture to egg mixture, whisking until smooth; stir in corn. Pour mixture into a lightly greased 13- x 9-inch baking dish.

3. Bake at 350° for 40 to 45 minutes or until set. Let stand 5 minutes.

Chocolate-Bourbon Pecan Pie

This is a perfect recipe to end a Derby Day celebration. Former Southern Living *staff member Cynthia Ann Briscoe, a Louisville native and ardent Derby fan, contributed this version.*

Makes 8 servings Hands-On Time 10 min. Total Time 1 hour, 10 min.

½	(14.1-oz.) package refrigerated piecrusts	½	cup firmly packed brown sugar
1½	cups chopped pecans	¼	cup bourbon or water
1	cup (6 oz.) semisweet chocolate morsels	4	large eggs
		¼	cup butter, melted
1	cup dark corn syrup	2	tsp. cornmeal
½	cup granulated sugar	2	tsp. vanilla extract
		½	tsp. table salt

1. Preheat oven to 325°. Fit piecrust into a 9-inch deep-dish pie plate according to package directions; fold edges under, and crimp.

2. Sprinkle pecans and chocolate evenly onto bottom of piecrust; set aside.

3. Combine corn syrup and next 3 ingredients in a large saucepan, and bring to a boil over medium heat. Cook, stirring constantly, 3 minutes. Remove from heat.

4. Whisk together eggs and next 4 ingredients. Gradually whisk about one-fourth hot mixture into egg mixture; add to remaining hot mixture, whisking constantly. Pour filling into prepared piecrust.

5. Bake at 325° for 55 minutes or until set; cool on wire rack.

Bourbon Balls

Small bites with a powerful punch, these sweet, no-bake treats are a favored gift and a perfect nibble for parties.

Makes about 5 dozen Hands-On Time 30 min. Total Time 55 min.

1	(12-oz.) package vanilla wafers, finely crushed	2	Tbsp. unsweetened cocoa
		½	cup bourbon
1	cup chopped pecans, toasted	2½	Tbsp. light corn syrup
¾	cup powdered sugar		Powdered sugar

1. Stir together first 4 ingredients in a large bowl until well blended.

2. Stir together bourbon and corn syrup until well blended. Stir together bourbon mixture and wafer mixture. Shape into 1-inch balls; roll in powdered sugar. Refrigerate in an airtight container up to 2 weeks.

If you're going to do Elvis while you're in Memphis, you should really go all out. And that means visiting during Elvis Week.

The annual event organized by Elvis Presley Enterprises is held at Graceland and coincides with the anniversary of Elvis Presley's death on August 16.

There are commemorative bingo games, tours of Graceland, candlelight vigils, a 5K run, and a tribute contest. More than 75,000 people showed up in 2012, the 35th anniversary of Elvis's passing and the first time Elvis's daughter, Lisa Marie, performed at Elvis Week.

Graceland is the second-most visited private residence in the country, behind only the White House. Opened to visitors in 1982 as a way for Elvis's estate to relieve a large tax burden, Graceland is a phenomenally successful attraction (more than 18 million people have visited) and a big moneymaker for the city.

Dr. and Mrs. Thomas D. Moore built the big house on a hill on nearly 14 acres of property originally owned by Memphis newspaper publisher S.E. Toof. Elvis bought the home, which is about 20 minutes from downtown Memphis, in 1957 for $102,000.

The tour includes a walk-through of at least some of Elvis's 23 rooms, among them the living room with its wall-to-wall white carpeting and the infamous Jungle Room with its wood paneling and green shag still intact. You can see his Army uniforms, his gold records, his favorite cars, and, outside, his grave.

"He was, after all, a poor country boy who drove a delivery truck, loved his mother, and ate bad food," the author Ann Patchett has noted of Elvis, "which means he had all the fundamental elements of Southern heroism."

The Fat Elvis

Makes 10 biscuits   Hands-On Time 15 min.   Total Time 30 min.

5   to 6 ripe bananas
2   cups all-purpose flour
1 ½ cups powdered sugar
2   tsp. baking powder
½   tsp. baking soda
½   tsp. table salt

½   cup honey-roasted peanuts, chopped
⅓   cup frozen butter
½   cup buttermilk
Peanut Butter Spread
10   cooked bacon slices, halved

1. Preheat oven to 450°. Cut 4 bananas into 2-inch pieces; halve each piece lengthwise. Mash remaining bananas to equal ½ cup. Sift together flour and next 4 ingredients in a large bowl; add mashed bananas and peanuts. Grate butter over flour mixture, using large holes of a box grater. Cut butter into flour mixture with a pastry blender or fork until crumbly. Add buttermilk, stirring just until mixture is slightly moistened.

2. Turn dough out onto a heavily floured surface; shape into a ball. Pat into a ½-inch-thick circle.

3. Cut with a floured 3-inch round cutter, and place biscuits 1 inch apart on a lightly greased baking sheet.

4. Bake at 450° for 10 to 12 minutes or until golden brown. Split warm biscuits; spread bottom halves of biscuits with Peanut Butter Spread. Top each with 2 bacon pieces and 2 banana slices. Cover with biscuit tops.

Peanut Butter Spread

Makes ½ cup   Hands-On Time 5 min.   Total Time 5 min.

⅓   cup creamy peanut butter
¼   cup powdered sugar

1   Tbsp. fat-free milk
¼   tsp. vanilla extract

1. Stir all ingredients together in a microwave-safe bowl. Microwave at HIGH at 30-second intervals until softened; stir until smooth.

Kimberly Pack
Knoxville, Tennessee

Southern Sweet Tea

If you like tea that's really sweet, add the full cup of sugar.

Makes 2 ½ qt.   Hands-On Time 5 min.   Total Time 25 min.

2 family-size tea bags	½ to 1 cup sugar

1. Bring 3 cups water to a boil in a saucepan; add tea bags. Boil 1 minute; remove from heat. Cover and steep 10 minutes.

2. Remove and discard tea bags. Add desired amount of sugar, stirring until dissolved. Pour into a 1-gal. container, and add 7 cups cold water. Serve over ice.

For Peach Iced Tea: Prepare Southern Sweet Tea using ½ cup sugar. Stir together 1 ½ qt. tea, 1 (46-oz.) bottle peach nectar, and 2 Tbsp. lemon juice. Serve over ice. Makes 3 qt.

Cheese Truffles

Pimiento cheese, rolled in chopped toasted pecans, parsley, or crumbled bacon, makes a delicious appetizer truffle.

Makes about 2 dozen   Hands-On Time 20 min.   Total Time 20 min.

Three-Cheese Pimiento Cheese	Chopped fresh parsley
Finely chopped toasted pecans	Cooked and crumbled bacon

1. Roll Three-Cheese Pimiento Cheese into ¾-inch balls. Roll balls in finely chopped toasted pecans, chopped fresh parsley, or cooked and crumbled bacon.

Three-Cheese Pimiento Cheese

A mixture of cheeses provides the base for this lightened-up pimiento cheese.

Makes about 2 ½ cups   Hands-On Time 10 min.   Total Time 10 min.

1 (8-oz.) block fat-free cream cheese, softened	2 tsp. finely grated onion
½ cup 1% low-fat cottage cheese	1 tsp. lemon juice
1 (4-oz.) jar diced pimiento, drained	Dash of hot sauce
2 tsp. coarse-grained mustard	1 (8-oz.) block 2% reduced-fat sharp white Cheddar cheese, shredded

1. Process cream cheese and cottage cheese in a food processor until smooth. Stir in next 6 ingredients. Add salt and pepper to taste.

Meet Chef
Kelly English

Memphis got a fresh blast of Louisiana-spiked haute cuisine in 2008, when Kelly English opened Restaurant Iris.

English had put himself through the University of Mississippi by cooking in restaurants, graduated with distinction from the Culinary Institute of America, and spent years training under the great New Orleans-based chef John Besh (more about Besh on page 82), when he happened upon and toured a restaurant space that was for sale in Memphis.

"Inside, there was a stained-glass fleur-de-lis [a New Orleans symbol], and I said, 'Oh my goodness.' We went outside, and there was a rainbow. I said, 'What's next, a unicorn?'" English recalled to *Food & Wine*. "Everything about it was exactly right."

Then and there, he decided to open Iris, a restaurant with a melting-pot cuisine he describes as French Creole. A year later, he won a prestigious *Food & Wine* Best New Chef award.

"Southern foods are so representative of the cultures that have come together to make them. The dishes that really speak to me incorporate old standbys with an influence from the New South in a way that people might not expect. This is one of my favorite examples of that." —Kelly English

Tempura Fried Okra

Makes 6 to 8 appetizer servings   Hands-On Time 15 min.
Total Time 15 min.

⅓ cup Greek yogurt	1 cup club soda
1 Tbsp. dark sesame oil	⅛ tsp. table salt
1 Tbsp. sorghum syrup	Canola oil
1¼ tsp. sambal oelek (ground fresh chile paste), divided	1 (16-oz.) jar pickled okra (20 okra pods)
1¼ tsp. lime zest, divided	½ tsp. toasted sesame seeds
1 Tbsp. fresh lime juice	Garnish: fresh cilantro leaves
1 cup all-purpose flour	

1. Stir together yogurt, sesame oil, sorghum syrup, 1 tsp. sambal oelek, 1 tsp. lime zest, and lime juice in a small bowl. In a separate bowl, whisk together the flour, club soda, and salt.

2. Pour canola oil to a depth of 1 inch in a large cast-iron skillet or Dutch oven over medium-high heat; heat to 400°. Test the oil with a drop of your batter; when it fries up nicely and releases from the pan, you are good to go.

3. Pat okra pods dry with paper towels. Working in batches, dip okra pods in the batter, making sure they are coated completely, and fry until golden brown on all sides (1 to 2 minutes). Drain on paper towels. Dot yogurt mixture with remaining ¼ tsp. sambal oelek; swirl with a spoon. Sprinkle with remaining ¼ tsp. lime zest and sesame seeds.

4. Serve okra immediately with yogurt mixture for dipping.

John Wills's Baby Back Ribs

This recipe won the Memphis in May World Championship Barbecue Cooking Contest. Taste it, and you'll learn why.

Makes 3 to 4 servings
Hands-On Time 30 min.
Total Time 8 hours, 40 min.

2   slabs baby back ribs (about 4 lb.)
3   Tbsp. Dry Spices
1   cup Basting Sauce
1   cup Sweet Sauce

1. Place ribs in a large, shallow pan. Rub Dry Spices all over ribs. Cover and chill 3 hours.

2. Prepare a hot fire by piling charcoal on 1 side of grill, leaving other side empty (for gas grills, light only 1 side). Arrange ribs over unlit side. Grill, covered with grill lid, 2 hours, basting sparingly with Basting Sauce (about every 30 minutes) and turning ribs occasionally. Brush ribs with Sweet Sauce the last 30 minutes.

Dry Spices

Makes 6 ½ Tbsp.   Hands-On Time 5 min.   Total Time 5 min.

3	Tbsp. paprika	1	tsp. dry mustard
2	tsp. seasoned salt	1	tsp. ground oregano
2	tsp. garlic powder	1	tsp. ground red pepper
2	tsp. ground black pepper	½	tsp. chili powder

1. Combine all ingredients in a small bowl.

Basting Sauce

Makes 4 ½ cups   Hands-On Time 5 min.   Total Time 8 hours, 5 min.

¼	cup firmly packed brown sugar	¼	cup Worcestershire sauce
1 ½	Tbsp. Dry Spices	½	tsp. hot sauce
2	cups red wine vinegar	1	small bay leaf

1. Stir together all ingredients and 2 cups water in a bowl. Cover and let stand 8 hours. Remove bay leaf.

Sweet Sauce

Makes 1 qt.   Hands-On Time 15 min.   Total Time 40 min.

1	cup ketchup	1	Tbsp. seasoned salt
1	cup red wine vinegar	1	Tbsp. paprika
1	(8-oz.) can tomato sauce	1	Tbsp. lemon juice
½	cup spicy honey mustard	1 ½	tsp. garlic powder
½	cup Worcestershire sauce	⅛	tsp. chili powder
¼	cup butter	⅛	tsp. ground red pepper
2	Tbsp. brown sugar	⅛	tsp. ground black pepper
2	Tbsp. hot sauce		

1. Bring all ingredients to a boil in a Dutch oven. Reduce heat, and simmer sauce, stirring occasionally, 30 minutes.

Take In
the Duck Parade
Like a Local

A Memphis institution opened by Colonel Robert Brinkley in 1869, the Peabody Hotel has long been known for its lavish appointments, the fact that it put up presidents and riverboat gamblers and plantation owners, and the big parties it held.

"If you stand near its fountain in the middle of the lobby ... ultimately you will see everybody who is anybody in the Delta," the author and historian David Cohn wrote in 1935.

But the thing it is perhaps most widely known for today is its daily duck parade.

The whole thing started as a lark in 1933. Hotel general manager Frank Schutt, returning from a hunting trip, put some live duck decoys in the lobby's grand marble fountain as a kind of grand prank. The 1930s version of a viral kitten video, the delightful duck episode caught hold. And it's been replayed daily for most of the past 80 years.

Every morning at 11 a.m., five North American mallards (one drake and four hens) march into the elevator from their roost on the roof and are escorted down to the lobby. And every evening at 5 p.m., they are taken back up again with considerable pomp. A set of steps is placed at the edge of the fountain, and a 50-foot red carpet is unrolled across the lobby. To the recorded strains of John Philip Sousa's "King Cotton March," the ducks parade single file down the carpet to the elevator.

The tradition survived the hotel's declaration of bankruptcy in 1975, when the Memphis economy tanked in the wake of Dr. Martin Luther King, Jr.'s, assassination. When the hotel reopened again in 1981, it had been painstakingly restored to the tune of $25 million, and the original Italian Renaissance architectural style had been revived. The duck theme abounds: Ducks are emblazoned on ties and slacks and belts for sale in the gift shops (though there are none on the restaurant menus).

Corn Chowder

Makes 11 cups
Hands-On Time 20 min.
Total Time 1 hour

2 medium-size red potatoes, peeled and diced
3 bacon slices
1 cup minced onion
2 (14 ¾-oz.) cans cream-style corn
2 cups milk
1 (12-oz.) can evaporated milk
1 cup chicken broth
½ tsp. table salt
⅛ tsp. ground nutmeg

1. Bring potato and 3 cups water to a boil in a large Dutch oven; reduce heat, and simmer 40 minutes or until tender. Set aside; do not drain.

2. Cook bacon in a skillet until crisp; remove bacon, reserving 2 Tbsp. drippings in skillet, and crumble bacon. Sauté onion in drippings until tender.

3. Stir bacon, onion, corn, and next 5 ingredients into Dutch oven.

4. Bring to a boil over medium heat; reduce heat, and simmer, stirring often, 10 minutes.

Carol Saucier
Memphis, Tennessee

The Bluegrass, Bourbon & Barbecue Trail

Welcome to
Nashville

There are lots of beautiful homes in Nashville, particularly in the leafy, lofty suburb of Belle Meade, where enormous lawns and garden clubs flourish. But the city is known for two homes of particular distinction.

The first is The Hermitage, where Andrew Jackson lived, died, and is buried. Jackson owned the property from 1804 to 1845 and lived there mostly after retiring from public service, turning what was essentially 1,100 acres of forest into a working farm. He installed gorgeous French wallpaper and a log kitchen in the original Federal-style brick house, built a distillery and a dairy on the land, and crafted a truly impressive two-story portico complete with six Doric columns. The mansion and grounds, open for tours, have been operated as a museum since 1889 and remain one of the best-preserved early presidential residences.

The second grand home to visit in Nashville is Cheekwood, otherwise known as the house built by Maxwell House. Yes, the coffee company. It all began in 1890 when two grocers, cousins Joel and Christopher Cheek, decided to concentrate on the coffee business. They established Nashville Coffee and Manufacturing, which created a prepared, roasted, and blended coffee at a time when most companies were selling green, unroasted beans.

As the coffee became more successful, the Cheeks expanded production, built a roasting plant, and managed to get their coffee into the dining room of Nashville's exclusive Maxwell House hotel. According to local legend, when President Theodore Roosevelt visited the hotel in 1907, he pronounced the coffee "good to the last drop." That story is disputed, but it's true that the Cheeks acquired the rights to market their coffee under the Maxwell House name, and the rest is (almost) history.

Postum (now General Foods) purchased Maxwell House's parent company, Cheek-Neal Coffee, for more than $40 million in 1928. With their share, the Cheeks bought 100 acres of land in West Nashville and commissioned an old-fashioned estate modeled on those in the English countryside. Cheekwood, designed by the architect Bryant Fleming and completed in 1932, is the result. In the 1950s, the family donated the limestone mansion and grounds as the site for a botanical garden and art museum. It has been open to the public since 1960.

The Hermitage
Nashville, Tennessee

~ A Recipe from a Local ~
Sorghum-Glazed Turnips

Makes 4 servings
Hands-On Time 50 min.
Total Time 50 min.

2	lb. small turnips, peeled and halved
2	Tbsp. butter
1	Tbsp. lemon juice
1 ½	tsp. sugar
½	tsp. table salt
2	tsp. sorghum syrup

Garnish: fresh thyme sprigs

1. Place turnips in a single layer in a 12-inch heavy skillet; add water to reach halfway up turnips (about 1 ½ cups). Add butter and next 3 ingredients. Cover and bring to a boil; reduce heat to medium-high, and simmer, stirring occasionally, 10 minutes. Uncover and cook, stirring often, 8 minutes or until turnips are tender and water evaporates. Cook, stirring often, 5 more minutes or until turnips are golden. Stir in sorghum and 3 Tbsp. water; toss to coat. Serve immediately.

Chef Tyler Brown, Capitol Grille
Nashville, Tennessee

Meet Singer and Survivor Naomi Judd

A native of Ashland, Kentucky, Naomi Judd was a single mother putting herself through nursing school when she began to sing with daughter Wynonna.

After moving to Tennessee, they were discovered by Nashville record producer Brent Maher. They recorded their first album in 1983 and have lived in and around Nashville ever since. Naomi and The Judds have sold more than 20 million albums, scored 15 No. 1 hits, and won six Grammy awards.

In 1991, when Naomi contracted Hepatitis C as the result of needles she handled in her nursing career, she gave up singing and has since become a public health advocate. Naomi also has written children's books and a couple of *New York Times* bestsellers, *Naomi's Breakthrough Guide* and *Naomi's Guide to Aging Gratefully.*

In addition, she has served as the national spokesperson for the National Liver Foundation. Long before her singing, however, Naomi was known for making good down-home Southern food. No accident there: Her mom, Polly, was a riverboat cook.

"Every good Southern cook has a deviled egg platter. Called 'church eggs,' they were expected at 'dinner on the ground' lunches after Sunday sessions. Since country churches didn't have space for banquets, families spread out quilts on church lawns to enjoy fried chicken, biscuits, 'tater salad,' watermelon, pie, and more."

—Naomi Judd

Polly's Deviled Eggs

These eggs get their special zing from drops of the hot pepper vinegar, Mom's (now-not-so-secret) secret ingredient.

Makes 12 servings   Hands-On Time 15 min.   Total Time 15 min.

1 dozen hard-cooked eggs, peeled	1 tsp. Worcestershire sauce
⅓ cup mayonnaise	6 drops liquid from hot peppers in vinegar, or to taste
1 Tbsp. prepared yellow mustard	½ tsp. table salt
½ cup sweet pickle relish, drained and squeezed in paper towels to remove excess liquid	¼ tsp. ground white pepper
	Paprika

1. Cut the eggs in half lengthwise with a long thin knife. Remove the yolks, and place them in a medium bowl; set the whites aside. Mash the yolks with a fork. Add the remaining ingredients except the paprika, and stir until the consistency of mashed potatoes. If the filling is too thick, add a little more pickle juice or mayonnaise. Spoon filling into the hollowed-out whites; sprinkle with paprika. Serve immediately, or refrigerate in an airtight container for up to 1 day.

Enjoy
Hot Chicken
Like a Local

It's hard to know precisely why a food trend takes hold: It could incite feelings of nostalgia. It could be irresistibly newfangled. Or, in the case of hot chicken and Nashville, it could just be too hot to handle.

Puns aside, "hot" chicken means spicy as hell—like incendiary. The goal, say aficionados, is a spiciness that goes all the way to the bone. Tradition dictates that it must be fried in a skillet, that the coating must contain cayenne, that the oil in which it's fried must be spiced, and that it be coated, either with more cayenne or hot sauce, after it's been cooked.

"Fried chicken is comfort food," say roving food reporting duo Jane and Michael Stern. "Hot chicken is discomfort food—in the best sense of the word."

Hot chicken generally is not served in fancy restaurants; it's served in no-frills chicken shacks, many of which are take-out only. The granddaddy of these is Prince's Hot Chicken Shack, on the north end of Nashville and in business for more than 50 years. Legend has it that hot chicken was invented here when original owner Thornton Prince's girlfriend got sick of his carousing and made his favorite dish, fried chicken, but doused it in hot sauce (which, as it turned out, he loved).

Still owned and operated by the Prince family, Prince's is small, crowded, and slow but delicious and cheap. Its hot chicken recipe is a closely guarded secret. The chicken is served on white bread with pickle slices and comes in four heat strengths (mild, medium, hot, and extra hot; medium being hot enough for most folks).

Another spot Nashvillians swear by for hot chicken is Bolton's Spicy Chicken & Fish, which is a bit spiffier inside, has a few more amenities (like actual drinks, as opposed to the vending machine at Prince's), and also serves "hot fish" (usually whiting or catfish with the same preparation).

Nashville's annual Music City Hot Chicken Festival, which includes an amateur hot chicken cook-off, is held on the Fourth of July.

Rock
East Nashville
Like a Local

Independent rock star Jack White, the Detroit native who founded The White Stripes, moved to Nashville in 2008.

White located his Third Man Records, a combination record store, label office, photo studio, and live music venue not downtown but in East Nashville.

The up-and-coming neighborhood across the Cumberland River has in recent years been a magnet for young creative types and the indie food businesses they enjoy.

East Nashville is home to the Olive & Sinclair Chocolate Co., a "bean-to-bar" maker of small-batch chocolates that are stone-ground from single-origin cacao beans.

You'll also find local favorites Las Paletas and Mas Tacos Por Favor in East Nashville. The former is a shop featuring intense and exotic fruit-based, Mexican-inspired gourmet frozen pops in flavors like hibiscus, honeydew, and Chai tea. The latter is the brick-and-mortar location of a long-popular taco truck that turns out killer fish tacos, *elotes* (Mexican-style grilled corn on the cob slathered in butter and cheese), and tortilla soup.

And you're likely to bump into White at any one of these places on a given day.

~ A Recipe from a Local ~

Roasted Butternut Squash Hash with Mulled Sorghum Glaze

The sorghum–apple cider glaze makes this squash an impressive side dish.

Makes 6 servings   Hands-On Time 30 min.   Total Time 50 min.

1	(3 ½-lb.) butternut squash, peeled and cut into ½-inch cubes	¼	tsp. ground black pepper
		½	cup sorghum syrup
		¼	cup apple cider
10	pearl onions	1	Tbsp. fresh orange juice
2	Tbsp. unsalted butter, melted	¼	cup cold butter, cubed
¾	tsp. table salt	1	Tbsp. chopped fresh sage

1. Preheat oven to 425°. Toss together first 5 ingredients. Place mixture in a single layer in a lightly greased roasting pan. Bake at 425° for 30 minutes or just until caramelized and fork-tender (al dente), stirring every 10 minutes.

2. Meanwhile, stir together sorghum, apple cider, and orange juice in a small saucepan. Bring to a boil over medium heat, stirring occasionally. Boil, stirring occasionally, 5 to 6 minutes or until mixture is reduced by half. Stir in cold butter until melted.

3. Toss together squash mixture, sorghum mixture, and sage in a serving bowl. Sprinkle with salt and pepper to taste.

Chef Tyler Brown, Capitol Grille
Nashville, Tennessee

Lemon-Roasted Vegetables

Makes 4 servings   Hands-On Time 15 min.   Total Time 35 min.

2	Tbsp. olive oil	1	yellow squash, cut into 1-inch pieces
1	Tbsp. fresh lemon juice		
1	garlic clove, minced	1	zucchini, cut into 1-inch pieces
½	tsp. table salt	1	Tbsp. chopped fresh basil
1	large red bell pepper, cut into 1-inch pieces		Freshly ground black pepper
1	large green bell pepper, cut into 1-inch pieces	⅓	cup sliced almonds, toasted

1. Preheat oven to 400°. Stir together first 4 ingredients in a large bowl; add vegetables, and toss to coat. Place in a single layer in an aluminum foil-lined jelly-roll pan.

2. Bake at 400° for 10 minutes; stir vegetables. Bake 10 more minutes or until tender.

3. Transfer vegetables to a large serving dish; toss with basil, season with pepper, and sprinkle with almonds.

Meet Singer
Trisha Yearwood

One of country music's best-selling artists and the author of two bestselling cookbooks, Trisha Yearwood often says she can't decide what she loves more, cooking or singing.

When it comes to singing, she's won three Grammy Awards, three Country Music Association Awards, and two Academy of Country Music awards. Her career highlights include performing at President Bill Clinton's inauguration and with Pavarotti at a concert in Italy.

And she can cook, too. Her cooking show, *Trisha's Southern Kitchen*, filmed at her home in Nashville, airs on the Food Network.

Yearwood divides her time between a ranch in Owasso, Oklahoma, and in Nashville with her husband, singer Garth Brooks.

"After discovering chicken pizza on a family beach trip, we decided to create it at home. We love this recipe because it's so different from traditional pizza—not a tomato in sight. Now we can all enjoy it more than once a year!"

—Trisha Yearwood

Chicken Pizza

Use fresh, unbaked pizza dough from the deli or bakery counter at your grocery store to make this tasty unsauced pizza.

Makes 4 servings   Hands-On Time 20 min.   Total Time 40 min.

1 lb. bakery pizza dough	½ green bell pepper, cut into thin strips
1 Tbsp. olive oil	
1 tsp. minced garlic	½ cup vertically sliced red onion
1 cup (4 oz.) shredded mozzarella cheese	2 cups chopped grilled chicken breast
1 cup (4 oz.) shredded sharp Cheddar cheese	3 cooked bacon slices, crumbled

1. Preheat oven to 400°. Roll pizza dough to a 15-inch circle on a lightly floured surface; place on a lightly greased pizza pan. Drizzle 1 Tbsp. olive oil and 1 tsp. garlic on pizza dough, followed by ½ cup each of the cheeses. Scatter the bell pepper, sliced onion, chicken, and bacon over pizza. Sprinkle remaining ½ cup of each of the cheeses over pizza.

2. Bake at 400° for 20 minutes or until the crust is lightly browned. Slice pizza into 8 pieces.

Smoky Steak or Chicken Barbecue Kabobs

Here's a backyard favorite with the flavor of Nashville: spicy, smoky, and with a unique twang.

Makes 8 servings   Hands-On Time 20 min.   Total Time 30 min.

2 lb. top sirloin steak, trimmed, or skinned and boned chicken breast
½ large red onion, cut into fourths and separated into pieces
1 pt. cherry tomatoes
8 (8-inch) metal skewers
Smoky Barbecue Rub
White Barbecue Sauce (page 47)

1. Preheat grill to 350° to 400° (medium-high) heat. Cut meat into 1-inch cubes. Thread steak, onion, and tomatoes alternately onto skewers, leaving a ¼-inch space between pieces. Sprinkle kabobs with Smoky Barbecue Rub.

2. Grill kabobs, covered with grill lid, 4 to 5 minutes on each side. Serve with White Barbecue Sauce.

Smoky Barbecue Rub

Makes about ¼ cup   Hands-On Time 5 min.   Total Time 5 min.

2 Tbsp. firmly packed dark brown sugar
2 tsp. garlic salt
1 tsp. chipotle chile powder
½ tsp. ground cumin
¼ tsp. dried oregano

1. Stir all ingredients together in a small bowl.

Catch a Flick at the Franklin Theatre Like a Local

Erected in 1937, this classic neighborhood movie theater was, well, out of a movie—complete with neon marquee, freshly popped popcorn, and an address on ... wait for it ... Main Street.

A beloved landmark in Franklin, Tennessee, about 20 minutes south of Nashville, the Franklin buckled to the mega-theater chains and rising rents in 2007 and shut its doors.

That left a sour taste in some locals' mouths, so they appealed to the Heritage Foundation of Franklin and Williamson County, a nonprofit preservation group. The foundation subsequently stepped in to buy and rehabilitate the historic landmark.

After four years and $8.7 million in renovations, and a serious polishing of the original Art Deco lobby fixtures, the 300-seat venue reopened in 2011.

It now shows all manner of revival movies from *The Wizard of Oz* to *Monty Python and the Holy Grail* (for five bucks a ticket!). It's also a live music venue for artists from Dr. John and Smash Mouth to Vince Gill and Amy Grant.

Meet Singer
Loretta Lynn

The second of eight children born to a poor coal miner, Loretta Lynn is a Kentucky native, a Nashville resident, a country singing sensation, and a serious home cook.

As chronicled in *Coal Miner's Daughter* (the 1980 movie about her life, starring Sissy Spacek), Lynn married Oliver "Doo" Lynn when she was just 14. She loved to sing, and Doo encouraged her to learn to play guitar and take singing gigs. During a talent contest, she so impressed Norm Burley that he started Zero Records just to record her.

To promote her single "I'm a Honky Tonk Girl," Doo and Lynn drove from station to station, asking them to play it. By the time they got to Nashville, the song was already a minor hit.

In the years since, she has had 52 top 10 hits, 16 of them ranked No. 1. She released an album in 2004 with indie rock star Jack White. Called *Van Lear Rose* (a reference to the Van Lear coal mines, where her father worked), it took home two Grammies. Her cookbook, *You're Cookin' It Country,* was also published in 2004.

Lynn marked her 50th anniversary as a Grand Ole Opry member in 2012. Her ranch in Hurricane Mills, Tennessee, remains one of the state's largest tourist attractions.

"One time, TV show host Dinah Shore and I fixed our favorite recipes (her potato soup and my chicken and dumplin's) to see which the audience liked better. When she poured her soup into a preheated pot, it shot clear up to the ceiling. It was the funniest darn thing. Anyway, I won."

—Loretta Lynn

Chicken and Dumplin's

Makes 8 to 10 servings   Hands-On Time 15 min.
Total Time 3 hours, 5 min.

CHICKEN
- 1 large fat hen (5- to 6-lb.), skinned
- 3 garlic cloves, crushed
- 1 tsp. table salt
- 1 tsp. freshly ground black pepper

DUMPLINGS
- 3 cups self-rising flour

- 1 tsp. table salt
- 1 large egg, lightly beaten
- ½ cup heavy cream
- 2 Tbsp. cornstarch
- 2 Tbsp. cold water

GARNISH
Chopped fresh flat-leaf parsley

1. Prepare the Chicken: In a large pot, boil the hen, garlic, salt, and pepper in water to cover for 2 hours. Add additional water as needed. Drain the hen, reserving the broth. Remove chicken meat from the skin and bones, and shred or cut the meat into bite-size pieces. Discard skin and bones.

2. Prepare the Dumplings: In a large bowl, sift together the flour and salt. Gradually add 1 cup of reserved chicken broth. Stir in the egg. Knead the dough thoroughly, and roll out to ¼-inch thickness on a floured surface. Cut the dough into 1½-inch-wide strips. Bring 6 to 8 cups of reserved chicken broth to a boil, and drop strips, a few at a time, into the boiling broth, stirring gently. Cover and simmer for about 15 minutes. Add the cream and chicken pieces, and simmer for 10 minutes longer. Dissolve cornstarch in cold water, and add to the pot to thicken broth, if needed.

Lemon-Mascarpone Icebox Tarts

Few things are dearer to Southern hearts than cool, creamy icebox desserts.

Makes 6 servings   Hands-On Time 30 min.
Total Time 6 hours, 20 min.

1. Preheat oven to 350°. Stir together first 4 ingredients; firmly press crumb mixture on bottom and up sides of 6 (3¾-inch) round tart pans with removable bottoms (about 6 Tbsp. per pan). Place tart pans on a baking sheet, and bake at 350° for 10 to 12 minutes or until lightly browned. Cool completely on baking sheet on a wire rack (about 30 minutes).

2. Whisk together sweetened condensed milk and next 3 ingredients until well blended; whisk in mascarpone cheese just until blended. Spoon mixture into prepared tart shells.

3. Bake at 350° for 12 to 15 minutes or until almost set. (The centers will not be firm but will set up as they chill.) Cool completely on wire rack (about 1 hour). Cover and chill 4 hours. Arrange berries and fruit decoratively over tarts just before serving.

2 ⅔ cups butter cookie crumbs
    (about 1 ½ [7.5-oz.] packages
    butter cookies)
⅓ cup butter, melted
¼ cup powdered sugar
½ tsp. almond extract
1 (14-oz.) can sweetened
    condensed milk
2 tsp. lemon zest
½ cup fresh lemon juice
6 egg yolks
1 (8-oz.) container mascarpone cheese
Toppings: fresh berries, sliced peaches or
    plums, fresh mint or thyme sprigs

~ A Recipe from a Local ~

Mint Tea Custard

Black tea, fresh mint, and quartered lemon combine with smooth custard for a dessert twist on sweet tea.

Makes 6 servings   Hands-On Time 10 min.   Total Time 1 hour, 45 min.

1. Cook milk in a small nonaluminum saucepan over medium-low heat, stirring once, 2 to 3 minutes or just until bubbles appear (do not boil); remove from heat. Add next 3 ingredients. Cover and steep 20 minutes. Remove and discard tea bags, without squeezing; discard mint sprigs and lemon quarters. Reserve 1 cup tea mixture.

2. Preheat oven to 300°. Whisk together sugar and eggs in a large bowl until mixture is thick and pale yellow. Gradually whisk in reserved 1 cup tea mixture and half-and-half until well blended. Pour mixture into 6 (4-oz.) custard cups or ramekins. Place custard cups in a roasting pan; add hot water halfway up sides of cups.

3. Bake at 300° for 40 to 50 minutes or until a knife inserted in center of custard comes out clean. Carefully remove from oven, and let stand in pan in water bath 30 minutes. Remove from water bath. Serve immediately, or cover and chill at least 2 hours.

1 ¼ cups low-fat evaporated milk
5 regular-size black tea bags
3 fresh mint sprigs, bruised
1 large lemon, quartered
½ cup sugar
4 large eggs
1 cup fat-free half-and-half
Garnishes: shaved chocolate, fresh
    mint sprigs

Lory Montgomery
Nashville, Tennessee

Owens-Thomas House
Savannah, Georgia

The Coastal South

The late American journalist Charles Kuralt famously observed that, thanks to the interstate highways, a person can cross the United States from coast to coast "without seeing anything." Transit along the Atlantic Coast, however, is a different story.

In fact, you don't need an interstate to travel between such seemingly disparate Southern locales as gritty and urban Baltimore, genteel and storied Charleston, romantic and gothic Savannah, and lively and artsy Miami. You could do it by boat. And, even if you did it by car, you'd be sure to see a whole lot of something in the Coastal South.

Avant-garde filmmaker John Waters says of his beloved **Baltimore, Maryland,** hometown: "You'll never discover a stranger city with such extreme style. It's as if every eccentric in the South decided to move North, ran out of gas in Baltimore, and decided to stay." Baltimore (BAWL-mer as the natives pronounce it) has long been considered the East Coast crossroads of North and South,

a place where the tastes of each pole and the seaside commingle to create a distinctive local flavor.

A port city in the only one of the original 13 colonies to be founded by Roman Catholics, Baltimore is where lawyer and author Francis Scott Key wrote "The Star-Spangled Banner." (Inspired by the bombardment of Fort McHenry, an entrance to Baltimore's harbor, during the Battle of Baltimore in 1814, the poem was set to music and designated in 1931 the American national anthem.)

The Chesapeake Bay was the source of the city's first trading fortunes, but railroads were also important to Baltimore's early growth. The country's first chartered railroad, the Baltimore & Ohio (the old B&O Railroad, which you might recall from playing the game Monopoly)

made its first run in 1830, helping lead the country's westward expansion and bringing jobs and money to the city. To this day Baltimore has an affinity for railroads. The B&O Railroad Museum—a national historic monument complete with a huge model railroad plus steam, electric, diesel, passenger, and freight trains—provides heaven-on-earth experiences for transportation junkies and model railroad enthusiasts.

In the early to mid-1800s, the rise of the American capital just 40 miles away in Washington, D.C., interrupted Baltimore's ascent as a national commerce center.

Some historians blame that development for Baltimore's legendary modern problems with crime and inner city blight, but, of course, no single factor is the reason Baltimore

257

Baltimoreans are justifiably proud of their entry into the canon of great American food. They seem to enjoy the tradition of pounding a mallet down on Old Bay-spiced steamed blue crabs just as much as the tourists.

became, by 1999, the country's leader in drug abuse and murders and the home of more than 40,000 abandoned buildings.

Former *Baltimore Sun* reporter David Simon chronicled this brilliantly in *The Wire*. The fictional HBO television series depicted Baltimore and its institutions—city hall, harbor stevedores, churches, the police department, the public school system, and the newspapers—as under siege, suffering from crime, drugs, decay, and corruption.

The Wire ran from 2002 to 2008. Coincidentally 2002 is the year that a group of concerned Baltimore business leaders launched their "Believe" campaign via billboards, TV commercials, T-shirts, signs on the sides of buses, you name it, to reawaken the city. With support from President Bill Clinton and the Maryland national congressional delegation, the "Believe" effort

helped put more police officers on the streets and pay them better, and it doubled funding for drug treatment.

A decade later, results started coming in: Baltimore now boasts the biggest crime reduction of any city in America. Its neighborhoods, even once-rough ones like Hampden and Highlandtown, are in a state of Brooklyn-esque rebuilding, complete with new bakeries, vintage clothing stores, art galleries, warehouse spaces, and relatively cheap rents.

As efforts continue, civic leaders note how broadminded and tolerant Baltimore is as a whole. The city's distinguished African-American community, an established part of Baltimore for more than century, produced Thurgood Marshall, the first African-American justice on the U.S. Supreme Court.

The Fells Point neighborhood, Baltimore's original seaport and one of the country's original shipbuilding

centers, was an early home to both enslaved and free blacks—and it's the place where famous abolitionist Frederick Douglass came of age.

Artists with an offbeat sensibility have always lived in and loved Baltimore. Billie Holiday grew up there, in great poverty and despair, gathering the material she would use in the jazz songs that made her a legend.

Filmmaker John Waters still resides in Baltimore and sets his movies there—including the blockbuster *Hairspray*, which pays homage to Baltimore's signature hairdo, the beehive, and the city's racially diverse history. (Waters also introduced the world to another Baltimore native, the late drag performer known as Divine.)

The newspaperman and social critic H.L. Mencken was born, thrived, and died here; a great man of words, he wrote such now-famous sentiments as: "Nobody ever went broke underestimating the taste of the American public."

There's a saying in Baltimore, which Mencken noted, that you can cook crab 50 ways, all of them good. Thanks to the Chesapeake Bay, the country's largest estuary, Baltimore is home to the distinctive blue crabs (*Callinectes sapidus*), as well as soft-shell crabs, Baltic clams, striped bass ("rockfish" on local menus), and oysters.

Baltimoreans are justifiably proud of their entry into the canon of great American foods, and they seem to enjoy the tradition of pounding a mallet down on Old Bay-spiced steamed blue crabs just as much as the tourists do. Some of the city's crab houses are quite old and famous, and all of them are extremely democratic—most likely because crab eating is the kind of roll-up-your-sleeves, messy process that invites camaraderie.

At places like L.P. Steamers, a beloved crab house across the street from a Little League field in South Baltimore, a bucketful is unceremoniously dumped before you on the brown paper that lines the tables, and you're given a mallet, a pick, a beer, and a job to do. But such reward!

The beer, by the way, has to be a "Natty Boh," also known as a National Bohemian. The beer has been a Baltimore brand since 1885 and a sponsor of the Orioles baseball team since the 1960s. Nobody seems to care that Pabst Brewing Company bought the brand or that it's currently brewed in North Carolina and Georgia; about 90 percent of all Natty Boh sales still take place in Baltimore.

If you travel farther down the Eastern Seaboard, you encounter

Cantler's Riverside Inn
Annapolis, Maryland

Cooper River
Charleston, South Carolina

in relatively quick succession two gems, cities that do more than their fair share to give the Southeast its well-mannered, genteel reputation: Charleston and Savannah.

Both are magnets for tourists, who come to experience the quaint streets, grand homes, and refined manner that both of these storied cities possess.

Charleston, South Carolina, is a small peninsular city nestled between the Ashley and Cooper Rivers where they merge with the Atlantic. It was first established by

the British, who arrived in 1670 and named the area "Charles Town" in honor of King Charles II.

The rivers that flank it were named for Anthony Ashley Cooper, an earl to whom King Charles granted land in the new colony. (If you sense an aristocratic attitude in Charleston, it's one that likely traces all the way back to the good earl, who served as lord proprietor of Charles Town.) The French Huguenot settlers came soon after, forging an alliance with the Brits.

These were lordly types, landed gentry who built magnificent Italianate and Greek Revival riverside

plantations and took up cotton, indigo, and rice farming. (A long-running and oft-repeated saying about Charlestonians is that they're like the Chinese: They eat rice and worship their ancestors.)

It's hard to explain the grandeur of plantations and manor homes to the uninitiated. When the French social critic and author Simone de Beauvoir visited Charleston in 1947, she called them "private Edens," and that's apt. Old Charlestonian families take enormous pride in keeping up their gardens, and for good reason: They are spectacular—ringed with

Spanish moss, scented with jasmine, and blooming with old roses.

The city's many home and garden tours allow glimpses into this private and spectacular world. Consider touring Drayton Hall, completed about 1744, to appreciate its porticos, its Tuscan and Ionic columns, and the elaborate detailing on its plaster moldings and ceilings.

Or take a stroll in the gardens at Middleton Place, the former home of Henry Middleton, the second president of the First U.S. Continental Congress and one of the South's wealthiest plantation owners. His plantation house is long gone, but his classical English gardens, a National Historic Landmark, remain in all of their glory—with terraces, grazing sheep, arching pink camellia bushes, mature magnolia trees, lakes, and canals.

Charleston has been an international port since its inception, and that tradition has only grown. Today it's the busiest container port in the South and the fourth busiest in the nation, which is remarkable when you compare its size to other major port cities like New York and San Francisco.

Before the Civil War, Charleston was a port of a different sort. Historians estimate that 40 percent of the Africans brought to the New World passed through Charleston. In keeping with the city's refined image, the ugly spectacle of selling slaves outdoors was prohibited in 1856, though the uglier-still practice continued indoors until the Civil War led to its abolishment.

Charleston's former slave auction hall reopened in 2007 as the Old Slave Mart Museum, complete with stirring exhibits honoring the suffering of those who passed through it.

Charleston saw plenty of Civil War action. The first shots of the Civil War were fired at Fort Sumter, the federal fort on Charleston Harbor, on April 12, 1861, and the battle raged for four years. Today the fort's ruins, accessible by boat, are a national monument and park with a Civil War history museum.

Charleston's recent history has included national recognition for its glorious food scene. The city has produced the 2008, 2009, and 2010 winners of the James Beard Award for Best Chef Southeast.

To call Charleston's brand of cuisine simply Southern is reductive. Charleston cooks put their collective stamp on the genre by adopting a "more is more" philosophy—not quite like the excesses of, say, Texas, but in an inclusive way.

Charleston chefs are influenced by both aristocratic and exotic tastes, so you find African and Caribbean influences, bold spices, and an interesting mix of high and low on most

Old Charlestonian families take enormous pride in keeping up their gardens, and they are spectacular—ringed with Spanish moss, scented with jasmine, and blooming with old roses.

The influence of the Gullahs—people of African descent whose practice involves communing with spirits—is sometimes palpable in Savannah, which celebrates its image as "America's Most Haunted City" with hearse rides and cemetery crawls.

menus. They also make the most of their native Lowcountry seafood: shrimp (in preparations like shrimp 'n' grits and the shrimp and rice casserole variously called *purloo, pulao, pilau, or perloo*); oysters (raw and in stews and pan roasts); crab (in the glorious sherry-spiked she-crab soup); plus tilefish, shad (when it's in season, of course), triggerfish, grouper, and vermillion snapper.

If it swims in their waters, Charlestonians have found a decadent way to enjoy it.

Like most of the rest of Georgia, **Savannah, Georgia,** was the brainchild of General James Oglethorpe, a British soldier and philanthropist. The Spanish had been in Georgia nearly two centuries earlier, but no one could make a proper town stick on Savannah's soil until Oglethorpe. Most historians agree it is because

he quickly made friends with the Native Americans, particularly the Yamacraw chief Tomochichi.

Founded in 1733, Savannah is Georgia's oldest city. Urban planners make much of its layout, which Oglethorpe designed himself: a grid of broad streets that covers 2 square miles and is punctuated by 24 squares.

Each of these miniature parks has its own character, and most were named for distinguished citizens or historical events. (Fun fact: The park bench scenes in the film *Forrest Gump* were filmed in Savannah's Chippewa Square.)

Despite its orderly design, things got more than a little topsyturvy for Savannah.

The city has seen war, yellow fever, hurricanes, fires, and pirates (yes, pirates—the curse of a thriving seaport). With all that arose the

notion that the area was cursed by its buried bodies and unsettled souls, earning it the nickname "America's Most Haunted City." In true Savannah style, the so-called curse is celebrated—more than 30 ghost tours of the town are offered on any given night, from haunted pub crawls and secret cemetery visits to tours by trolley or hearse.

Like Charleston, Savannah has its share of swampy lowlands, perfect for farming rice, and its share of grand plantations. Savannah's architecture is its own, though, and not just when it comes to private homes: Every public building seems to boast a buttress or a vault or an arch of some significance.

The influence of the Gullahs— people of African descent who settled in the coastal South and whose practices involve communing with spirits—is sometimes palpable.

Savannah, Georgia

(The term "Gullah" comes from the language they speak, a kind of patois of English and West African dialects.) That the Gullah culture thrives in Savannah is testament to its African-American history.

The First African Baptist Church, organized in 1773 and "constituted as a body of organized believers" in 1777, lays claim to the country's longest continually active African-American congregation. The Second African Baptist Church, a relative late-bloomer opened across town in 1802, is where Union General William Tecumseh Sherman read the Emancipation Proclamation promising every freed slave "40 acres and a mule."

Savannah has spirit—a big personality for such charming and seemingly restrained environs. Its flair for celebration, especially between Thanksgiving and New Year's Day, may actually date to the end of the Civil War. General Sherman mounted his final siege on the Confederacy in late 1864, marching through the South and burning everything in sight. "I can make Georgia howl!" he reportedly cried before torching Atlanta.

Having thoroughly dismantled the rebel army by the time he reached Savannah on December 21, he offered the city as a Christmas gift to President Abraham Lincoln.

Ever since, the city's residents have taken up partying as their mission—perhaps in gratitude, perhaps in noble defeat, perhaps just because.

Oh, are there any American cities that have changed more in the past 30 years than **Miami** and **Miami Beach, Florida?** In the 1960s, comedian Lenny Bruce described Miami Beach as "the place where neon goes to die." Now it's the place where people from around the world flock for honest-to-goodness art. The area's burgeoning art scene is no

Miami Beach, Florida

Vizcaya Museum and Gardens
Miami, Florida

Thanks to its irresistible combination of beautiful
weather and stunning beaches, the Miami area has been a
tourist destination almost as long as it has existed.

joke. The repurposed warehouses in Miami's Wynwood Art District contain some of the country's largest collections of work from cutting-edge artists like Cindy Sherman and Keith Haring. And Miami Beach contains the country's largest collection of Art Deco buildings in the country.

All of these are celebrated at Art Basel, an offshoot of a European modern and contemporary art show. What began with a handful of galleries in 2002, is now an annual show that includes more than 250 galleries and a weeklong party that attracts actors, music stars, the international jet set, serious collectors, and tourists.

The amalgam of cultures in Miami and Miami Beach includes the seriously fashionable, the seriously poor, and everything in between. The Caribbean-born and Latin American-born contingencies do much to give the area its flavor.

The range includes very wealthy Venezuelan and Colombian business-men and jet-setting models, Latin American expatriates, and fresh-off-the-boat immigrants living hand to mouth.

At the heart of the area's Latin experience is Miami's Little Havana. The neighborhood name is apt. Since Fidel Castro took over Cuba in 1959, Cubans have been fleeing to Miami any way they could.

Half the Cubans in the United States live in the Miami-Dade County area. Miami's Little Havana is home to cigar factories, monuments to fallen Cuban heroes, shops selling hand-embroidered guayabera shirts, salsa dancing, music clubs, and *Viernes Culturales*, a street party held on the last Friday of every month.

The Miami area has been a tourist destination almost as long as it has existed, thanks to its irresistible combination of beautiful weather

and stunning beaches. When the Florida East Coast railroad came in 1896, it brought tourists in droves to Coconut Grove, Miami's oldest community and the site of the area's first hotel.

The Grove is home to the historic Vizcaya Museum and Gardens, the former faux Renaissance winter estate of the industrialist James Deering, which was completed in 1916. The Gilded-Age-meets-Jazz-Age-meets-Venice villa with its striped dock poles makes a spectacular tour stop.

To many, Miami means South Beach, and South Beach means clubs, bashes, and late-night shenanigans. Some may not realize South Beach is actually part of Miami Beach, a separate city across Biscayne Bay from mainland Miami. The party playground at its southernmost end, known as SoBe, features beaches lined with imported Bahamian sand

and irresistible pastel pieces of Art Deco eye candy.

The beach has undergone at least two major booms. The first was when Indiana-born businessman Carl Fisher, who made his fortune selling cars and headlights and taillights, came to Miami on a friend's recommendation in 1909. Fisher liked it so well that he bought a vacation home.

Eventually he decided he wanted to turn present-day Miami Beach, then a mangrove swamp with a few homes, into a tropical paradise. In a story of tremendous American ingenuity, by gum he did! In no time at all, there was a wooden boardwalk lined with Art Deco hotels and well-heeled vacationing Yankees. Titans of American industry built mansions there.

Trendy destinations come and go and come again. Miami Beach became a place where people retired, and when they moved out by the mid-1960s, Miami Beach was mostly dilapidated, a beloved spot only for locals who remembered its former splendor.

Massive revitalization efforts began in the early 1980s and spurred a renaissance. The Army Corps of Engineers made a commitment to dredge the beach and erect a new beachfront. Local design enthusiasts restored the old Art Deco buildings. And the TV program *Miami Vice*, largely filmed in Miami Beach, premiered in 1984, making the area look downright sexy.

Sexy it has stayed, with its boutique hotels, its clubs, and the rappers and fashion models it attracts. By recent estimates, more than 1,500 models live and work in Miami. Today, the area is about as modern and edgy as any in the country, proof that the South is its

Marlin Hotel
Miami, Florida

own melting pot, an amalgam of cultures, flavors, and traditions old and new.

It's a reminder that, even though they are always evolving, the places we hold sacred also stay the same. Our hometowns exist in our hearts

and minds just the way they were when last we saw them.

And the best way to bring both the past and present of a place into focus is to endeavor to reproduce the flavors its people know and love best. There is truly no taste like home.

Inner Harbor
Baltimore, Maryland

ᘉᘉ
Welcome to
Baltimore
ᘉᘉ

You can't talk about Baltimore without mentioning crabs. But there are two other serious points of pride: the Inner Harbor and Johns Hopkins.

Start with the Inner Harbor, a former working seaport whose grand makeover into a kind of mass-market retail complex culminated with the opening of the Harborplace in 1980. The big deal: It's home to the excellent National Aquarium and its 16,000 sharks, birds, frogs, turtles, jellyfish, snakes, crocodiles, sea turtles, and other harbor and water creatures.

It's also just a few blocks away from the historic Fells Point, a cobblestoned waterfront area brimming with locally owned bakeries, bars, galleries, and real Bawlmer flavor.

Johns Hopkins University and Johns Hopkins Hospital are less tourist destinations than beacons of Baltimore accomplishment. Both bear the name of the man who gave the money to build them—a Quaker, lifelong bachelor, and one-time grocer who made his fortune in railway shipping, banking, and insurance.

Established in 1876 as America's first research university, Johns Hopkins University still perennially ranks amongst its best. Some 36 Nobel Prize winners have ties to the school.

Johns Hopkins Hospital and its School of Medicine pride themselves on offering extremely high-quality treatment for patients, advanced education for health-care providers, and cutting-edge medical research.

Fried Soft-Shell Crab Benedicts

You need no mallet to unlock the delectable flavor of the soft-shell crab. The Chesapeake staple stars in this Baltimore brunch favorite.

Makes 6 servings   Hands-On Time 30 min.   Total Time 40 min.

Vegetable oil
1   (12-oz.) can evaporated milk
7   large eggs
6   soft-shell crabs
1½ tsp. seasoned salt
1½ cups self-rising flour
6   (¾-inch-thick) French bread loaf slices
2   Tbsp. butter, melted

1   (0.9-oz.) envelope hollandaise sauce mix
1   cup milk
1   Tbsp. lemon juice
½   tsp. white vinegar
2   cups loosely packed baby arugula
2   Tbsp. chopped fresh chives

1. Pour oil to depth of 3 inches in a Dutch oven; heat to 360°. Whisk together evaporated milk, 1 egg, and ¼ cup water in a large bowl.

2. Rinse crabs, pat dry, and sprinkle with seasoned salt. Dredge crabs in flour; dip in evaporated milk mixture, and dredge in flour again. Fry crabs, in 2 batches, in hot oil 2 minutes on each side or until golden brown. Drain on a wire rack over paper towels. Keep warm.

3. Preheat oven to 375°. Brush 1 side of each bread slice with butter. Bake bread slices, buttered sides up, 5 minutes or until toasted.

4. Prepare hollandaise sauce mix according to package directions, omitting butter and using 1 cup milk and lemon juice.

5. Pour water to depth of 2 inches in a large saucepan. Bring to a boil; reduce heat, and maintain at a light simmer. Add vinegar. Break remaining 6 eggs, and slip into water, 1 at a time, as close as possible to surface. Simmer 3 to 5 minutes or to desired degree of doneness. Remove with a slotted spoon. Trim edges, if desired.

6. Top bread slices with arugula, fried crabs, poached eggs, and hollandaise sauce. Sprinkle with chives and table salt and freshly ground black pepper to taste.

Mini Crab Cakes with Garlic-Chive Sauce

Makes 16 cakes   Hands-On Time 15 min.   Total Time 40 min.

1	(8-oz.) package fresh lump crabmeat, drained
3	whole grain white bread slices
⅓	cup light mayonnaise
3	green onions, thinly sliced
1	tsp. Old Bay seasoning
1	tsp. Worcestershire sauce
2	large eggs, lightly beaten
	Garlic-Chive Sauce
	Garnish: lemon slices

1. Pick crabmeat, removing any bits of shell. Pulse bread slices in a blender or food processor 5 times or until finely crumbled (yield should be about 1½ cups).

2. Stir together mayonnaise and next 4 ingredients in a large bowl. Gently stir in breadcrumbs and crabmeat. Shape mixture into 16 (2-inch) cakes (about 2 Tbsp. each).

3. Preheat oven to 200°. Cook cakes, in batches, on a large hot griddle or nonstick skillet coated with cooking spray over medium-low heat 4 minutes on each side or until golden brown. Season with salt to taste. Keep cakes warm in oven up to 30 minutes; serve with Garlic-Chive Sauce.

Note: We tested with Sara Lee Soft & Smooth Whole Grain White Bread

Garlic-Chive Sauce

Makes 1 cup   Hands-On Time 5 min.   Total Time 35 min.

¾	cup light sour cream or light mayonnaise
1	garlic clove, minced
1	Tbsp. chopped fresh chives
¾	tsp. lemon zest
1 ½	Tbsp. fresh lemon juice
¼	tsp. table salt
⅛	tsp. black pepper

1. Stir together all ingredients in a small bowl. Cover and chill 30 minutes before serving.

Buy, Make, and Eat Crab Cakes Like a Local

Mystery novelist and former *Baltimore Sun* reporter Laura Lippman has said, "Anyone can love a perfect place. Loving Baltimore takes some resilience." Let's say the crab cakes help.

Crab cakes are the epitome of regional American food, a dish that sprang up in and around Baltimore in the 1820s and by 1939 was so well known that it was served at the World's Fair in New York.

Crab cakes are essentially composed of four things: crabmeat, binding (usually egg or mayonnaise), seasonings (various herbs, spices, and minced vegetables such as onions or bell peppers), and filler (breadcrumbs or cracker crumbs).

Crabmeat is expensive, especially the jumbo lump, and fillers and binders are cheap, so bad crab cakes that rely too heavily on filler seem to abound. But a good crab cake is a crowning achievement, an irresistibly savory and scrumptious treat. And you can find very good ones in Baltimore.

Locals swear by those made and sold in Lexington Market by Faidley Seafood, a family-owned business that dates to 1886.

Meet Actress Mo'Nique

That this amazingly talented and tell-it-like-it-is actress, comedienne, and author also knows how to cook is no surprise. Mo'Nique seems to know how to do everything.

A Baltimore native and former telephone company employee, Monique Angela Hicks took the professional name Mo'Nique and quickly established it in comedy.

She joined the professional comedy circuit and appeared on *Showtime at the Apollo* and *Def Comedy Jam.* Her career took what she calls a "quantum leap" when she was asked to appear on *The Parkers,* the UPN television program about a single mom who attends college with her daughter. Mo'Nique won an Academy Award for her portrayal of Mary Jones, an abusive, mentally ill mother in the film *Precious,* based on the novel *Push* by Sapphire.

Along the way, she became a sort of unofficial spokesperson for plus-size women, authoring *Skinny Women Are Evil* and *Skinny Cooks Can't Be Trusted.* More recently, she's inspired fans with her weight loss. Through it all, she's remained fabulous.

"F.A.T. means Fabulous And Thick, Full And Tasty, Fluffy And Tender." —Mo'Nique

F.A.T. Green Beans

There are green beans with bacon, and then there's bacon with green beans. This would be the latter.

Makes 8 servings   Hands-On Time 30 min.   Total Time 45 min.

4 lb. fresh green beans	4 garlic cloves, smashed
1 lb. sliced bacon	Juice of 1 lemon
1 large Vidalia onion, chopped	3 Tbsp. salted butter

1. Cut the ends off of the green beans (or snap them like the old folks did, and remove the string), if desired. Wash and drain the beans. Cut the bacon into small cubes, and set it aside with the onion and garlic until ready to use.

2. Bring a large pot of salted water to a boil (about 2 Tbsp. salt to 1 gallon of water). Add the beans and the lemon juice; let this boil gently for 7 to 10 minutes or until the beans are tender. Drain the beans, reserving about 2 cups of the cooking liquid.

3. In a large sauté pan, cook the bacon for 7 minutes. Then add the onion and garlic; cook over low heat 7 to 10 minutes or until onions are softened. Add the beans and the reserved cooking liquid to the bacon mixture; stir to combine. Add the butter, season with kosher salt and freshly ground black pepper, and cover. Simmer for 10 minutes over low heat. Serve immediately.

Cornbread-and-Crab-Stuffed Fish

Crab-stuffed seafood is a tradition along the Chesapeake Bay. In season you may substitute rockfish, a Bay-area favorite, for the bass or snapper.

Makes 6 servings   Hands-On Time 30 min.   Total Time 1 hour, 45 min.

1	(6-oz.) package buttermilk cornbread mix	2	white bread slices, toasted and cut into cubes (about 1 cup)
1	cup fresh lump crabmeat, drained (about ½ lb.)	1	Tbsp. chopped fresh parsley
2	Tbsp. butter	¼	tsp. lemon zest
¼	cup chopped celery	½	cup chicken broth
¼	cup chopped onion	1	(3- to 5-lb.) striped bass or red snapper, dressed
1	tsp. Old Bay seasoning, divided		Kitchen string

1. Preheat oven to 350°. Prepare cornbread mix according to package directions. Cool 30 minutes; crumble into a large bowl.

2. Meanwhile, pick crabmeat, removing any bits of shell.

3. Melt butter in a large skillet over medium heat; add celery and onion, and sauté 10 to 12 minutes or until tender. Stir in ½ tsp. Old Bay seasoning. Stir celery mixture, crab, bread cubes, parsley, and lemon zest into crumbled cornbread, stirring gently until blended. Add broth, and stir gently until moistened.

4. Sprinkle cavity of fish with remaining ½ tsp. Old Bay seasoning. Spoon stuffing mixture into fish, and secure with kitchen string. Place fish in a large, lightly greased roasting pan.

5. Bake at 350° for 45 to 50 minutes or until fish flakes with a fork.

Chesapeake Chowder

Makes 8 cups   Hands-On Time 25 min.   Total Time 1 hour, 10 min.

½	lb. unpeeled, medium-size fresh shrimp	2 ½	cups chicken broth
½	lb. fresh crabmeat	1	cup dry white wine or chicken broth
1	onion, chopped	1	(8-oz.) bottle clam juice
3	garlic cloves, minced	5	red potatoes, peeled and diced
2	celery ribs, chopped	1	Tbsp. Old Bay seasoning
1	Tbsp. olive oil	½	cup heavy cream
¼	cup all-purpose flour		

1. Peel shrimp; devein, if desired. Drain and flake crabmeat, removing any bits of shell. Set seafood aside.

2. Sauté onion, garlic, and celery in hot oil in a Dutch oven over medium-high heat 8 minutes or until tender. Stir in flour, and cook, stirring constantly, 1 minute. Stir in broth and next 4 ingredients. Bring to a boil; cover, reduce heat, and simmer, stirring occasionally, 30 minutes or until potatoes are tender.

3. Stir in shrimp, crabmeat, and heavy cream; cook over low heat 5 minutes or just until shrimp turn pink.

Watch a Game at Camden Yards Like a Local

The Baltimore Orioles have been a big deal in Baltimore from the get-go.

Before the team came to the city in 1954, Baltimoreans had had only a minor league franchise—nothing worth bragging about to their big-city relations.

It took many years for the Orioles to get good, many years spent in the shadow of the all-powerful Yankees. "Baltimore, of course, has better fans," wrote Baltimore native and movie director Barry Levinson. And the Orioles also actually have a better park.

Oriole Park at Camden Yards is, as *The New York Times* put it, "the ballpark that forever changed baseball." The first modern baseball stadium of any real architectural distinction, it opened in 1992 as a throwback to a time when watching a baseball game was a warm and inclusive experience (as opposed to an anonymous foray into hooliganism).

Camden Yards is on the old B&O Railroad yards on the city's outskirts. With its arched facades of red brick and cast stone and ornate clock over the scoreboard, it remains a marvelous place to spend an afternoon, especially with a Natty Boh Brat from Polock Johnny's, a Baltimore institution since 1921.

Maryland Black Walnut Cake

Black walnut trees are native to Maryland and much of the eastern United States. A black sheep of the tree world, they are toxic to some other landscape plants and messy when in leaf. But their wood is prized for furniture and cabinets, and their notoriously difficult-to-crack nuts have a rich, distinctive flavor beloved by local bakers and others who've acquired a taste for them.

Makes 12 servings   Hands-On Time 20 min.   Total Time 1 hour, 10 min.

1. Preheat oven to 350°. Pulse black walnuts in a food processor 8 to 10 times or until finely ground; set aside.

2. Beat butter at medium speed with an electric mixer until creamy; gradually add granulated sugar, beating until light and fluffy. Add egg yolks and vanilla, beating just until blended.

3. Sift together flour, baking powder, and salt; add to butter mixture alternately with milk, beginning and ending with flour mixture. Beat batter at low speed just until blended after each addition.

4. Beat egg whites at medium speed with an electric mixer until stiff peaks form; fold into batter. Fold ground walnuts into batter. Spoon batter evenly into a greased and floured 10-inch Bundt pan.

5. Bake at 350° for 50 minutes or until a wooden pick inserted in center comes out clean. Cool in pan on a wire rack 10 minutes; remove from pan, and cool completely on wire rack. Sprinkle evenly with powdered sugar. Serve with vanilla ice cream and sliced fresh strawberries, if desired.

John Shields, Chesapeake Bay Cooking
Baltimore, Maryland

1 ½ cups chopped black walnuts
1   cup butter, softened
1 ½ cups granulated sugar
3   large eggs, separated
1   tsp. vanilla extract
2   cups all-purpose flour
1   Tbsp. baking powder
¼   tsp. table salt
¾   cup milk
¼   cup powdered sugar
Vanilla ice cream (optional)
Sliced fresh strawberries (optional)

Chesapeake Bay Party Nuts

Makes 2 cups   Hands-On Time 10 min.   Total Time 45 min.

2   Tbsp. butter, melted
2   tsp. Old Bay Seasoning
2   Tbsp. Worcestershire sauce
½   tsp. garlic powder
¼   to ½ tsp. hot sauce
2   cups pecan halves or whole almonds

1. Preheat oven to 300°. Stir together melted butter, Old Bay Seasoning, Worcestershire sauce, garlic powder, and hot sauce; add pecans or almonds, tossing to coat. Place nuts in an aluminum foil-lined 15- x 10-inch jelly-roll pan.

2. Bake seasoned nuts at 300° for 30 minutes, stirring twice. Cool completely. Store in an airtight container.

Meet Chef
Duff Goldman

Better known as "the ace of cakes," Jeffrey Adam "Duff" Goldman is the Baltimorean who opened the amazing Charm City Cakes bakery in Baltimore in 2002.

Known for his over-the-top architectural and thematic cakes—he made a Hogwarts Castle cake for the Warner Bros. premiere of *Harry Potter*, for example—the cutting-edge baker got his start selling bagels at a mall shop when he was 14. After turns in cooking schools and the kitchens of high-end restaurants, Goldman found his niche marrying art and cake.

His incredible cake sculptures garner massive attention. *Ace of Cakes*, the reality show about his bakery, aired on the Food Network for 10 seasons. He's since developed his own line of baking gear, including specialty pans, icings, and glazes, plus innovations like "cake tattoos" and "cake graffiti."

"OK, secret pastry chef knowledge about to be revealed, forever getting me banned from the secret pastry chef conference on world domination: Coffee is to chocolate like salt is to beef. Adding just a smidge of coffee to a chocolate dessert will make that flavor really burst." —Duff Goldman

Charm City Chocolate Cake

Makes 8 servings   Hands-On Time 30 min.   Total Time 3 hours

Vegetable cooking spray
Parchment paper
DRY INGREDIENTS
3   cups all-purpose flour
3   cups sugar
1   cup unsweetened cocoa
2   tsp. baking soda
1 ¼ tsp. table salt
¾   tsp. baking powder
WET INGREDIENTS
1 ½ cups buttermilk

¾   cup canola oil
½   cup hot brewed coffee
3   oz. dark chocolate baking bar, melted
3   large eggs, at room temperature
ADDITIONAL INGREDIENTS
4   cups Easy Kahlúa-Chocolate Buttercream or other chocolate frosting
Caramel sauce

1. Preheat oven to 350°. Coat 2 (9-inch) round cake pans with cooking spray. Line bottoms of pans with parchment paper, and coat paper with cooking spray.

2. Beat all dry ingredients at low speed with a heavy-duty electric stand mixer, using whisk attachment, until blended. Whisk together wet ingredients; gradually add to dry ingredients, beating on low speed until blended, stopping to scrape bowl as needed. Pour batter into prepared pans.

3. Bake at 350° for 35 to 40 minutes. Cool in pans on wire racks 10 minutes; remove from pans to wire racks, and cool completely (about 1 hour). Level layers if needed with a long serrated knife. Spread Easy Kahlúa-Chocolate Buttercream between layers and on top and sides of cake. Drizzle with caramel sauce, and enjoy!

Easy Kahlúa-Chocolate Buttercream

To reinforce the flavors in Duff Goldman's cake, we spiked a tasty Southern Living *chocolate frosting recipe with coffee liqueur.*

Makes 4 cups   Hands-On Time 10 min.   Total Time 20 min.

1. Microwave chocolate in a microwave-safe bowl at HIGH 1 to 1½ minutes or until melted and smooth, stirring at 30-second intervals. Cool 10 minutes.

2. Beat butter at medium speed with an electric mixer until creamy; gradually add powdered sugar, beating until blended. Add melted chocolate; beat on low speed until blended, stopping to scrape bowl as needed. Add Kahlúa, beating just until blended.

8 (1-oz.) semisweet chocolate
   baking squares
1½ cups butter, softened
3½ cups powdered sugar
2 Tbsp. Kahlúa or coffee liqueur

Welcome to
Charleston

In most cities, a horse-and-carriage ride is considered tourist bait. In Charleston, with its charming cobblestone streets and secret hidden-from-street-view gardens, carriage rides are a bona fide tradition.

Charleston's got the carriage ride down to a science: You show up on Anson Street a block north of the City Market, and you enter a lottery of sorts among the five major companies that offer this service: Carolina Polo & Carriage Company, Old South Carriage Company, Olde Towne Carriage Company, Classic Carriage Works, and Palmetto Carriage Company. Each offers comprehensive one-hour tours of the city. Because this is a competitive business for tourist dollars, the licensed guides are wonderfully (and uniformly) knowledgeable and funny. They know all about the lore of the city and old families who made it so. They'll take you down to the mansions on the Battery and up to the city's oldest churches.

There are also walking tours, harbor tours, garden tours, and culinary tours. The Gullah tour, led by a former schoolteacher and local legend named Alphonso Brown, takes visitors through the African-American experience in Charleston, including a stop at the neighborhood that was the inspiration for George Gershwin's classic musical *Porgy and Bess*.

Charleston, South Carolina

Heirloom Tomato Salad

Use your best summer tomatoes in this eye-catching salad.

Makes 8 servings
Hands-On Time 15 min.
Total Time 50 min.

4   lb. assorted heirloom tomatoes
2   small Kirby cucumbers, sliced
1   small red onion, halved and sliced
Lady Pea Salsa
Fresh basil leaves

1. Cut tomatoes into wedges or in half, depending on size. Gently toss tomatoes with cucumbers and onion. Top with Lady Pea Salsa and basil.

Lady Pea Salsa

This colorful salsa makes a delicious topping for sliced tomatoes, grilled chicken, or steak.

Makes about 4 cups
Hands-On Time 20 min.
Total Time 35 min.

1   cup diced unpeeled nectarine
2   jalapeño peppers, seeded and minced
1   Tbsp. sugar
3   Tbsp. fresh lime juice
2   tsp. orange zest
2   tsp. grated fresh ginger
2   cups cooked fresh lady peas
½   cup chopped fresh cilantro
⅓   cup diced red onion

1. Stir together first 6 ingredients in a large bowl; let stand 15 minutes. Add peas and next 2 ingredients, and gently toss to coat. Serve immediately, or refrigerate in an airtight container up to 24 hours.

Lowcountry Shrimp-and-Okra Pilau

For the most authentic version, serve this stew over Carolina Gold rice browned in butter and simmered until tender in stock made from the shrimp shells.

Makes 4 servings   Hands-On Time 50 min.   Total Time 1 hour, 25 min.

1. Peel shrimp; reserve shells for stock, and devein, if desired.

2. Cook sausage in a large Dutch oven over medium-low heat, stirring often, 5 minutes or until golden brown. Remove sausage, reserving drippings in Dutch oven. Melt butter in drippings. Stir in onion and garlic, and sauté 3 minutes or until tender. Add celery, and cook 2 minutes. Stir in tomatoes and chicken broth; bring to a boil. Reduce heat to low, and simmer 30 minutes.

3. Stir in shrimp, sausage, and okra; cook 5 minutes. Stir in parsley and next 4 ingredients. Season with salt and freshly ground black pepper to taste. Serve over hot cooked rice; top with green onions.

Note: We tested with Conecuh Hickory Smoked Sausage.

Chef Sean Brock, McCrady's and Husk
Charleston, South Carolina

1	lb. unpeeled, large raw shrimp
1	cup diced smoked sausage
2	Tbsp. butter
1	cup diced sweet onion
1	garlic clove, chopped
½	cup diced celery
4	large plum tomatoes, peeled, seeded, and chopped (about 1 ¼ lb.)
2	cups chicken or shrimp broth
1	cup sliced fresh okra
3	Tbsp. chopped fresh parsley
1	Tbsp. fresh lemon juice
1	tsp. dried crushed red pepper
2	tsp. hot sauce
1	tsp. Worcestershire sauce
4	cups hot cooked rice
3	green onions, thinly sliced

Garnish: grilled halved okra

~ You've Gotta Try ~
Perloo, Pilau, Pulao, or Purloo

By any of its various names, perloo is a classic Southern rice dish that belongs in the same family as gumbo and jambalaya but has a flavor all its own.

The base: rice that is browned in butter or oil before it's cooked in a rich and flavorful stock, a technique that helps keep the grains distinct. (All those spellings, by the way, are Lowcountry riffs on the word "pilaf.") Depending on where it's served, it may be finished with tender chicken, seafood, or sausage.

The dish emerged in the South in places like Charleston and New Orleans, where African and Caribbean immigrants prepared it with the proteins and vegetables at hand.

In Charleston it's often made with Carolina Gold rice, the beautiful extra-long-grained variety cultivated in the 17th century by slaves, now a Lowcountry staple and counted among the best-tasting rice varieties in the world.

No matter what you call it, the dish is a distinctly homey, rustic, and comforting totem of coastal Southern cooking.

The Coastal South

Meet Author
John Martin Taylor

They say you can never be from Charleston unless you were born in Charleston, but John Martin Taylor is one notable exception.

He won his way into this storied city's heart by tackling its stomach.

For many years Taylor's culinary bookshop, Hoppin' John's, was the place in town to find out what to cook and how, and Taylor himself became a notable cooking teacher running it.

He is the author of four ground-breaking cookbooks on Southern food, including *Hoppin' John's Lowcountry Cooking: Recipes and Ruminations from Charleston & The Carolina Coastal Plain* and *The New Southern Cook*.

"This meal is a celebration of late summer's bounty."

—John Martin Taylor

Hoppin' John's Frogmore Stew

This recipe gets its name from an island settlement between Charleston and Savannah that once was called Frogmore, after an ancestral English country estate, but is now just called St. Helena. The dish is less a stew and more the Lowcountry version of a summer seafood boil.

Makes 8 servings   Hands-On Time 20 min.   Total Time 30 min.

⅓ cup dry shrimp-and-crab boil seasoning

3 Tbsp. table salt

2 lb. spicy smoked link sausage, cut into 2-inch pieces

12 ears freshly shucked corn, broken into 3- to 4-inch pieces

4 lb. unpeeled large raw shrimp

1. In a large stockpot, add the shrimp-and-crab boil seasoning and salt to 1½ gal. water, and bring to a boil. Add the sausage, and boil, uncovered, for 5 minutes. Add the corn, and cook 5 minutes. Add the shrimp, and cook 3 minutes (do not wait for the liquid to come to a boil when timing the corn and shrimp). Drain immediately, and serve.

Cemetery at St. Phillip's Episcopal Church
Charleston, South Carolina

Enjoy the Spoleto Like a Local

When Italian composer and librettist Gian Carlo Menotti founded a musical festival in Spoleto, Italy, in 1958, it probably wasn't clear how the city of Charleston would fit in.

But Menotti, who toured the world performing his operas, imported the idea of the festival here in 1977.

Each spring since, Charleston has hosted Spoleto (spo-LAY-toe), a 17-day extravaganza of jazz, opera, theater, dance, visual arts exhibitions, and musical acts from orchestras to indie rock bands.

The key venue is the Dock Street Theater, an intimate 450-seat space in the historic district. Organizers make it easy to get involved, selling tickets to individual events and packages of them, and it's thrilling for Charlestonians to see international critics and enthusiasts flying into their city.

Alongside the main festival, an important offshoot has developed: Piccolo Spoleto ("Little Spoleto"), an arts event with an exclusive focus on regional and local performers. Its events are low cost or free, and many are kid friendly.

Sizzling Flounder

Flounder is a Charleston favorite, but you can use any firm-fleshed fish, such as tilapia, grouper, or catfish. Adjust the cooking time according to the thickness of the fish.

Makes 4 servings   Hands-On Time 10 min.   Total Time 25 min.

½ cup butter	¾ tsp. table salt
¼ cup grated Parmesan cheese	¼ tsp. black pepper
1 tsp. paprika	2 Tbsp. fresh lemon juice
4 (6-oz.) flounder fillets	

1. Place 1 oven rack 5 inches from heat; place a second rack in middle of oven. Preheat oven to 450°. Heat butter in a broiler-safe 13- x 9-inch baking dish in oven 8 minutes or until butter melts and begins to brown.

2. Meanwhile, combine Parmesan cheese and paprika. Season fish with salt and pepper. Place fish in hot butter, skin sides up.

3. Bake at 450° on middle oven rack 10 minutes. Carefully flip fish, and baste with pan juices. Sprinkle with lemon juice and Parmesan cheese mixture. Bake 5 more minutes or just until fish flakes with a fork. Remove from oven; increase oven temperature to broil.

4. Broil fish on oven rack 5 inches from heat 2 to 3 minutes or until bubbly and golden brown.

Field Peas with Okra and Andouille Sausage

This dish, perfect for midsummer when field peas and okra are in season, comes together in just one pot.

Makes 8 to 10 servings   Hands-On Time 10 min.   Total Time 40 min.

½ lb. andouille sausage, cut into ¼-inch-thick slices	½ lb. small, fresh whole okra
6 cups assorted fresh or frozen field peas	12 fresh basil leaves, torn

1. Sauté andouille in a Dutch oven over medium heat 5 minutes or until lightly browned.

2. Add field peas and water to cover 1 inch above peas; bring to a boil. Cover, reduce heat to medium-low, and simmer 20 minutes. Add okra; cover and simmer 5 minutes or until okra and peas are tender. Stir in basil and salt and pepper to taste. Transfer to a serving dish; serve with a slotted spoon.

~ A Recipe from a Local ~

Lowcountry Red Rice

Makes 6 to 8 servings   Hands-On Time 15 min.
Total Time 1 hour, 30 min.

1. Cook bacon slices in a large skillet over medium-high heat until crisp. Remove bacon, and drain on paper towels, reserving 2 Tbsp. drippings in skillet. Crumble bacon, and set aside.

2. Preheat oven to 350°. Sauté chopped onion in hot drippings in skillet over medium-high heat 3 minutes or until tender. Add tomato paste to skillet, stirring until mixture is smooth. Gradually stir in chicken broth, stirring to loosen particles from bottom of skillet. Stir in sugar, salt, and pepper. Bring to a boil; reduce heat, and simmer, stirring occasionally, 10 minutes.

3. Stir uncooked long-grain rice into tomato mixture in skillet, and bring to a boil. Stir in bacon pieces. Pour mixture into a lightly greased ovenproof Dutch oven; bake at 350° for 1 hour or until rice is tender.

Bishop England High School
Charleston, South Carolina

9   bacon slices
1   small onion, chopped
1   (12-oz.) can tomato paste
3 ½ cups chicken broth
2   tsp. sugar
1   tsp. table salt
½   tsp. freshly ground black pepper
2   cups uncooked long-grain rice
Garnish: chopped fresh parsley

~ You've Gotta Try ~
Benne Seeds

The sesame (*Sesamum indicum*), first grown wild in Africa, is an herb whose small seeds, which may be white, yellow, brown, or black depending on variety, have an almond-like flavor that deepens and becomes intensely rich and earthy when it's roasted or toasted.

Historians say that the seed made its way out of Africa because its pods split easily when ripened, which allowed them to scatter (hence the phrase "open sesame," which originally appeared in *"Ali Baba and the Forty Thieves"*). The first sesame seeds came to America in the 17th century along with the slaves from West Africa.

Ever since, they have been a food of the South, where they are called *benne* seeds, from an African word for seed. They were adopted in New Orleans and Charleston in particular for use in a type of cookie called a benne wafer; there are also benne brittle and benne balls (sesame seeds bound with corn syrup and brown sugar).

They happen to be very healthy—sesame seeds are considered a "complete protein," meaning they provide the full complement of amino acids. They're also an excellent source of copper and manganese, and they're high in lignans, a type of fiber that may help lower cholesterol.

Benne Brittle

Makes about 1 lb.   Hands-On Time 20 min.   Total Time 40 min.

1 ¼ cups benne (sesame) seeds   1   tsp. vanilla extract
2   cups sugar

1. Cook benne seeds in a large heavy skillet over medium heat, stirring often, 8 minutes or until seeds begin to turn brown. Remove from skillet.

2. Cook sugar and 2 Tbsp. water in skillet over low heat, stirring constantly, 10 minutes or until sugar melts. Quickly stir in benne seeds and vanilla. Pour onto a well-buttered baking sheet. Quickly spread to ⅛-inch thickness, using a metal spatula. Cool completely (about 20 minutes). Break into pieces, and store in an airtight container.

Adapted from *Charleston Receipts*

~ *A Recipe from a Local* ~

Sparkling Charleston Cosmopolitan

Boost your spirits with this Southern take on the Cosmo.

Makes 1 serving   Hands-On Time 5 min.   Total Time 5 min.

1   cup crushed ice   1   Tbsp. white cranberry juice
3   Tbsp. vodka   2   lemon wedges
1½ Tbsp. peach nectar   2   Tbsp. sparkling white wine
1   Tbsp. orange liqueur   Garnish: orange slice (optional)

1. Combine crushed ice, vodka, peach nectar, orange liqueur, and white cranberry juice in a cocktail shaker. Squeeze juice from lemon wedges into shaker. Place wedges in shaker. Cover with lid, and shake vigorously until thoroughly chilled (about 30 seconds). Strain into a 6- to 8-oz. glass; discard lemon wedges and ice. Top with sparkling white wine.

Note: We tested with Absolut Vodka.

**Bar Manager Ken Maciejewski, Tristan
Charleston**

Welcome to
Savannah

Inescapable in any conversation about Savannah that has taken place since 1994 is what residents call simply The Book.

John Berendt's "nonfiction novel," *Midnight in the Garden of Good and Evil*, centers on the murder of 21-year-old handyman and hustler Danny Hansford by his rumored lover Jim Williams, a Savannah fixture and antiques dealer who lived in the painstakingly restored Mercer House. Tried four times for the murder; Williams was eventually acquitted shortly before his death.

The book, which depicts the city's eccentricities and buried bodies, spent 216 weeks on *The New York Times* best-seller list. After its publication, overnight stays in Savannah more than tripled. The Mercer-Williams House Museum, now owned by and the residence of Williams's sister Dorothy Kingery, is open for tours.

Construction on the home began in 1860 for General Hugh Mercer, the great-grandfather of the legendary composer Johnny Mercer, and was finished in 1868. Williams bought the house in 1969, after it had been vacant and fallen into disrepair. He undertook a two-year renovation effort, and the results are something else.

The white marble fireplaces have mantels that were hand-carved in Italy, there is a formal courtyard, and the second floor has a dome made of Edwardian-era Murano glass. "Don't think for a second that questions about Williams's sexuality, his promiscuity, or the murder will be engaged," *The New York Times* warns. "Guides firmly advise before tours even begin that these are AAA Tours (including only questions about art, architecture, and antiques)."

Georgia Peach Deviled Eggs

Makes 2 dozen   **Hands-On Time 20 min.**   **Total Time 30 min.**

12 large eggs	1 tsp. Dijon mustard
⅓ cup fat-free Greek yogurt	½ tsp. apple cider vinegar
2 oz. ⅓-less-fat cream cheese	¼ tsp. black pepper
¼ cup finely chopped country ham	⅛ tsp. table salt
3 Tbsp. peach preserves	Sliced fresh peaches
1 Tbsp. chopped fresh parsley	Chopped toasted pecans
1 tsp. grated Vidalia onion	

1. Place eggs in a single layer in a stainless steel saucepan. Add water to depth of 3 inches. Bring to a rolling boil; cook 1 minute. Cover, remove from heat, and let stand 10 minutes. Drain.

2. Place eggs under cold running water until just cool enough to handle. Tap eggs on the counter until cracks form; peel.

3. Slice eggs in half lengthwise, and carefully remove yolks. Mash together yolks, yogurt, and next 9 ingredients until smooth using a fork. Spoon yolk mixture into egg white halves. Top with sliced fresh peaches and chopped toasted pecans. Serve immediately, or cover and chill 1 hour before serving.

Forsyth Park
Savannah, Georgia

Hoppin' John Hush Puppies

A Lowcountry field-pea dish turns into a crispy, satisfying fritter in this recipe—proof that you can make a hush puppy out of just about anything. (Read more about hush puppies and how they got their name on page 81.)

Makes about 2 dozen   Hands-On Time 40 min.   Total Time 55 min.

Peanut oil
1   (15-oz.) can seasoned field peas and snaps, drained and rinsed (about 1 cup)*
1   cup yellow self-rising cornmeal mix
¾   cup buttermilk
½   cup all-purpose flour
½   cup chopped country ham
½   cup cooked long-grain rice
½   cup sliced green onions, light green parts only
1   jalapeño pepper, seeded and diced
2   garlic cloves, pressed
1   tsp. baking powder
1   tsp. freshly ground black pepper
2   large eggs, lightly beaten
Green Tomato-Corn Relish

1. Pour oil to depth of 3 inches in a large, heavy skillet or Dutch oven; heat over medium-high heat to 350°.

2. Meanwhile, stir together field peas and next 11 ingredients in a large bowl.

3. Scoop pea mixture by rounded tablespoonfuls, in batches, and drop into hot oil. Fry 3 to 4 minutes or until hush puppies are golden brown. Drain on paper towels; keep warm. Serve with Green Tomato-Corn Relish.

Note: 1 (15.5-oz.) can seasoned black-eyed peas may be substituted.

Green Tomato-Corn Relish

Ready-made relish and fresh corn make this an easy add-on.

Makes 1 cup   Hands-On Time 10 min.   Total Time 10 min.

1   thick bacon slice
1   cup fresh corn kernels (about 1 ear)
1   garlic clove, pressed
1   (8-oz.) jar green tomato relish
2   tsp. hot sauce
¼   tsp. table salt

1. Cook bacon in a medium skillet over medium-high heat 3 minutes or until crisp; remove bacon, and drain on paper towels, reserving 1 Tbsp. drippings in skillet. Crumble bacon.

2. Sauté corn and garlic in hot drippings 3 minutes or until tender. Stir in tomato relish, next 2 ingredients, and bacon. Serve immediately.

Celebrate St. Patrick's Day Like a Local

On March 17, 2013, more than 300,000 people flooded the streets of Savannah for one of the country's largest St. Patrick's Day parties, second only to New York's.

Irish singers, bagpipe bands, and military units show up annually for a parade that has been a city tradition since 1813.

In early days the parade was held as a kind of military celebration, a chance for Irish soldiers to come out and march together in honor of Saint Patrick of Ireland and have some fun. Now it lasts more than three hours and features more than 350 floats.

The festivities actually begin two weeks in advance and include a Catholic Mass and the greening of the fountain in Forsyth Park. All the action culminates on River Street, where the bars and restaurants throw open their doors for the revelry. You'll see the obligatory "Kiss Me I'm Irish" T-shirts, green beer in the bars, and green grits in some restaurants (fusion food if ever there was).

Meet Food TV Star
Bobby Deen

It can be hard to follow in your parents' footsteps, but perhaps not if you're Bobby Deen, son of Savannah's own Paula Deen.

Bobby, Paula's younger son, went to work for his mom at age 18 as the deliveryman for The Bag Lady, the now-legendary business that saved the family from homelessness and launched Paula on the road to success.

Bobby brought "lunch-and-love-in-a-bag" to the customers and their praise to Paula.

The business would soon grow into a restaurant, called The Lady and Sons, where Bobby Deen helped manage the front of the house and took care of the customers, leaving his mom to run the kitchen.

With The Lady and Sons firmly established, Bobby and his brother, Jamie, began appearing to rave reviews on their mother's Food Network cooking shows and then launched their own. By mid-2011, the Deen brothers had published four cookbooks. Bobby's latest show, *Not My Mama's Meals*, focuses on lightening up Southern classics and debuted on the Cooking Channel in 2012.

"The key to tender, delicious fried chicken is a good long soak in buttermilk. As it turns out, the same holds true for this roasted version of fried chicken. What you'll end up with is moist, delicious chicken on the inside, and a crunchy, crispy coating." —Bobby Deen

Crispy Oven-Fried Chicken

Makes 4 servings   Hands-On Time 10 min.   Total Time 1 hour, 15 min.

⅔ cup low-fat buttermilk	½ tsp. table salt
½ cup finely chopped fresh chives	½ tsp. freshly ground black pepper
2 tsp. Dijon mustard	1 cup panko (Japanese breadcrumbs)
½ tsp. hot sauce	Garnish: chopped fresh chives
4 (12-oz.) skinned, bone-in chicken breasts	

1. In a medium bowl, whisk together the buttermilk, chives, mustard, and hot sauce. Add the chicken to the bowl, and let it soak for at least 30 minutes or (covered, in the fridge) overnight.

2. Place a jelly-roll pan in oven. Preheat oven to 450°.

3. Remove chicken from the marinade, and season with salt and pepper. Place the breadcrumbs in a wide, shallow bowl. Dredge the chicken into the breadcrumbs, pressing to adhere.

4. Remove pan from oven; coat with cooking spray. Immediately place the chicken on the pan; spray the chicken generously with cooking spray. Bake at 450° for 40 to 45 minutes or until chicken is just cooked through (at least 165° when tested with a meat thermometer).

Note: To make this dish just a little more decadent without adding too many more calories, I like to grate some Parmesan or Pecorino Romano cheese into my breadcrumbs. About 2 Tbsp. should give you a nice cheesy flavor in your crust.

Wynwood Art District
Miami, Florida

Moore Building, Design District
Miami, Florida

Welcome to
Miami

Two seemingly disparate locales, each stunning in its own way, anchor Miami.

Everglades National Park, established in 1947 and only 38 miles from downtown, includes four sites and more than 1.5 million acres that offer the totality of the Florida outdoor experience: bird watching, hiking, biking, canoeing, camping, boat and tram wildlife tours, and fishing in the marshes, alligator holes, and mangrove and palm groves.

The Ten Thousand Islands area of the park includes the largest protected mangrove forest in the Western Hemisphere, which offers visitors the chance to see bald eagles, manatees, dolphins, flamingos, and peacocks.

A different sort of peacock haunts Miami's lauded Design District, also known as "one square mile of style." You can find fashion, furniture, and high art galore in the showrooms and galleries surrounding the hub, the intersection of Northeast First Avenue and Northeast 40th Street. All of the top international fashion brands are there—Hermes, Prada, Dior, Cartier—plus high-end furniture showrooms and chic restaurants.

The District's key landmark is the four-floor Moore Building, once the flagship of pineapple farmer turned furniture tycoon T. W. Moore. Area developer Craig Robins has converted the top two floors of the 1921 building into artists' work-residence studios.

The nearby Wynwood Art District is home to more than 70 galleries.

Spicy Mango Shrimp

This quick and colorful skillet sauté topped with toasted coconut offers a light, innovative take on the sweet-hot flavor of fried coconut shrimp.

Makes 6 to 8 servings   Hands-On Time 20 min.   Total Time 35 min.

Coconut-Lime Rice
1 ½ lb. peeled, large raw shrimp
3   Tbsp. olive oil, divided
1   cup chopped green onions
1   cup diced red bell pepper
2   garlic cloves, minced
1   Tbsp. grated fresh ginger
½   to 1 tsp. dried crushed red pepper

1   cup chopped fresh mango
¼   cup chopped fresh cilantro
¼   cup soy sauce
2   Tbsp. fresh lime juice
Topping: toasted sweetened flaked coconut

1. Prepare Coconut-Lime Rice.

2. Meanwhile, sauté half of shrimp in 1 Tbsp. hot oil in a large skillet over medium-high heat 2 to 3 minutes or just until shrimp turn pink. Remove shrimp from skillet. Repeat procedure with 1 Tbsp. hot oil and remaining shrimp.

3. Sauté onions and next 4 ingredients in remaining 1 Tbsp. hot oil over medium-high heat 1 minute. Stir in mango and next 3 ingredients, and cook 1 minute; stir in shrimp. Serve over hot cooked Coconut-Lime Rice; top with toasted coconut.

Coconut-Lime Rice

Light coconut milk and a splash of fresh citrus give jasmine rice a tropical edge.

Makes 6 servings   Hands-On Time 10 min.   Total Time 35 min.

1   cup light coconut milk
½   tsp. table salt
1½ cups uncooked jasmine rice

1   tsp. lime zest
1½ Tbsp. fresh lime juice

1. Bring coconut milk, salt, and 2 cups water to a boil in a saucepan over medium heat. Stir in rice; cover, reduce heat to low, and simmer, stirring occasionally to prevent scorching, 20 to 25 minutes or until liquid is absorbed and rice is tender. Stir in lime zest and juice.

"Your guests might assume that there's a lot of cream in this, but there's not a drop. The luscious texture comes from grinding the almonds with the other ingredients, and then emulsifying the mixture with good extra virgin olive oil." —Michelle Bernstein

White Gazpacho

Makes 6 cups   **Hands-On Time 10 min.**   **Total Time 40 min.**

1 ½ cups salted Spanish Marcona almonds	1 Tbsp. chopped fresh dill weed
½ tsp. minced garlic	1 ½ cups vegetable broth
½ Tbsp. minced shallot	1 Tbsp. sherry vinegar
2 cups English or other cucumbers, peeled and chopped	2 Tbsp. dry sherry
2 cups seedless green grapes	½ cup extra virgin olive oil
	Garnishes: sliced grapes, crushed almonds, dill sprigs

1. Place almonds, garlic, shallot, cucumber, grapes, dill weed, and broth in a blender. Puree until very smooth.

2. While blender is running, add the sherry vinegar and sherry. Drizzle in the olive oil. Add salt and black pepper to taste.

3. Refrigerate in an airtight container until chilled (about 30 minutes).

Meet Chef Michelle Bernstein

National audiences know her from her many appearances as a guest judge on the reality TV show *Top Chef*.

But Michelle Bernstein has been wowing Miami's diners for years with her modern take on Latino flavors.

A Miami native of Jewish and Latin descent and a James Beard Foundation Award-winning chef, Bernstein is known for her spunky, vivacious energy.

Her restaurant Michy's is a bright blue-and-orange temple of hip and innovative cooking, a style Bernstein describes as "luxurious comfort food."

Cubano Sandwiches

This Miami staple, a good use of leftover pork, and a favorite for midnight snacking after a night of dancing, is made with distinctive Cuban bread. The loaves look like long, slightly flattened French bread, though the texture is often a bit finer and softer, owing to a touch of lard or shortening in the dough. Look for Cuban bread at better grocery stores and Latin markets.

Makes 4 servings   Hands-On Time 10 min.   Total Time 25 min.

1   (12-oz.) Cuban bread loaf, cut
    in half crosswise
6   to 8 Tbsp. yellow mustard
⅓   lb. thinly sliced pork loin roast
    or smoked pulled pork
⅓   lb. thinly sliced baked ham
⅓   lb. thinly sliced provolone cheese
¼   to ⅓ cup dill pickle chips
2   Tbsp. butter, softened

1. Cut bread halves lengthwise, cutting to but not through opposite side. Spread mustard on cut sides of bread. Layer with pork and next 3 ingredients. Close sandwiches, and spread outsides with butter.

2. Place 1 sandwich in a large skillet over medium heat; place a heavy skillet on top of sandwich. (You can also use a panini press.) Cook 2 to 3 minutes on each side or until cheese melts and sandwich is flat. Repeat with remaining sandwich. Cut each sandwich in half, and serve immediately.

Note: To get a jump start on the party and achieve extra-flat Cubanos, assemble the sandwiches, wrap tightly in plastic wrap, and place under a heavy pan in the refrigerator up to 1 day ahead, and cook as directed in Step 2.

Yuca with Garlic-Lime Mojo

Pronounced YOO-kuh, this starchy root vegetable, also known as cassava, is beloved in Latin cultures and tastes similar to red potatoes. Mojo (pronounced MO-ho) is a sort of vinaigrette flavored with garlic and lime or orange juice.

Makes 8 servings   Hands-On Time 15 min.   Total Time 50 min.

2   lb. yuca, peeled, halved, and cut
    into 3- to 4-inch pieces*
3   tsp. table salt, divided
6   garlic cloves, pressed
1   large sweet onion, finely chopped
½   cup extra virgin olive oil
⅓   cup fresh lime juice
    Sliced onion rings (optional)
    Garnish: lime zest

1. Bring yuca with water to cover and 2 tsp. salt to a boil in a large Dutch oven over medium-high heat. Cover, reduce heat to medium-low, and simmer 25 minutes or until tender. Drain well. Transfer yuca to a large bowl or serving platter, and keep warm.

2. Stir together remaining 1 tsp. salt, garlic, and next 3 ingredients in saucepan over medium heat; cook, stirring occasionally, 8 to 10 minutes or until onion is translucent. Spoon garlic mixture evenly over yuca; top with onion rings, if desired, and serve immediately.

Note: 1 (24-oz.) package frozen yuca, thawed, may be substituted for fresh. Check the produce section for yuca, which looks like a large sweet potato with a thick, brown skin, or order it online at www.melissas.com.

Yolanda Mellon
Miami, Florida

Visit Versailles Like a Local

No, not *that* Versailles. This one is a restaurant and the premier gathering place for Cuban society in Miami's Little Havana.

From politicians to street vendors, they all come to this cavernous, crystal-chandeliered faux palace, the self-proclaimed "most famous Cuban restaurant in the world," for all the authentic favorites—arroz con pollo, ropa vieja, guava-stuffed sweets, Cubano sandwiches, and lively gossip and carousing.

The popular venue opened in 1971 and became the heart of the Cuban exile community, a safe place to espouse politics over café con leche. The last bit is important: Cubans are justifiably proud of their strong coffee. All over Miami you can find the signature café Cubano, a very intense shot of espresso brewed with sugar. Bitter and sweet all at once, it's no joke. After you've tasted it you'll understand why it's been compared to rocket fuel—and then you'll want some more.

Meet Rapper
Vanilla Ice

"If you got a problem, yo, I'll solve it," Vanilla Ice rapped, becoming the first hip-hop singer to top the singles charts.

The Miami native skyrocketed to fame in 1990 with his "Ice Ice Baby" ditty and will probably go down in the annals of pop culture as "the white rapper." In his heyday, he was a pop idol on the scale of Justin Bieber. His album *To the Extreme* sold more than seven million copies.

Before he was Ice, though, Robert Van Winkle grew up in both South Florida and South Dallas. A motocross enthusiast and a great dancer, he was discovered while dancing in a Dallas club. He became a household name with record speed.

The inevitable drop in popularity brought about some rough "finding himself" years involving drug addiction and depression. He experimented with careers in pro jet-skiing and real estate.

Now a celebrated "house-flipper," his renovation exploits are documented on *The Vanilla Ice Project* on the DIY Network. He lives with his wife, Laura, and their two daughters in South Florida.

"You know how some people can have a bunch of cheeseburgers and get high cholesterol? Mine was hereditary. I tried being vegetarian for three months, and it brought my cholesterol from over 300 to 133 without drugs ... It opened up a whole new menu to me. I love it." —Vanilla Ice

Vegetarian Chiles Rellenos

The ideal Vanilla Ice meal starts with these stuffed peppers and ends with cinnamon–dusted apple pie with pecans and, you guessed it, vanilla ice cream.

Makes 8 servings   Hands-On Tim: 30 min.   Total Time 55 min.

8 small whole poblano peppers (about 2 lb.)	1 cup canned organic sweet potato puree (unsweetened)
¼ cup minced fresh onion	½ cup (2 oz.) shredded Monterey Jack cheese
1 tsp. vegetable oil	
3 garlic cloves, minced	½ cup (2 oz.) shredded sharp Cheddar cheese
1 tsp. ground cumin	
1 tsp. dried Mexican oregano	16 frozen phyllo sheets, thawed
⅛ tsp. ground cinnamon	Toppings: salsa, sour cream, guacamole
1 (16-oz.) can vegetarian refried beans	

1. Preheat broiler with oven rack 5 inches from heat. Broil peppers on an aluminum foil-lined baking sheet for 12 minutes or until peppers look blistered, turning every 3 minutes. Place peppers in a zip-top plastic freezer bag; seal and let stand 10 minutes to loosen skins. Peel peppers, and cut a lengthwise slit in each pepper; discard stems and seeds. Reduce oven temperature to 400°, and return oven rack to middle position.

2. Sauté onion in hot oil in a large nonstick skillet over medium heat 3 minutes or until tender. Add garlic, cumin, oregano, and cinnamon; sauté 1 minute. Stir in refried beans and sweet potato puree; cook, stirring often, 2 minutes or until warm. Remove from heat; stir in cheeses.

3. Carefully spoon ⅓ cup refried bean mixture evenly into peppers, and reshape them, pressing cut edges of each pepper together to seal.

4. Place 1 sheet of phyllo on a damp towel (keep the rest covered, or it will be impossible to use). Spray phyllo with cooking spray. Top with another sheet of phyllo. and spray with cooking spray. Place 1 stuffed pepper, centered, at 1 narrow end of phyllo; roll up stuffed pepper in phyllo until pepper is enclosed, stopping about halfway through length of phyllo sheets. Fold edges of phyllo to center over top of pepper; continue to roll up stuffed pepper to end of phyllo sheet. Place, seam side down, on baking sheet. Repeat procedure with remaining phyllo and stuffed peppers.

5. Coat tops of chiles rellenos with cooking spray. Bake at 400° for 15 minutes or until phyllo is crisp and golden brown, rotating pan in oven after 8 minutes. Serve with toppings, if desired.

Elegant Citrus Tart

The Florida-grown Ruby Red grapefruit, pink grapefruit, and navel oranges atop this dessert are as vibrant as a Miami sunset.

Makes 8 servings   Hands-On Time 20 min.
Total Time 10 hours, 5 min.

1. Preheat oven to 350°. Bake coconut in a single layer in a shallow pan 4 to 5 minutes or until toasted and fragrant, stirring halfway through; cool completely (about 15 minutes).

2. Pulse coconut, flour, and powdered sugar in a food processor 3 to 4 times or until combined. Add butter and coconut extract, and pulse 5 to 6 times or until crumbly. With processor running, gradually add 3 Tbsp. water, and process until dough forms a ball and leaves sides of bowl.

3. Roll dough into a 12½- x 8-inch rectangle (about ¼ inch thick) on a lightly floured surface; press on bottom and up sides of a 12- x 9-inch tart pan with removable bottom. Trim excess dough, and discard.

4. Bake at 350° for 30 minutes. Cool completely on a wire rack (about 40 minutes).

5. Spread Buttery Orange Curd over crust. Top with citrus sections.

Note: To make a round tart, roll dough into a 10-inch circle (about ¼ inch thick) on a lightly floured surface; press on bottom and up sides of a 9-inch round tart pan with removable bottom. Trim excess dough, and discard. Bake as directed.

⅓	cup sweetened flaked coconut
2	cups all-purpose flour
⅔	cup powdered sugar
¾	cup cold butter, cut into pieces
¼	tsp. coconut extract
	Buttery Orange Curd
9	assorted citrus fruits, peeled and sectioned

Buttery Orange Curd

Makes about 2 cups   Hands-On Time 20 min.
Total Time 8 hours, 15 min.

1. Combine sugar and cornstarch in a 3-qt. saucepan; gradually whisk in orange juice. Whisk in egg. Bring to a boil; boil, whisking constantly, 3 to 4 minutes.

2. Remove from heat; whisk in butter, zest, and salt. Place heavy-duty plastic wrap directly on curd (to prevent a film from forming), and chill 8 hours. Store leftovers in refrigerator up to 3 days.

Note: We tested with Simply Orange 100% Pure Squeezed Orange Juice.

⅔	cup sugar
2 ½	Tbsp. cornstarch
1 ⅓	cups orange juice
1	large egg, lightly beaten
3	Tbsp. butter
2	tsp. orange zest
	Pinch of table salt

Meet Restaurateur Ingrid Hoffmann

Miami's Ingrid Hoffmann is one of the hippest Latina cooks around.

A Colombian-American television personality and restaurateur, Hoffmann currently hosts *Simply Delicioso*, which first aired on the Food Network and now is part of the Cooking Channel lineup, and the Spanish-language cooking and lifestyle show *Delicioso* on Galavisión.

She was raised in Colombia and Curaçao, the island country (part of the Kingdom of the Netherlands) off the coast of Venezuela. She later moved to Miami and opened La Capricieuse, a luxury boutique in Coconut Grove, in the mid-1980s.

Shortly thereafter she opened Rocca, the first restaurant to feature tabletop cooking on heated lava rocks. Television executives discovered her while she was doing promotional appearances for that restaurant—and the rest is history.

"Every Latin American country does their own version [of cooking]. Mine is the Colombian, and I say it's better because Colombia is passion. And anything you do with passion is better." —Ingrid Hoffmann

Arroz Con Pollo

This traditional dish is a staple of Latin American cuisine.

**Makes 8 servings (14 cups)   Hands-On Time 30 min.
Total Time 2 hours, 10 min.**

1 (3- to 4 ¼ -lb.) chicken, cut in 8 pieces	1 cup fresh or frozen sweet peas
1 medium yellow onion, quartered, plus ½ medium yellow onion, thinly sliced	1 cup ketchup
	1 tsp. table salt
	2 medium carrots, finely diced
6 garlic cloves, roughly chopped	8 oz. fresh green beans, trimmed and quartered
5 cups (homemade or canned reduced-sodium) chicken broth	3 Tbsp. unsalted butter
1 cup light beer, such as lager	½ red bell pepper, cut into thin strips
¼ cup Delicioso Adobo Seasoning	½ green bell pepper, cut into thin strips
3 Tbsp. Worcestershire sauce	1 cup pimiento-stuffed Spanish olives
1 cup chopped fresh cilantro, divided	
3 cups uncooked long-grain rice	

1. Place the chicken, quartered onion, garlic, chicken broth, beer, Delicioso Adobo, Worcestershire sauce, and ½ cup of the cilantro in a large stockpot over high heat. Bring to a boil, reduce heat to medium-low, cover, and simmer 35 minutes or until the chicken is cooked through. Remove the chicken to a plate, and set aside to cool. Strain the broth into a bowl through a fine-mesh sieve, discarding the onion pieces.

2. Pour the broth into a large measuring cup to measure 6 cups of liquid, adding water if needed. Return the broth to the stockpot, and bring to a boil. Add the rice, peas, ketchup, salt, carrots, and green beans; stir well, and bring to a boil. Cover, reduce heat to low, and simmer 35 minutes or until the rice is tender and fully cooked.

3. Meanwhile, melt the butter in a large skillet over medium heat. Add the bell peppers and the sliced onions, and cook 8 minutes or until they're tender. Shred the cooked chicken meat, discarding the skin and bones, and add the chicken to the vegetables. Cook 2 to 3 minutes or until heated through, 2 to 3 minutes. Fluff the rice with a fork and add the chicken, bell pepper, and onion to it. Stir in the olives, sprinkle with the remaining ½ cup cilantro, and serve immediately.

Delicioso Adobo Seasoning

Makes ½ cup   Hands-On Time 5 min.   Total Time 5 min.

1 Tbsp. table salt	1 Tbsp. dried parsley flakes
1 Tbsp. garlic powder	1 Tbsp. lemon pepper
1 Tbsp. onion powder	1 Tbsp. achiote or annatto powder
1 Tbsp. dried oregano	1½ tsp. ground cumin

1. Combine all ingredients in a small glass jar with an airtight lid,
and shake to blend. Store in an airtight container in a cool, dry
place up to 2 weeks.

The Coastal South

Rum Cake

This moist, rich rum cake is great to make ahead for special occasions or as a food gift. It tastes even better the next day.

Makes 10 to 12 servings   Hands-On Time 20 min.
Total Time 2 hours, 20 min.

1½	cups butter, softened	3	cups all-purpose flour
1½	cups granulated sugar	2	tsp. baking powder
3	large eggs	½	tsp. baking soda
1	egg yolk	⅛	tsp. table salt
2	tsp. vanilla extract	1	cup whipping cream
2	Tbsp. lemon zest		Rum Syrup
½	cup dark rum		Powdered sugar
¼	cup banana liqueur		

1. Preheat oven to 350°. Beat butter and granulated sugar at medium speed with an electric mixer until light and fluffy. Add eggs, egg yolk, and vanilla, beating until blended. Add lemon zest, beating until blended. Gradually add rum and banana liqueur, beating until blended. (Batter will look curdled.)

2. Stir together flour and next 3 ingredients; add to batter alternately with whipping cream, beginning and ending with flour mixture. Beat batter at low speed just until blended after each addition. Pour batter into a greased and floured 10-inch Bundt pan.

3. Bake at 350° for 55 to 60 minutes or until a long wooden pick inserted in center of cake comes out clean.

4. Cool in pan on a wire rack 15 minutes. Pierce cake multiple times using a metal or wooden skewer. Pour Rum Syrup evenly over cake. Let stand 45 minutes. Remove from pan; cool completely on a wire rack. Sprinkle evenly with powdered sugar before serving.

Note: ¼ cup dark rum may be substituted for banana liqueur.

Rum Syrup

Makes about 1 cup   Hands-On Time 5 min.   Total Time 30 min.

10	Tbsp. butter	¼	cup dark rum
¾	cup sugar	¼	cup banana liqueur

1. Melt butter in a 2-qt. saucepan over medium-high heat; stir in remaining ingredients. Bring to a boil, stirring often; reduce heat to low, and cook, stirring often, 8 to 10 minutes or until slightly thickened. Remove from heat, and cool 10 minutes.

Note: ¼ cup dark rum may be substituted for banana liqueur.

Three Guys from Miami Cook Cuban
Miami, Florida

Meet Comedian Wayne Brady

Emmy Award-winning and Grammy-nominated comedian Wayne Brady was born in Columbus, Georgia, to West Indian parents.

He grew up in Florida, and began his career working for the Disney World and Universal theme parks in Orlando.

His career took off in 1998, when he joined the ABC improv comedy show *Whose Line Is It Anyway?* Brady went on to host his own syndicated talk/variety show *The Wayne Brady Show* and *Don't Forget the Lyrics* on Fox, as well as the CBS daytime game show *Let's Make a Deal.*

His paternal grandmother, Valerie Petersen, a native of the U.S. Virgin Islands, raised him in Orlando. Brady says the food she cooked was always homemade and the perfect mix of "Southern-Islands" cuisine.

One of his absolute favorite recipes is her red velvet cake. For special occasions, because she knows Brady loves peanut butter, she adds peanut butter chips to the frosting or presses finely crushed Nutter Butter cookies into the frosting on the sides.

"My grandmother still makes red velvet cake for every holiday and any special occasion. I've never tasted one that compares to hers." —Wayne Brady

Miss Valerie's Islands Red Velvet Cake

Makes 8 to 10 servings   Hands-On Time 30 min.
Total Time 2 hours, 15 min.

2 cups all-purpose flour	1 cup buttermilk
2 Tbsp. unsweetened cocoa	2 tsp. vanilla extract
1 tsp. baking soda	1 (1-oz.) bottle red food coloring
1 tsp. baking powder	½ cup brewed coffee, at room
1 tsp. table salt	temperature
2 cups sugar	1 tsp. white vinegar
1 cup vegetable oil	Cream Cheese Frosting
2 large eggs	

1. Preheat oven to 350°. In a medium bowl, whisk together flour, cocoa, baking soda, baking powder, and salt; set aside. In a large bowl, whisk together the sugar and vegetable oil. Whisk in the eggs, buttermilk, vanilla, and red food coloring until combined. Whisk in the coffee and white vinegar. Add the wet ingredients to the dry ingredients, whisking until combined. Generously grease and flour 2 (8-inch) round cake pans. Pour the batter evenly into each pan.

2. Bake at 350° on the middle rack for 30 to 35 minutes or until a wooden pick comes out clean (check at 30 minutes; do not overbake as cake will continue to cook as it cools). Cool in pans on wire racks 10 minutes. Slide a knife or offset spatula around the inside of the pans to loosen the cake from the pans. Remove the cakes from the pans, and cool completely on a cooling rack (about 1 hour).

3. Frost when the layers have cooled completely.

Cream Cheese Frosting

Makes 4¼ cups   Hands-On Time 7 min.   Total Time 7 min.

2 (8-oz.) packages cream cheese, softened	2 tsp. vanilla extract
½ cup butter, softened	4 cups powdered sugar

1. Beat together cream cheese, butter, and vanilla in a large bowl at medium speed with an electric mixer until well combined. Add half the powdered sugar; beat until combined. Add the remaining powdered sugar; beat until smooth, using a spatula to scrape down the side of the bowl.

Metric Chart

The recipes that appear in this cookbook use the standard U.S. method for measuring liquid and dry or solid ingredients (teaspoons, tablespoons, and cups). The information in the following charts is provided to help cooks outside the United States successfully use these recipes. All equivalents are approximate.

Metric Equivalents for Different Types of Ingredients

A standard cup measure of a dry or solid ingredient will vary in weight depending on the type of ingredient. A standard cup of liquid is the same volume for any type of liquid. Use the following chart when converting standard cup measures to grams (weight) or milliliters (volume).

Standard Cup	Fine Powder (ex. flour)	Grain (ex. rice)	Granular (ex. sugar)	Liquid Solids (ex. butter)	Liquid (ex. milk)
1	140 g	150 g	190 g	200 g	240 ml
¾	105 g	113 g	143 g	150 g	180 ml
⅔	93 g	100 g	125 g	133 g	160 ml
½	70 g	75 g	95 g	100 g	120 ml
⅓	47 g	50 g	63 g	67 g	80 ml
¼	35 g	38 g	48 g	50 g	60 ml
⅛	18 g	19 g	24 g	25 g	30 ml

Useful Equivalents for Dry Ingredients by Weight

(To convert ounces to grams, multiply the number of ounces by 30.)

1 oz	=	¹⁄₁₆ lb	=	30 g
4 oz	=	¼ lb	=	120 g
8 oz	=	½ lb	=	240 g
12 oz	=	¾ lb	=	360 g
16 oz	=	1 lb	=	480 g

Useful Equivalents for Length

(To convert inches to centimeters, multiply the number of inches by 2.5.)

1 in					=	2.5 cm	
6 in	=	½ ft			=	15 cm	
12 in	=	1 ft			=	30 cm	
36 in	=	3 ft	=	1 yd	=	90 cm	
40 in					=	100 cm	= 1 m

Useful Equivalents for Liquid Ingredients by Volume

¼ tsp						=	1 ml	
½ tsp						=	2 ml	
1 tsp						=	5 ml	
3 tsp	=	1 Tbsp			= ½ fl oz	=	15 ml	
		2 Tbsp	=	⅛ cup	= 1 fl oz	=	30 ml	
		4 Tbsp	=	¼ cup	= 2 fl oz	=	60 ml	
		5⅓ Tbsp	=	⅓ cup	= 3 fl oz	=	80 ml	
		8 Tbsp	=	½ cup	= 4 fl oz	=	120 ml	
		10⅔ Tbsp	=	⅔ cup	= 5 fl oz	=	160 ml	
		12 Tbsp	=	¾ cup	= 6 fl oz	=	180 ml	
		16 Tbsp	=	1 cup	= 8 fl oz	=	240 ml	
		1 pt	=	2 cups	= 16 fl oz	=	480 ml	
		1 qt	=	4 cups	= 32 fl oz	=	960 ml	
					33 fl oz	=	1000 ml	= 1 l

Useful Equivalents for Cooking/Oven Temperatures

	Fahrenheit	Celsius	Gas Mark
Freeze water	32° F	0° C	
Room temperature	68° F	20° C	
Boil water	212° F	100° C	
Bake	325° F	160° C	3
	350° F	180° C	4
	375° F	190° C	5
	400° F	200° C	6
	425° F	220° C	7
	450° F	230° C	8
Broil			Grill

Recipe Index

Regional Guide

The Heart of Dixie

Welcome to
Athens, 36
Atlanta, 18
Birmingham, 46
Decatur, 30
Oxford, 58

People to Meet
Actress Donna D'Errico, 44
Author Susan Rebecca White, 28
Chef Frank Stitt, 52
Chef John Currence, 66
Chef Kevin Gillespie, 24
Chef Richard Blais, 20
Country Singer Sara Evans, 54
Journalist John T. Edge, 62
Pitmaster Myron Mixon, 34
Songwriter Matthew Sweet, 38

Things to Do Like a Local
Appreciate the Blues, 61
Experience the Cyclorama, 23
Order a "Meat-and-Three," 51
Visit the Moto-Museum, 57

Foods You've Gotta Try
Alabama White Barbecue Sauce, 47
Coca-Cola Cake, 27
Vidalia Onions, 23

Cajun Country

Welcome to
The Bayou, 78
Bird Heaven, 106
The Boudin Trail, 88

People to Meet
Actress Angela Kinsey, 92
Cajun Maven Kay Robertson, 100
Chef Emeril Lagasse, 86
Chef John Besh, 82

Things to Do Like a Local
Say "Praline", 108

Foods You've Gotta Try
Crawfish, 96
Gumbo, 85

Big, Bold Texas

Welcome to
Austin, 148
Dallas, 118
Houston, 130
San Antonio, 138

People to Meet
Actress Eva Longoria, 140
Chef John Tesar, 124
Choreographer Judy Trammell, 120
Country Star Miranda Lambert, 128
Journalist Robb Walsh, 136

Things to Do Like a Local
Eat Frito Pie, 144
Eat Puffy Tacos, 147
Remember LBJ and Lady Bird, 156
Shop at Boggy Creek Farm, 153
Shop at Neiman Marcus, 123

Foods You've Gotta Try
Houston Vietnamese Food, 132
King Ranch Chicken Casserole, 152

The Piedmont & the Mountains

Welcome to
Asheville, 192
Charlottesville, 184
The Triangle, 166

People to Meet
Actress Andie MacDowell, 202
Author Charles Frazier, 198
Chef Andrea Reusing, 170
Chef Ashley Christensen, 178
Chef Katie Button, 194
Chefs Dean and Erin Maupin, 190
Reality Star Emily Maynard, 174
Scholar Marcie Cohen Ferris, 182

Things to Do Like a Local
Cheer On the Durham Bulls, 173
Dig Hoops, 181
Visit Malaprop's, 205
Enjoy Virginia Wine, 186

Foods You've Gotta Try
Carolina Barbecue, 172

The Bluegrass, Bourbon & Barbecue Trail

Welcome to
Louisville, 214
Memphis, 230
Nashville, 240

People to Meet
Chef Kathy Cary, 226
Chef Kelly English, 234
Singer and Survivor Naomi Judd, 242
Singer Loretta Lynn, 252
Singer Trisha Yearwood, 248

Things to Do Like a Local
Catch a Flick at Franklin Theatre, 251
Do the Kentucky Derby, 218
Enjoy Hot Chicken, 245
Rock East Nashville, 246
Take in the Duck Parade, 238

Foods You've Gotta Try
Kentucky Hot Brown, 220
Mint Julep, 215

The Coastal South

Welcome to
Baltimore, 266
Charleston, 278
Miami, 294
Savannah, 288

People to Meet
Actress Mo'Nique, 270
Author John Martin Taylor, 282
Chef Duff Goldman, 276
Chef Michelle Bernstein, 296
Comedian Wayne Brady, 308
Food TV Star Bobby Deen, 292
Rapper Vanilla Ice, 300
Restaurateur Ingrid Hoffmann, 304

Things to Do Like a Local
Buy, Make, and Eat Crab Cakes, 269
Celebrate St. Patrick's Day, 291
Enjoy the Spoleto, 284
Visit Versailles, 299
Watch a Game at Camden Yards, 273

Foods You've Gotta Try
Benne Seeds, 286
Perloo, Pilau, Pulao, or Purloo, 281

©2013 by Time Home Entertainment Inc.
135 West 50th Street, New York, NY 10020

ISBN-13: 978-0-8487-3962-1
ISBN-10: 0-8487-3962-0
Library of Congress Control Number: 2013944408

Printed in the United States of America
First Printing 2013

Oxmoor House
Editorial Director: Leah McLaughlin
Creative Director: Felicity Keane
Senior Brand Manager: Daniel Fagan
Senior Editor: Rebecca Brennan
Managing Editor: Elizabeth Tyler Austin

No Taste Like Home
Editor: Nichole Aksamit
Project Editor: Megan McSwain Yeatts
Senior Designer: Melissa Clark
Recipe Developers and Testers: Wendy Ball, R.D.;
    Victoria E. Cox; Tamara Goldis, R.D.; Stefanie Maloney;
    Callie Nash; Karen Rankin; Leah Van Deren
Recipe Editor: Alyson Moreland Haynes
Food Stylists: Margaret Monroe Dickey,
    Catherine Crowell Steele
Photography Director: Jim Bathie
Senior Photographer: Hélène Dujardin
Photo Stylist: Mindi Shapiro Levine
Assistant Photo Stylist: Mary Louise Menendez
Senior Production Manager: Sue Chodakiewicz
Production Manager: Theresa Beste-Farley

Contributors
Assistant Editor: Ashley Strickland Freeman
Project Editor: Julia Sayers
Recipe Developers and Testers: Kathleen Royal Phillips
Copy Editors: Donna Baldone, Julie Bosche, Barry Smith
Proofreader: Rebecca Benton
Indexer: Mary Ann Laurens
Interns: Frances Gunnells, Susan Kemp, Sara Lyon,
    Staley McIlwain, Jeffrey Preis, Maria Sanders
Photo Stylists: Lisa Powell Bailey, Mary Clayton Carl,
    Missie Neville Crawford, Annette Joseph,
    Amy Burke Massey, Leigh Anne Montgomery,
    Lydia Degaris Pursell, Caitlin Van Horn, Amy Wilson
Food Stylists: Simon Andrews, Marian Cooper Cairns,
    Cynthia Groseclose, Ana Kelly, Angie Moiser,
    William Smith, Mariana Velasquez

Time Home Entertainment Inc.
Publisher: Jim Childs
Vice President, Brand & Digital Strategy:
    Steven Sandonato
Executive Director, Marketing Services: Carol Pittard
Executive Director, Retail & Special Sales: Tom Mifsud
Director, Bookazine Development & Marketing:
    Laura Adam
Executive Publishing Director: Joy Butts
Associate Publishing Director: Megan Pearlman
Finance Director: Glenn Buonocore
Associate General Counsel: Helen Wan

Southern Living®
Editor: M. Lindsay Bierman
Creative Director: Robert Perino
Managing Editor: Candace Higginbotham
Art Director: Chris Hoke
Executive Editors: Rachel Hardage Barrett,
    Hunter Lewis, Jessica S. Thuston
Food Director: Shannon Sliter Satterwhite
Senior Food Editor: Mary Allen Perry
Deputy Food Director: Whitney Wright
Test Kitchen Director: Robby Melvin
Recipe Editor: JoAnn Weatherly
Test Kitchen Specialist/Food Styling: Vanessa McNeil Rocchio
Test Kitchen Professionals: Norman King, Pam Lolley,
    Angela Sellers
Photographers: Robbie Caponetto, Laurey W. Glenn,
    Melina Hammer, Hector Sanchez
Senior Photo Stylist: Buffy Hargett
Editorial Assistant: Pat York

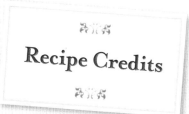

Photography Credits

Erin Adams: 233; **Gio Alma:** 296 (top left); **Ralph Anderson:** 149 (top), 164 (top right), 257 (top center); **Cedric Angeles:** 71 (right) 72 (top right) 74 (top center), 78, 160 (top left); **B.B. King Museum and Delta Interpretive Center:** 210 (center); **Bobby Badger:** 120 (top left); **Iain Bagwell:** 42 (inset), 89 (bottom), 119 (bottom), 257 (top left); **Barber Vintage Motorsports Museum:** 57 (inset); **Kristin Barlowe:** 242 (top left); **Biltmore House:** 192 (top); **Birmingham Botanical Gardens:** 11 (center); **Justin Fox Burks:** 234 (top left); **Joshua Carpenter:** 159 (top right); **Mary Margaret Chambliss:** 74 (top left); **Van Chaplin:** 56, 156 (top), 291 (top right); **Gary Clark:** 34 (top left), 61 (inset), 72 (top left), 106 (top left) 115 (center), 206, 218 (top left), 264 (right), 237 (top right); **John Currence:** 66 (inset); **Cyclorama:** 23 (inset); **Jennifer Davick:** 19, 43 (inset), 72 (center), 86 (top left), 102 (inset), 103 (inset), 128 (bottom right), 143 (inset), 172 (bottom), 193, 246 (top left), 250, 254, 268, 279, 295 (inset), 302; **Donna D'Errico:** 44 (inset); **Joseph De Sciose:** 204; **Peter Frank Edwards/Redux Pictures:** 186 (top left), 256; **Everett Collection:** 252 (top left), 270 (top left); **Marcie Cohen Ferris:** 182 (top left); **Ben Fink Photography:** 292 (top left); **Squire Fox:** 262 (top right), 263; **Jim Franco:** 187 inset, 287; **Andrew Geiger:** 111 (top center);

Heidi Geldhauser: 20 (top left) **Georgia Department of Economic Development:** 10; **Chris Granger:** 82 (top left); **David Hanson:** 36 (top right and middle); **Michael Hanson:** 76 (top right), 209 (top center) 210 (top left), 212 (top left); **Russ Harrington:** 54 (top left), 248 (top left); **David Hillegas:** 11 (top left); **Beth Hontzas** 167 inset; **Jody Horton:** 116 (top center and right), 148; **Chris Howard:** 100 (top left); **Cary Jobe:** 110, 112 (top right); **Jeff Katz Photography:** 308 (top left); **John Kernick:** 134, 151 (inset), 154, 170 (top left); **Sarah Kerver:** 115 (bottom left); **Angela Kinsey:** 92 (inset); **Ryan Kurtz:** 7 (top left), 207 (top right); **Thien La:** 174 (top left); **Lilly's Restaurant:** 226 (top left); **Becky Luigart-Stayner:** 31, 68 (inset), 69, 111 (top right), 133, 135 (inset), 186 (bottom right), 217, 267, 289 (bottom), 290; **Kevin Mann:** 205 (top right); **Greg Martin:** 198 (top left); **Dean Maupin:** 190 (inset); **Meg McKinney:** 288; **Andrew Meade/Chica Worldwide:** 304 (top left); **Art Meripol:** 6 (bottom center and right), 7 (top center), 12 (top left and right), 14-15, 18, 46 (top left), 70, 71 (top left), 73, 75 (bottom left, center and right), 76 (top center), 77 (top left and right), 88 (top and bottom), 99 (inset), 108 (top left), 112 (top left), 113, 116 (top left), 117 (bottom left), 118, 129, 158, 164 (top left), 165 (bottom center) 196, 207 (top center), 208, 209 (top

right), 210 (top right), 211 (bottom), 212 (top right), 214, 238 (top left), 251 (top right), 260 (top), 265, 294 (top); **Miami Design District:** (294 (bottom); **Gregory Miller:** 30 (bottom right); **Dorothy O'Connor:** 28 (top left); **John O'Hagan:** 209 (top left); **Michael Ochs Archives:** 230; **Jackson Riley Parker/DIY Network:** 300 (top left); **Allan Rokach:** 262 (left); **Chris Rogers:** 11 (top right), 59 (bottom), 71 (top center), 78, 98, 160 (top center), 162 (top center), 258 (top left and right), 284 (top left); **John Russo:** 140 (top left); **Mark Sandlin:** 115 (bottom right) **Blake Sims:** 106 (top); **Allison V. Smith:** 124 (top left); **Laurie Smith:** 136 (top left); **Owen Stayner:** 220 (left); **Frank Stitt:** 52 (inset); **Scott Suchman:** 2, 7 (top left), 257 (top right), 259, 264 (top center) 266 (top left); **David Swanson/San Antonio Convention and Visitors Bureau:** 1114 (inset); **Matthew Sweet:** 38 (inset); **Daniel Taylor:** 112, 122, 127, 130, 145, 146; **John Martin Taylor:** 282 (top left); **Eugenia Uhl:** 71 (right), 74 (top right) **Stacey Van Berkel:** 160 (top right), 161, 173 (top right); **Jason Wallis:** 162 (top left); **Charles Walton:** 153 (top right); **John Warner Photography:** 194 (top left); **Scott Wiseman:** 299 (top right); **Ann-Marie Wyatt:** 62 (top left). All other photos provided by *Southern Living* or Oxmoor House.

Recipe Credits

Richard Blais recipe (20) adapted from *Try This at Home: Recipes from My Head to Your Plate* by Richard Blais (Clarkson Potter, 2013).

Bobby Deen recipe (292) adapted from *From Mama's Table to Mine: Everybody's Favorite Comfort Foods at 350 Calories or Less* by Bobby Deen and Melissa Clark (Ballantine, 2013).

John T. Edge recipe (62) adapted from *The Southern Foodways Alliance Community Cookbook* (University of Georgia Press, 2010).

Kevin Gillespie recipe (24) adapted from *Fire in My Belly: Real Cooking* by Kevin Gillespie with David Joachim (Andrews McMeel Publishing, 2012).

Marcie Cohen Ferris recipe (182) adapted from *Matzoh Ball Gumbo: Culinary Tales of the Jewish South* by Marcie Cohen Ferris (UNC Press, 2010).

Emeril Lagasse recipe (86) from *Emeril's Kicked-Up Sandwiches* by Emeril Lagasse.

Copyright © 2012 by Emeril/MSLO Acquisitions Sub, LLC. Adapted and reprinted by permission of HarperCollins Publishers.

Eva Longoria recipe (140) adapted from *Eva's Kitchen: Cooking with Love for Family and Friends* (Clarkson Potter, 2011).

Loretta Lynn (252) recipe adapted from *You're Cookin' It Country: My Favorite Recipes and Memories* (Thomas Nelson Inc., 2004).

Myron Mixon recipe (34) adapted from *Smokin' with Myron Mixon: Recipes Made Simple, from the Winningest Man in Barbecue* by Myron Mixon and Kelly Alexander (Ballantine Books, 2011).

Andrea Reusing recipe (170) adapted from *Cooking in the Moment: A Year of Seasonal Recipes* by Andrea Reusing (Clarkson Potter, 2011).

Mo'Nique recipe (270) from *Skinny Cooks Can't be Trusted* by Mo'Nique with Sherri McGee

McCovey. Copyright © 2006 by Mo'Nique and Sherri McGee McCovey. Adapted and reprinted by permission of HarperCollins Publishers.

Robb Walsh recipe (136) adapted from *Legends of Texas Barbecue Cookbook: Recipes and Recollections from the Pit Bosses* (Chronicle Books, 2002).

Susan Rebecca White recipe (28) adapted from *A Place at the Table: A Novel* (Touchstone, 2013).

Trisha Yearwood recipe (248) adapted from *Home Cooking with Trisha Yearwood: Stories and Recipes to Share with Family and Friends* by Trisha Yearwood (Clarkson Potter, 2010).

All other recipes previously published by *Southern Living* and/or Oxmoor House or newly submitted by their credited authors for use in this book. All recipes tested by *Southern Living* or Oxmoor House test kitchens.

Whiskey River Landing
Breaux Bridge, Louisiana

Acknowledgments

In putting together *No Taste Like Home*, I have been inspired by some of the best minds and tomes on the subject of Southern food. These are writers who apply scholarship and enthusiasm to the history, lore, customs, and ceremonies behind what we eat, and these are the works I've not only liberally consulted but also heartily recommend as useful and exciting additions to any cookbook collection:

Matzoh Ball Gumbo: Culinary Tales of the Jewish South by Marcie Cohen Ferris

Southern Food: At Home, On the Road, In History by John Egerton

Biscuits, Spoonbread, and Sweet Potato Pie by Bill Neal

Smokestack Lightning: Adventures in the Heart of Barbecue Country by Lolis Eric Elie

Legends of Texas Barbecue Cookbook: Recipes and Recollections from the Pit Bosses by Robb Walsh

Who's Your Mama, Are You Catholic, and Can You Make a Roux: A Cajun/Creole Family Album Cookbook by Marcelle Bienvenu

Chef Paul Prudhomme's Louisiana Kitchen by Paul Prudhomme

I would also like to acknowledge two of my forebears in the world of food writing. The late R.W. Apple, Jr., was uncommonly kind and generous. And then there's Colman Andrews, my friend and mentor, whose exhaustive, scholarly, and often wryly humorous words on food inspire me most of all. In my opinion, no serious food enthusiast should be without these titles: *Apple's Europe: An Uncommon Guide* and *Apple's America: The Discriminating Traveler's Guide to 40 Great Cities in the United States and Canada* by R.W. Apple, Jr.; and *The Country Cooking of Ireland, The Country Cooking of Italy, Catalan Cuisine*, and *Ferran: The Inside Story of El Bulli and the Man Who Reinvented Food* by Colman Andrews.

It has been my great good luck to have worked with the *Southern Living*/Oxmoor House team on this book, and I would like to thank my editor, Nichole Aksamit, for her uncommon devotion to telling good stories about Southern food and her commitment to getting all of the attendant details exactly right. Her team, including copy editor Norma Butterworth-McKittrick and the inestimable Oxmoor House test kitchen and photo and design professionals, went above and beyond to make this a beautiful, historically accurate, and utterly precise cookbook.

I would like to thank my agent, Michael Psaltis, for encouraging me to write this book in a way that applies literary convention to food traditions and recipes, and my research team: expert celebrity wrangler Janet Elbetri and the great Dallas-based food reporter Carol Shih (you'll see her name in the cookbook aisles some day in the future, I'm sure of it).

Finally, I would like to thank my family—my husband, Andrew, and my sons, Louis and Dylan—whose love and support makes it all possible.

—Kelly Alexander

About the Author

Food writer Kelly Alexander grew up in a boisterous Southern-Jewish family in Atlanta, Georgia.

She is co-author of the *New York Times* bestselling cookbook *Smokin' with Myron Mixon* (Ballantine, 2011) and author of the critically acclaimed *Hometown Appetites: The Story of Clementine Paddleford, the Forgotten Food Writer Who Chronicled How America Ate* (Gotham, 2008).

Her magazine work, which has covered everything from obsessive collectors of Fiestaware to the cross-cultural significance of brisket, earned her a James Beard Foundation journalism award. She was a senior editor at *Saveur* and editor at *Food & Wine* and *Boston* magazines. Her writing also has appeared in *The New York Times, The New Republic, Gourmet, New York* magazine, *Real Simple, Newsweek, Slate,* and *Travel + Leisure,* among others.

Alexander teaches food writing and narrative nonfiction writing at the Center for Documentary Studies at Duke University and can be heard chronicling food customs on *The State of Things,* which airs on North Carolina Public Radio and NPR stations across the country.

A graduate of Northwestern University's Medill School of Journalism, she lives in Chapel Hill, North Carolina, with her husband, two sons, a dachshund, a calico cat, and a box turtle.